# Paper
# Shadows

## A Chinatown Childhood

# Wayson Choy

**VIKING**

VIKING
Published by the Penguin Group
Penguin Books Canada Ltd, 10 Alcorn Avenue, Toronto, Ontario,
Canada M4V 3B2
Penguin Books Ltd, 27 Wrights Lane, London W8 5TZ, England
Penguin Putnam Inc., 375 Hudson Street, New York, New York 10014, U.S.A.
Penguin Books Australia Ltd, Ringwood, Victoria, Australia
Penguin Books (NZ) Ltd, cnr Rosedale and Airborne Roads, Albany, Auckland
1310, New Zealand

Penguin Books Ltd Registered Offices: Harmondsworth, Middlesex, England

First published 1999
10 9 8 7 6 5 4 3 2

Printed and bound in Canada on acid free paper ∞

Text design by Laura Brady

CANADIAN CATALOGUING IN PUBLICATION DATA

Choy, Wayson
    Paper shadows: a Chinatown childhood

ISBN 0-670-87709-3

1. Choy, Wayson, 1939–    – Childhood and youth. 2. Novelists, Canadian
(English) – Biography.*  3. Chinese Canadians – British Columbia –
Vancouver – Biography.*  4. Chinatown (Vancouver, B.C.) – Biography.
I. Title.

PR8555.H6658Z53 1999    C813'.54    C99-931576-5
PR9199.C49672473 1999

Visit Penguin Canada's website at **www.penguin.ca**

# Author's Note

THIS MEMOIR IS A work of creative non-fiction. In order to re-create past times and personalities, I had to select details and various points of view, and I am solely responsible for these choices. No doubt, other views and opinions exist about the same persons and events. This book is, however, about the people and stories as I remember them — from my own life.

I am also responsible for any final rendering of Chinese phrases and complex kinship terms into English equivalents, and for the adoption of the different sets of rules for the spelling and transliteration of Chinese words and names.

Portions of this book in different form have appeared in *The Globe and Mail; Icon Magazine; Writing Home, A Pen Canada Anthology;* and *The Vancouver Institute Anthology: An Experiment in Public Education.* My thanks to the editors for their original interest.

Grateful acknowledgement is extended to the Canada Council for their research and travel grant; the Writers' Trust of Canada for a lecture grant; and to Humber College, Toronto, and the Humber School for Writers, for allowing me both the time and circumstance to complete Paper Shadows.

# Photo Credits

FROM THE AUTHOR'S collection, pictures illustrating Chapters Two, Three (photo by Leong Ding Bong), Five, Six, Seven, Nine, Thirteen (by Chew Begg Studio), Fourteen, Fifteen, Sixteen (by Larry Wong), Eighteen, Twenty, Twenty-One (by Yucho Chow Photo Studios), Twenty-Four, Twenty-Two, Twenty-Five, and Epilogue (by Yucho Chow Photo Studios).

Other pictures are reprinted through the courtesy of the following persons or institutions, for which the author expresses his thanks: for the picture illustrating Chapter One, the Vancouver Public Library Archive; Chapter Four, the Victoria Yip Collection; Chapter Eight, the Nancy Hee and Larry Wong Collections; Chapters Ten, Eleven, Twelve and Twenty-Three, the Toy and Mary Lowe Collection; Chapter Seventeen, the John Atkin Collection; and Chapter Nineteen, the David Lee Family Collection. For the author's most recent portraits, thanks to photographers Robert Mills and Tony Fong.

# Dedication

In Remembrance:
Always with me, never gone:

Bob Brankley

Nancy Cole

Thomas Cottrell

Rev. Glen Eagle, Sr.

Stella Grier

Jack Harris

Philip Mah

Mary McNeil

Chris Morton

Dr. Kasper Naegele

Earl Reidy

Felix Sannes

Cherie Smith

三歲定八十

*"At three, at eighty—the same."*
—Cantonese saying

# Part One

# One

*Chinatown*

"I SAW YOUR MOTHER LAST WEEK."

The stranger's voice on the phone surprised me. She spoke firmly, clearly, with the accents of Vancouver's Old Chinatown: "I saw your *mah-ma* on the streetcar."

Not possible. This was 1995. Eighteen years earlier I had sat on a St Paul's Hospital bed beside Mother's skeletal frame while she lay gasping for breath: the result of decades of smoking. I stroked her forehead and, with my other hand, clasped her thin, motionless fingers. Around two in the morning, half-asleep and weary, I closed my eyes to catnap. Suddenly, the last striving for breath shook her. I snapped awake, conscious again of the smell of acetone, of death dissolving her body. The silence deepened; the room chilled. The mother I had known all my life was gone.

Eighteen years later, in response to a lively radio interview about my first novel, a woman left a mysterious message: URGENT WAYSON CHOY CALL THIS NUMBER.

Back at my hotel room, message in hand, I dialled the number and heard an older woman, her voice charged with nervous energy, insist she had seen my mother on the streetcar.

"You must be mistaken," I said, confident that this woman would recognize her error and sign off.

"No, no, not your mother"—the voice persisted—"I mean your *real* mother."

"My first crazy," I remember thinking. *The Jade Peony* had been launched just two days earlier at the Vancouver Writers' Festival, and already I had a crazy. My agent had, half-whimsically, warned me to watch out for them. The crazies had declared open season upon another of her clients, a young woman who had written frankly of sexual matters. I was flattered, but did not really believe that my novel about Vancouver's Old Chinatown could provoke such perverse attention. Surely, my caller was simply mistaken.

"I saw your *real* mother." The voice emphatically repeated the word "real" as if it were an incantation.

My *real* mother? I looked down at the polished desk and absently studied the Hotel Vancouver room-service menu. My real mother was dead; I had witnessed her going. I had come home that same morning eighteen years ago and seen her flowered apron folded precisely and carefully draped over the kitchen chair, as it had been every day of my life. I remember quickly hiding the apron from my father's eyes as he, in his

pyjamas and leaning on his cane, shuffled into the kitchen. Seeing that the apron was missing from the chair, he began,
"She's ... ?" but could not finish the question. He stared at the
back of the chair, then rested his frail eighty-plus years against
me. Unable to speak, I led him back to his bed.

The voice on the hotel phone chattered on, spilling out details
and relationships, talking of Pender *Gai*, Pender Street, and noting how my novel talked of the "secrets of Chinatown."

I suddenly caught my family name, pronounced distinctively
and correctly: *Tuey*. Then my grandfather's, my mother's and my
father's formal Chinese names, rarely heard, sang into my consciousness over the telephone.

"Those are your family names?" the voice went on.

"Yes, they are," I answered, "but who are you?"

"Call me Hazel," she said.

She had an appointment to go to, but she gave me a number
to call that evening.

"Right now, I can't tell you much more."

"Oh," I replied lamely, "I understand."

I did not understand. I meant it as a pause, a moment in which
to gather my thoughts. I wanted to learn more. Provoked and
confused, I said what came immediately into my head:

"Where should I begin?"

The line went dead. Hazel was gone.

That afternoon, in my fifty-seventh year, a phone call from a
stranger pushed me towards a mystery. The past, as I knew it,
began to shift.

WHEN I THINK OF my earliest memories, I do not worry about family history, nor do I think of the *five-times-as-hard* hard times my parents endured.

I think, instead, of first hauntings.

At the age of four, something vivid happened to me. I woke up, disturbed by the sound of a distant clanging, and lifted my head high above the flannelled embankment that was my mother's back to see if a ghost had entered the room. Mother rolled her head, mouth partially open, sound asleep. I rubbed the sleep from my eyes to survey the near-darkness. What I saw, reflected in the oval mirror above the dresser, was the buoyant gloom alive and winking with sparks. A cloud of fireflies.

The wonder of it jolted me fully awake.

The clanging began again. Then it ceased.

For a moment, I forgot about the noise. Mother's soft breathing pulled at the silence, stealing away a bit of my nameless fear. As I shook Mah-ma to wake her so she could see the fireflies, there was a rush of wind. I turned my head to look at the windows. A strong breeze lifted the lace curtains and fluttered one of the three opaque pull-down shades. Pinpoints of outside light sprayed across the room and spangled gems across the ceiling. I looked back at the wide, tilted mirror, at the reflected lights dancing within. I remembered how fireflies came together to rescue lost children in the caves of Old China. Mah-ma, her back to me, mumbled something, then receded into sleep.

I sank into the bed and leaned tightly against Mah-ma's great warmth. The clanging grew louder. A monster was approaching. My mind conjured a wild, hairy creature, eyes like fire, heaving itself, and the chains it was dragging, towards our bedroom cave. I turned to stone.

My child's wisdom said that Mah-ma and I had to lie perfectly still, or the monster would veer towards our bed, open its hideous wet mouth and devour us. Rigidly, I watched the pinpoints of light crazily dancing up the wall and across the ceiling.

Suddenly the wind died.

The blind hung still, inert.

I looked up. A ceiling of stars shimmered above me. The monster would be dazzled by the stars. It would be fooled. It would turn away from us. We were sky, not earth. I shut my eyes and whispered, "Go away, monster! Go away!"

There was rattling and banging, a clinking, and then a crescendo of sharp, steady *clip-clop, clip-clop*s.... The monster, now frustrated by the lack of prey, shuddered—and turned into the milkman's old chestnut horse, its chains into *clink-clank*ing bottles.

When I told Grandfather the next day how Mah-ma and I had escaped the hairy monster, he laughed. He said I was very smart to lie very still and not wake Mah-ma, who had been working two shifts and was tired. When I told Fifth Aunty, who often took care of me, she smiled, pinched my cheeks and said, "You lucky boy. Fireflies and stars always fortunate."

This haunting, Grandfather and Father both assured me, was only a child's dream. Many years later, Fifth Aunty reminded me of the old horse, how one late morning, when the milkman came to her alleyway door to sell her a strip of milk tickets, she had lifted me up to the animal's large, snorting head, and I, squirming in her arms, trembling, let it snatch a carrot stump from my palm.

"Only an old mare." She laughed.

Fifth Aunty told everyone how I had wiped the horse saliva on her face. I remembered none of it.

AT FIVE, I HAD MY second haunting. This one, I recall clearly.

The distant clattering and clanging began again. I knew by now it was the sound of the approaching milkman. I lay still, listened for the comforting sound of the old horse, its hooves going *clip-clop, clip-clop* on the cobblestones, a rhythmic drumming that I can still hear today.

I sat up, not letting go of Mah-ma. She stirred and her breath deepened. My mother and I were utterly alone in the island kingdom of the double bed. Father was away again, on one of his frequent alternating three- and five-week stints as a cook on a Canadian Pacific steamship liner.

For my own amusement, I dared to imagine a slimy three-eyed monster somewhere in the dark outside, coming towards us, dragging its clanking chains.

I was lucky. I was brave. At will, I could render the great monster harmless and go back to sleep in the comfort of my own created magic. The chain's rattling had become as familiar as the sound of a chopstick hitting a milk bottle.

But that morning, for a reason I could not understand, I did not go back to sleep. From somewhere within me, a nameless fear slithered up my spine and gripped me by the nape of my neck. Then it began to pull me down. During the summer evening, the blanket and sheet had been pushed away. My pyjama top, rolled up, exposed my back. I could not reach the bedding wadded below my feet. I clung to Mah-ma, my cheek tight against her flannel nightgown. Her body heat and sweet salty smell anchored me.

As the morning sun began to bleach the darkness from the ceiling, the pinpoints of light faded. I needed to pee. But I did not get up and go down the hall, as I had been taught to do. An odd feeling fettered me, made me feel inadequate, like a helpless baby. And yet I knew that a big boy doesn't cry out for his *mah-ma*.

Carefully, I sat up.

A faint, distant clattering came through the open window: the milk wagon was lumbering down the street. I pushed myself off the big bed. The cold linoleum floor tickled my soles. I listened. The milk wagon halted. Except for Mother's breathing, and a scattering of birdsong, there was no sound. The world seemed to me to have suddenly altered, slipped into enchantment, like in a Grimm fairy tale.

In the near-dark, the scratched oak dressing table stood with squat authority. On its polished top lay a cluster of bottles filled with mysterious amber liquid, tortoiseshell combs, silver-topped jars, and fancy cylinders holding fragrant talc. I resolved to go there, pull out the seat, and climb up and play with the bottles. But then the single opened window dispatched a rapid tattoo of clopping hooves. The wind rose. The window shade lifted like a hand and beckoned me.

I was tall enough to lay my head on the window sill. Standing there, I then turned my head and stuck my tongue out to lick the rough, paint-flaked wood. It was real enough. I stared at the pullcord ring swinging from the blind. When the wind faltered, the beige wooden ring *click-click*ed against the glass. Outside, the milkman's horse whinnied and shook its bells. The wagon stopped, started, stopped, started. My heart thumped against my chest. But I was not afraid of the milk wagon. It was something else I feared.

I turned my head and glimpsed, in the dresser mirror, my mother, a length of warm shadow stretched out along the far edge of the bed. From where I stood, I could not see the rise and fall of her back. Suddenly, I could not breathe: she seemed too still.

I swallowed hard and stared at her.

The milk wagon clattered on, the bump, bump, bump of the wheels on the cobblestones fading into nothingness. I did not cry out.

This is all I know of the second haunting.

---

TO THIS DAY, THE vision of that moment—me with my head on the window sill, breathless, watching my sleeping mother—has not left me. Whenever this image comes to me, unbidden, my heart pounds, my lungs constrict. I taste a second or two of panic, then, catching my breath, I tell myself I am being foolish.

Years after that moment, at the age of thirty-seven, I was at my mother's funeral, and Fifth Aunty was saying how pleased my mother must be that her last ride was in a Cadillac, and that Father had bought her such a fine oak casket.

"The lid good enough for a dining table, Sonny," she said, using my English name. "First class!"

Fifth Aunty leaned on my arm as we walked to my cousin's car. She looked up at the bright, cloudless sky and frowned. She had almost tempted the gods: if she made the funeral sound too perfect, the gods would humble us. She had to find something wrong. She stopped, casually curved her finger into her mouth and popped out her ill-fitting false teeth. They dropped into a Baggie. The handbag snapped shut. Fifth Aunty sighed; she was stalling, thinking how to tell me (as family should tell each other) what had gone wrong. She would have to be diplomatic, yet frank.

"Oh, but if you win the lottery, Sonny, you remember: I want a horse-drawn hearse. More fancy." She stopped, cleared her throat carefully. "Everything should take longer, Sonny. Cadillac so fast! Service too fast! Even your dear *mah-ma*, why so fast! Today everything too fast."

I laughed—exactly what Aunty wanted me to do. She went on, cheeks flapping. "If up to me, I order, you know, an *old* horse and a shining first-class wagon with lace curtains!"

Fifth Aunty touched my shoulder with her cane and giggled. Death never scared her. She had seen too much death in Old Chinatown. I told her that, if I won the big lottery, I would see her ride into the sunset in the grandest, and slowest, horse-drawn hearse.

"Remember that day you little boy and saw your very first one, Sonny?" she said. Aunty always went back to the old days.

"No, I don't," I said. "I remember big milk wagons."

"Yes, yes, you remember," she insisted. "We stand on Hastings Street, I hold your hand, and your aunty finally tell you that black thing no fancy milk wagon." Fifth Aunty broke into toothless laughter. "Oh, you looked so surprised that people died, just like your goldfish."

"What did I say?"

"You cry out, '*Mah-ma won't die!*'"

I think of that morning of the second haunting, when I was five years old—the haunting that has never left me. In my mind's eye, the looking-glass reflects half the bed where my mother lies; its cool surface mirrors the dappled wall where my shadow first ambled towards the morning light.

As Fifth Aunty gets into the car, I know now why I stood there at the window, unable to speak. My cousin's car drives away.

I listen.

There is birdsong.

There is silence.

———

THAT EARLY MEMORY, that haunting, sends me on a search for
other remembered moments. Some come in dreams, mere fragments, weighted with a sense of mystery and meaning. At such
times, a sadness pervades me. I close my eyes: older, long-ago
faces, a few of them barely smiling, push into my consciousness.
I hear voices, a variety of Chinatown dialects, their sing-song
phrases warning me: "You never forget you Chinese!"

Now I am a child stumbling against Mother in an alley barely
wide enough for two people, my three-year-old legs scooting two
or three steps ahead of her. I am jerked backwards. "Walk properly," Mother says. I jump a few steps more, her arm extends and
she tugs me back. I look up at the wintry strip of sky. We are
going to visit someone who lives up the stairs at the back of the
building.

"Remember what I told you to say," Mother cautions.

I nod, laughing.

"No"—her tone is solemn—"*no laughing.*"

At the end of the narrow alley, Mother stops walking and
kneels beside me. She wets her fingers and brushes down my
cowlicks. Other people angle themselves to pass us. A damp
wind whistles above us. Mother pulls me closer to her. A man
wearing a black fedora pats my head and tells me I'm a good boy.
Two women push by us. Each speaks a few words to Mother, and
their long, dark coats brush against my face. Everyone is going in
the same direction. Mother shakes me to get my attention.

"Whisper to me what you are going to say."

I whisper. Every word. Clearly.

"Good," Mother says, wetting her fingers to push back a lock
of hair that has fallen over my eye. "Remember. No laughing."

We follow some people up the stairs to the second or third
floor of the building. A long hallway holds cardboard boxes the
size of me; the cartons are piled on top of each other against one

wall. As Mother and I walk down the dim corridor, the two women in the dark coats, single-file ahead, look back at us, as if to make sure we are safely following them. I do not laugh. It does not feel like a place for laughing.

"She's in here," one of the women murmurs to Mother, and the two women step aside to let us through. Mother holds my hand as we enter a tiny room that smells of incense and medicine. On one side, a big woman bends over someone on a bed and whispers, "He's here."

Mother lifts me up. I see a lady with damp black hair straining to raise her head and focus her eyes on me. The pillow is embroidered with flowers. Mother says, "What do you have to say, Sonny?"

I gulp. I know what I have to say, but I can't understand why the lady does not ask me anything. I am not afraid, but what I was told to say sounds, to me, like an answer. And an answer needs a question. Finally, the lady on the bed smiles and nods at me. I am satisfied.

"I'm fine," I say. "My name is Choy Way Sun and I'm a good boy."

The lady on the bed breathes heavily and closes her eyes. Mother puts me down. Whatever was to be done is done. We walk out of the room and down the two or three flights of stairs, pushing against people coming the opposite way.

"My, my," a voice exclaims. There is whispering.

Mother says nothing, only pulls me along and back out onto Pender Street. I blink.

The street is filled with a bluish light.

———

AFTER THAT STRANGE VISIT, Mother bought me an ice-cream cone and a paper snake with a wiggling clay head. At Ming Wo's hardware store, I sat on the oak counter in my new clothes, and Helena Wong popped a hard candy into my mouth. She distracted me with some nails she was weighing out for a customer. While my head was turned, another lady came and took Mother's place.

"Where's Mah-ma?" I ask.

Mother is not beside me, but I feel safe with Chulip Sim, one of Mother's best friends. She always smells of perfume and gives me squeezing hugs, and makes funny faces until I laugh aloud.

"Your mother will be right back," Chulip Sim says, but she does not hug me or make any funny faces. She holds me, as we both stare at Mother climbing quickly up the mezzanine staircase. I remember that I did not lick the ice-cream cone or even notice the paper snake bobbing its head. I remember watching Mother wipe her eyes with a handkerchief.

"I'm fine," I whisper. "I'm Choy Way Sun and I'm a good boy."

Chulip Sim gives me a big hug.

---

THESE ARE THE DOCUMENTED facts that I have known all my life: I was born Choy Way Sun, on April 20, 1939, in Vancouver, in the province of British Columbia, to Nellie Hop Wah, age thirty-eight, and Yip Doy Choy, age forty-two, the *gai-gee meng*, the *false-paper names*, officially recorded in my parents' immigration documents. A midwife, listed as Mrs Eng Dick, attended the birth.

"We waited a long time for you," Father used to say to me. Mother always pointed to my baby picture, that pudgy baby that was me, and shook her head.

"You were *soooo* big!" she would say. "Weighed eight or nine pounds!"

"Why didn't you have more?" I'd ask.

"You were enough." Then Mother would laugh. "I was too old to try for another one!"

Father always joined in the laughter.

Years later, after I knew something about how babies arrived into the world, I asked Mother about my delivery. How did she manage with an eight- or nine-pound baby? The year was 1967 and I was twenty-eight; my friend Donna Alexander and I were talking about a mutual friend who had endured a difficult labour. Mother was cutting up the home-made upside-down cake Donna had brought us for tea. The fresh pink roses my friend had brought for the house perfumed our kitchen.

"Were there any problems?" I asked. "Was it a difficult birth?"

"*Ho-naan wahtak teng,*" Mother continued in Toisanese. "*Not easy to say for certain.*" Mother handed me a slice of cake. "*Aiihyaah: too long ago!*"

I translated into English for Donna.

"Sonny, your mother has small, delicate hips," she said, and gently laughed. "You don't have to ask your poor mom if it was difficult."

Mother never liked to discuss bodily matters of any kind, so I wasn't surprised she would rather not remember. She looked down, hesitated, then shifted the conversation.

"You remember how you got your name?"

———

"THINK ABOUT YOUR Chinese name," Mother always said to me, tapping my head. "Think what it means. Your grandfather came from Victoria to give you your name."

Six weeks after my birth, Grandfather left Grandmother and his family in Victoria and took the overnight ferry to Vancouver, where he proudly pronounced the formal name he had selected for his first grandson:

"Choy Way Sun."

A half-dozen jade and gold baby bracelets ringed my crib as he said my new name aloud three times to a gathering of friends and relatives.

The two Chinese characters Grandfather selected for my name form a political motto: "*Way Sun*," that is, "*to rehabilitate*," was an epigram in Old China, a promise "to reform old ways through peaceful means."

When Grandfather informed my parents of the name he intended to give me, Mother mentioned to him, very gently, how it seemed too distinctive, too unlike the usual names for boys; Father as well politely hinted that the reform sentiments might prove to be more of a burden than a blessing for his First Son. Even Third Uncle came on his day off to suggest that "Way Sun" was perhaps too idealistic for a *Gim San*, a *Gold Mountain*, child. The name "Gold Mountain," what the Chinese, during the fabled gold-rush days, called North America, was a symbol for those who craved or dreamed of earning lucky fortunes. No one in our family had had any such luck.

Grandfather did not reply. With an air of authority, he picked up his brush and dipped it into the prepared ink stone. With exquisite strokes of black ink, Grandfather slipped onto the surface of the vermilion-coloured paper the two characters of my name. He held the lucky-coloured sheet up for all to witness. At once, everyone, even Third Uncle, joined in the chorus of approval:

"Yes, yes! Fine, very fine!"

Grandfather's generation believed that names were potent, significant. In Old China, the act of naming a First Son, a First Grandson, involved the advice of numerologists and astrologers, fortune-tellers divining appropriate meanings and symbols. The "right" name assigned to the "right" child is an invocation against bad fortune. Grandfather's naming me, following tradition, could not have been a shallow or pointless act. But I wonder if the old man had reflected upon his own failed dreams in naming me, or if he had just looked to his heart and simply knew: *this name and no other.*

On my desk, I have a family photograph from 1939, taken in Chinatown's Yucho Chow Photo Studio, shortly after the naming ceremony.

The chubby three-month-old baby propped cozily against his mother is Choy Way Sun, soon to be called by his English nickname, "Sonny," because his parents had been fond of Al Jolson's rendition of "Sonny Boy," and because, as a child, he had a sunny disposition.

Looking beautiful, Lilly Choy (also Nellie Hop Wah), her make-up fresh, is holding her son securely on her lap.

Toy Choy (also Yip Doy Choy), stands proudly behind his wife and his new son, their only child. In the tradition of Old China— for the child's long life and for his good fortune—a jade bracelet encircles the tiny wrist.

# Two

*Mah-ma*

"YOU REMEMBER THAT HOUSE in the three-hundred block Keefer?" Fifth Aunty asked.

"Yes," I said. I remembered. "The house with the ghost."

After three years of living on the third floor of the Kam Yen Jan Chinese sausage factory, in overcrowded rooming-house conditions, Mother had demanded of Father that we rent a house all to ourselves. I was getting to be a handful, banging my toys in the hallway and always crying for attention. When I had just turned three, we moved into the narrow pine house on Keefer Street that was also home to a sort of ghost.

Years later, Mother told me Father took that house because it was so cheap. No one else wanted to live in it. Mother was desperate to escape the confines of the sausage factory, desperate to live in her own home. Ghost or not, Father went to the bank and showed the manager his seasonal-work contract with the Canadian Pacific Railway. He came home with the rent deposit and told Mother to start packing. He might even have said, "Beggars can't be choosers."

We left our cramped quarters at 223 Keefer Street and moved into my parents' first house, a block east of the sausage factory. Father and Mother had finished the packing, and Third Uncle had helped us settle in. Mother's adopted sister, whom I called *Dai Yee, Great Aunty*, helped, too. Dai Yee and Mother had met on the ship coming over and swore they would take care of each other in Gold Mountain, like sisters. Dai Yee always stiffened her face and narrowed her eyes at any of the misbehaving children at the sausage factory, and scared us straight. Her daughter, Lena, was my favourite sitter, but I always had to behave when her stern-faced mother showed up. Dai Yee was two years older than my mother; she had a strong voice and a tough attitude, and her eyes never let you forget that.

Everyone worked. Unpacking straw-filled boxes of dishes. Organizing stacks of shoeboxes stuffed with documents and letters. Emptying two steamer trunks and three suitcases of camphor-scented clothes. Washing floors and walls. My job, Father said, was to keep out of the way, and I mostly did. Dai Yee would just look at me, start narrowing, and I'd immediately grab my tin trucks and run them through a wall of alphabet blocks and over my lead soldiers.

Third Uncle and the sausage factory's supervisor, Jim Lee, borrowed a delivery truck from the factory and helped Father transport our few pieces of furniture. Mother and Dai Yee set up my second-hand foldaway child's cot. Dai Yee had heard the rumours about the ghost, and she was not too happy about the house, but Father told her not to worry. Father went away to do a three-week shift for the CPR, leaving Mother to unpack, and to clean up the mess. I had new rooms to explore.

———

OUR HOUSE WAS THE second in a tight row of detached old two-storey houses on Keefer Street, just a few blocks east from the heart of Chinatown. They all had small alcove porches jutting out at varying angles, and matching second-storey windows topped by pitched cedar-shingled roofs. Gingerbread trim sheltered nesting birds and gnawing grey squirrels. Each house had its own rickety wooden steps leading from the sidewalk to the porch and, whenever it rained, slippery snail-silvered lines trailed across the planks.

Before my father ended his shore leave, my parents must have discussed how secure Mother might feel, living in a house for three or five weeks alone with a three-year-old, and with a ghost.

During the war years, Chinatown women left alone commonly feared strangers appearing at their front doors, especially at night. Stories were told of wayward drunks slamming themselves against closed doors, clever hoodlums picking flimsy locks, immigration officials showing up unannounced. One could never be too cautious.

Our front door had one key lock; one inside chain lock; and two bolts, one ten inches from the top of the door and the other six inches from the bottom. Mother sometimes used to let me play a game with her at bedtime: *On your mark, get set . . .* and on my shout of GO! we would race to lock the door. She raised her arm high to pull the top bolt and I yanked shut the bottom one. She always let me win by seconds.

If a stranger knocked, and if Mother felt insecure about peering through the glass panel in the front door, she would very quietly take me upstairs with her and, together, we would look down to see who was knocking. We rarely were able to see any faces.

"Is that Third Uncle's hat?" she would ask me.

If we couldn't recognize the caller, Mother would kneel and hold me close to her and whisper, "*Shhhhh,* no noise." And I understood from the intensity of her grip that I should keep as still as possible, to outwit the stranger with silence.

Slim notebook in hand, a stranger might ask too many questions. Immigration officials chasing *gai-gee yung, false-paper citizens,* or city health inspectors hunting TB cases might come knocking at our door. Mother's responses to English speakers were limited to "Thank you," "No, thank you," "Yes," "No," or a blank fixed smile if the English words came too quickly at her.

Because of the war, the door's single six-by-ten-inch panel of glass was blocked by a thick curtain. Blackout flats, as well as curtains and blankets, darkened all the front windows. The demons in the sky could drop their bombs on Vancouver if they saw our lights. That was why, Father told me, the Japanese people were moved away from *Hahm-sui-fauh, Salt Water City,* the Chinese name for Vancouver.

Mother went to great trouble to protect the city. A length of heavy towelling was draped over the mail slot, to prevent someone peering through the opening and to keep the light from betraying us to the enemy. I remember a few evenings when the air-raid sirens sang out and Mother rushed me into the kitchen to stand with her by the back door.

"Here," she said. "We can get out fast."

She must have assumed that, if the enemy landed, they would come through the front door. Or that bombs falling from the sky would be aimed at the road, blasting through our parlour or front bedrooms, like the torn fronts of huge buildings in England shown on the newsreels.

When the sirens screamed, Mother lit a candle and shut off all the lights, slumping into a chair in the dim, stove-lit kitchen to sit and wait. She rubbed my ears, which I suppose was intended to distract me from sensing her fear, but it just hurt. Once I was awakened from a nap, and Mother, holding me tightly against her warmth, was shaking the ashes at the bottom of the stove. She lifted me up and told me not to worry. All the blackout curtains, draped blankets and black-papered flats, were on our windows, even the street lights were out—the dark, a shield against sudden death.

I was not scared. Using an iron handle, Mother hooked the round fitting on the stove-top and set it aside so I could see the fire. Flickering flames from the burning sawdust tinted the kitchen walls with an orange-yellow glow. The fire snapped and crackled. Everything felt dream-like until Mother began a sing-song refrain—*Hm-mo pah, hm-mo pah . . . No worry, no worry*—absent-mindedly rubbing my ears. I wailed.

After the first series of blackout nights, the fear that enemy planes all the way from Japan would bomb Vancouver dissipated and we were allowed to take the blackout frames down. Not sure whom to trust, having seen too many newsreels of the bombing of Shanghai and Nanking, Mother kept the flats standing beside every window. After a Japanese submarine shelled Estevan Point on June 22, 1942, rumours flared around Chinatown: the Japanese were ready to land at any minute.

The blackout curtains went up again. Only when Father was

home, or when we had visitors, did Mother let in the daylight. Otherwise, the front of the house was in a constant gloom.

In our new house, I would dream of the Cantonese opera and wake Mother up with my singing, or I would dream of the trick-playing Monkey and the shape-changing Fox from the ghost stories Great Aunty used to tell me at the Kam Yen Jan factory. The creature-ghosts made me kick my feet. But, because of Father, I was not too afraid of ghosts.

In Old China, when Father was a thirteen-year-old student in the village district of Sunwui, a fortune-teller had told him he had a special gift: malevolent spirits were afraid of him. The fortune-teller, a village crone, had observed wild dogs running away from him. And wild dogs, as everyone knew, were often the manifestation of evil spirits.

Though Father meant the circling, growling dogs no harm, as he hurried to school he would stop and look at them directly, staring each one down.

"The dogs would scatter," Father told me, still astonished, "their tails between their legs."

Few men were born with a *chee*, an *aura*, like this.

"Nothing to be afraid about," Father assured Mother, as he also assured Great Aunty when he told her this story. Great Aunty repeated it twice to me, and whenever I grew too frightened of her ghost stories, she would say, "No worry." Then with a laugh and a roll of her narrow eyes: "You like your father. Demons scare of you."

Throughout Vancouver at night during the war years, the street-cars and other vehicles had their headlights taped up, so that only a slit of light shone through. No one was allowed to drive faster than fifteen miles an hour. Glowing slit-eyes prowled city streets like unknown creatures, tail-lights like the red eyes of tigers. In the distance, snake-long trains rumbled; fog horns wailed; a patrolman sometimes blew his whistle sharply. Gradually, silence wrapped around our tiny house. I slept, and no bombs fell.

But a ghost came.

———

THE ROOMS OF THAT house I recall most vividly were the small front parlour, and the smaller dining room, with its shelved rows of wedding-gift silver, ornamental china, and English serving plates ranked according to size. On a middle shelf, collectable British bone-china teacups sat in a row. Some of the cups, with their delicate wing-like handles, were gifts celebrating Mother's marriage to Father, and a half-dozen or so came from birthdays and anniversaries. Many of them came from the first-class store called Birks, on Granville. Whenever Chinatown ladies saw the familiar blue box from that store, their eyes would light up.

Neatly dividing this glittering collection of Mother's English-style teacups in two was my oversized clay piggy bank, a gift from Aunty Freda. I had insisted Piggy share the same space with Mother's prized Royal Doulton porcelain cups and saucers and, after some discussion, there it sat, a grinning pink pig among the flowery Staffordshire and Crown Derby cups. At night, as I waited for sleep, I imagined it sauntered about the lavish pasture of delicate Spode and Minton florals. Piggy, after all, had a hand-painted flower on each pink flank. It belonged.

Father always gave me some of his coins and lifted me up so that I could drop money into Piggy.

"Be careful," Father would say. "Don't knock over Mother's teacups."

The English teacups glittered in the morning light, as fragile as butterflies. I'd take Father's hand and we'd go down the hall-way, then turn and climb the stairs.

As he pushed open a second-floor window, Father's eyes shone with satisfaction at the sight of similar houses built on higher ground across the street.

"Good air," he said.

Standing beside him, I took a deep breath. Father stood so assertively, looked so boldly, that I imagined yelping four-legged demons darting away.

One day, Dai Yee brought us a bag of red apples, three oranges and a rare pomegranate. "Not to worry," she said. "Eat, eat, eat." When she saw Piggy on the shelf among Mother's collection of English teacups, she gave me three nickels and lifted me up to feed him.

"Careful," Mother said, watching my fist wavering over her prized collection.

"Not to worry," Dai Yee said. "Bless the house with good fortune, Sonny."

I slipped the nickels into Piggy.

"Don't worry?" Mother said. "I thought I heard something last night."

Dai Yee lost her stern look.

"What do you mean, Lilly?"

"At the front door," Mother said.

Dai Yee raised an eyebrow. Mother looked at my big ears and said nothing more.

There was a small kitchen in the back of the house. Against one wall, a great iron-black stove sat on thick-clawed legs. It had two rings of gas jets on one end, and, on the other, widely separated by a lampblack top and a steel-edged oven door, a sluggish sawdust feeder that burped loudly when you banged it during cold days. A pot of heated water always sat on the sawdust-burning side of the stove. Whenever Mother readied to turn on one of the gas elements, her mouth tight with tension, I always told her to wait. I liked to see the tiny blue pilot flame *poof* into a halo of fire and to watch Mother jump back.

---

BUT HOW UTTERLY small that first house was!

To my three-year-old eyes, accustomed to exploring the long hallways and endless rooms of Kam Yen Jan, I suspect everything seemed lacking in that first house.

Shortly after we moved to that Keefer Street house, Mother took me to a family celebration held in the Wing Sang Block, a three-storey, bay-windowed building fronting on Pender Street that belonged to one of the richest merchant families in Chinatown. It must have been a truly festive occasion, an anniversary of sorts, for almost all the Chinatown families were invited to attend. There were tables and tables of food, and colourful paper chains and lanterns hanging over everything. Incense was burned, and the children, me included, got red packages of lucky money.

The man who built the Wing Sang Block, Yip Ch'un Tien, or Yip Sang, was a successful, shrewd, and obviously astute and extraordinary man. Yip Sang held together a complex of business ventures and, with amazing harmony, supported three wives in Vancouver, his first wife having died in China. He eventually fathered an official count of twenty-three children—nineteen sons and four daughters. These local-born sons and daughters eventually married, and many of them lived in the building with their children, some of whom were around my age.

The older children played games that imitated our working parents, games like Laundry Man, Cook or Waiter. They played Grocery Store or Herbal Store, or they pretended to be behind the ornate iron-grilled counter, like the clerks at Wing Sang, and made us younger children line up to buy steamship or railway tickets, or pick up our mail or send remittances back to China.

In one of the many Wing Sang family rooms, Mother sat at a table to gossip and play mah-jong with the Yip women she knew, while I was merrily tempted away by a trio of their older daughters to play House with them. In exchange for being their play child, I got to explore what seemed to be an emperor's palace of countless rooms. One "room" was actually an auditorium/gymnasium. From there, the three older girls, myself and one other dawdling boy roamed through long hallways, storage areas piled high with sealed trunks and hemp-tied boxes smelling of dried herbs, sacks of rice and silvered tins with colourful labels. Turning ill-lit corners and heading down deeper hallways, we eventually found a door that opened into a mysterious room with long windows. Panes of glass portioned off rooftops and bright sky. A strong arm gathered me up and lifted me so I could see. I gripped a thin wooden ledge, leaned way out, and glimpsed how high the open window stood above Pender Street. At first, I leaned heavily against the slim body that prevented me from falling away and dropping into the street. I caught my breath and giggled with wide-eyed wonder.

"Let go," the girl said to me. "I've got you." My fingers detached from the ledge and my hands flew skyward. I had never been up so high or felt so precarious.

Arms out, I gazed across at the windows of smaller buildings, watched a few men looking back to wave at me. I could see the whole length of Chinatown stretching east, towards Main Street, a vista dotted with straw hats and vegetable wagons, open stalls, and rows and rows of awnings billowing in the breeze like red and green sails.

In the distance were merchant ships docked like toys in blue slices of False Creek. Above Chinatown, the sky was streaked with a green and yellow chemical smog from the refineries. Seagulls launched upon unseen currents of wind and floated above us, their beaks pointing left, then right, wings outstretched. If only I could fly!

Suddenly, the Yip girl jerked me forward as if she were going to toss me out the window. I burst into tears.

"Oh, don't be a cry-baby," she said, pulling me down from the window and making it clear that our fun was over.

Without a second's thought, I abruptly lifted my foot, kicked her and sprinted away. I could not fly, but I giggled with the freedom of a child. There was nothing to be afraid of, except being called a cry-baby.

I was caught, of course, by a big boy coming down the stairs who lifted me up, laughed and turned me over to my chaperone.

"Don't be such a brat," she said, limping. I could sense she had decided to treat me with some caution. After all, I might squeal on her.

"Do you want to see more?" She took the hand of the other little boy.

"Yes," I said. "Everything."

We were friends again.

At Wing Sang, there were numerous front, side and back staircases to climb, and multiple household kitchens to visit for what seemed like endless treats. Some pantries were small enough to contain only a hotplate and cupboards; others were much larger than our own kitchen: the one built for the preparation of banquets was at least ten times the size of our own tiny scullery. There were bedrooms of every size and condition; what I assumed were playrooms, but probably were storage areas, filled with mysterious boxes smelling of camphor, and oily machinery that had moving arms, iron chains with hooks, and iron wheels; and rooms with padded doors I was told were forbidden for children to enter. From some rooms came the sound of a Victrola playing big-band music. A king and queen lived here, I thought.

A pleasant mixed scent of damp wood, pungent herbs, ointments and jasmine incense drifted after us as we walked from room to room. There were motes of dust floating in the rays of sunlight that crossed our path. We stopped to rest in one of the smaller family rooms.

"I live here," the boy holding the Yip girl's hand said to me.

It was my first taste of envy. A little boy just like me lived in this wonderful maze of rooms, and could dash about adventurously and see the world from high above Pender Street, higher even than our second-floor window. I wanted to live in countless rooms and roam miles of hallways and staircases—in a building like Wing Sang.

"You live here?" I said to the boy, incredulous. When he nodded so vigorously, the paper lanterns blinking triumphantly over his head suddenly made me want to cry. Instead, I punched him.

Mother took me away, dragging me down long flights of steps while I tried to get away. I would never forget Wing Sang.

———

VISITING WING SANG HAD seeded me with dissatisfaction, but all that changed when I learned why our house had stood empty for so long before we moved in, with no one willing to rent it. I overheard Mother telling Dai Yee our house had a ghost.

"Does Wing Sang have any ghosts?" I asked.

Dai Yee narrowed her eyes and said, "Of course, plenty of ghosts in Wing Sang!" and Mother said, "Chulip Sim saw one in the storage room in the basement!"

I never quite longed to live in Wing Sang again. If our tiny house held a single ghost, a possible demon ghost, how many more must haunt that vast building?

I could have boasted of "our" ghost to the little boy I'd met at Wing Sang, but I was too scared and perplexed to dwell on the mysteries of the unseen world. And, really, no one in their right mind, especially not a child of Chinatown, would dare to talk to just anyone about seeing ghosts. That was for adults. When they told stories and plunged us into those other worlds of talking wolves and form-changing foxes, all of the children listened. Watched. Paid attention.

It wasn't until many years later—when I was fifteen and living in Belleville, Ontario, and had just watched a movie about a haunted house—that I even considered asking Mother about our Keefer Street ghost.

———

WHAT HAPPENED BETWEEN Father and Mother—and the tumbling, wall-shaking crashing that resulted—made us the talk of our neighbours.

Will Toy and Lilly Choy separate?

What will happen to their boy, Sonny?

The neighbours might have blamed the incident on Mother's decision to stay out late playing mah-jong that night, or on Father's bad temper and his return from work a day early. These were reasonable interpretations, and wholly inadequate for me when I was a child. Even today, I can't imagine there was not a more significant cause, one that ran deeper than the mundane facts.

The house, after all, had an actual wraith, a ghost, that I could clearly hold culpable. I would have regarded sombre explanations such as "Your parents weren't getting along" or "Mother and Father had a misunderstanding" as a mockery of my universe. To me, our first big family disturbance was as startling as a typhoon or a volcanic eruption—calamitous, but a natural disaster, like any other.

Nearing my fifth birthday, I was already deeply influenced by Chinatown stories of ghosts and hauntings. I took it for granted that the Keefer house had a *kwei*, a *ghost*, that had provoked Father to turn into a demon.

In Chinatown, there were at least two categories of ghosts. The Chinese who died in Vancouver became harmless, familiar ghosts and belonged to the first category.

"Ghosts everywhere," Fifth Aunty told me. "All the time ghosts. Not to worry."

Generally, Dai Yee and Third Uncle told me these spirits were "lost China people."

"Why don't they go away?"

"They wait," Third Uncle explained, "for their bones to be ship back home."

"Home," of course, was always a village or city in Old China, the place where you were raised, where they still wanted you, even dead; where you belonged. For ever.

"Canada no want you," Dai Yee said, matter-of-factly, remembering both her and Mother's welcome-to-Canada three-week confinement together in the "Pig House" customs building in Victoria.

"Canada say, 'Go home, chinky Chinaman!'" Mother tapped my head, the better for me to remember. "You worry about being Chinese."

Dai Yee agreed with Mother. "*Gay-gai quaw kwei-ah?*" Dai Yee said. "*Why worry about ghosts?*"

But the two women furrowed their brows, and I guessed why they worried. Dai Yee and Mother both knew that our Keefer Street house was possessed. Our house had a *bak kwei*, a ghost from the second category—a *white man's ghost*, an apparition full of spiteful trickery.

————

THE *bak kwei* IN OUR HOUSE made its appearance only when Father wasn't home.

Years later, whenever Mother's mind grew hungry for the past, she would say, "Remember that ghost?"

And if I were being tolerant about such superstitious non-sense—for I had grown up by then and supposed every ghost story had a logical explanation—I would answer, "I remember that loud knocking downstairs."

With a sigh, Mother would begin: "Yes, you were only four then."

I never forgot. That banging downstairs. It was frantic. We agreed about that.

"Mommy?" I muttered, half-awake. "What's that?"

"*Shhhhhhhhh . . .*"

Cushioned by darkness, Mother lifted me up and we eased over to the window ledge, my thin arms clutched about her neck. We both peered through the sheer curtains, studying the glim-mer of moonlight that touched the alcove of our porch. There was no one there.

No one.

I clung even tighter as Mother bent down to see if whoever had been knocking might have stood aside. My head bumped the glass. Nothing.

Pushing aside another inch of window shade, Mother lifted up a bit of curtain. We looked again.

"Do you see anyone?" she whispered. Floorboards. Nothing more. Wooden planks and the moonlit metal grin of our mail slot. I rubbed my eyes and began to sniffle. When the doleful banging started again, Mother said, "It's just the wind."

But on all the nights that the banging occurred, there was barely any wind. Sometimes a draught, barely lifting the edges of the curtains. But no wind—at least not that either of us could recall.

When I was in my twenties, I decided this incident with Mother had a logical explanation. Vancouver is located on a fault line. The earth moves. The noise was the house settling, the foundation shifting.

"Think what you like," Mother said, unable or unwilling to let go of the *bak kwei*.

Years before we moved in, a labourer had been walking home from a shift late at night. Unknown to him, a robber with a knife had been following him. The man jumped the workman. A struggle followed. The knife plunged deeply—once . . . twice. Bleeding profusely, the wounded man managed to struggle up the staircase at our house on Keefer, to the front door, and banged, *banged* for help. No one would open the door, and he died.

"Was there a newspaper report?" I asked.

Mother grew impatient. I was old enough to be dogged about evidence. Mother was dismissive. We were the fifth tenants in three years who reported to the landlord these strange night bangings. Why was I so thick-headed? Was I still missing the point?

"It was a white man. That's all anyone ever said."

A white man. What else was there to know? Dai Yee had told her that a white man's ghost meant a curse.

"The Wongs next door said it was the *bak kwei* making all that noise," Mother said. "Even they heard the banging sometimes."

I turned the pages of *Time*. Everyday facts. Everyday reality.

People were sometimes knifed in city streets. Often there were earth tremors.

"Have it your way." Mother sighed. "It was the house."

Of course, I knew when I was four it was not the foundation or the earth shifting. If I had not grown up, I would have agreed with Mother: it was the *bak kwei*.

———

"I HEARD IT AGAIN last night," Mother reported to Mrs Chew, our neighbour across the street.

"Yes, yes," Mrs Chew said, nodding. "But why worry? No harm came to you or Sonny. The Wongs told me they heard something, too."

When she told Father, he laughed contentedly. "You see," he said. "Nothing to worry about. Mrs Chew says so, too."

"This time it woke Sonny," Mother said. "I don't like being by myself in this house."

"Then go out. You stay home too much."

As usual, Father and Mother stopped talking when I began to pay attention.

When Father suggested Mother "go out," he meant that she should mix more with her new friends, go out for an hour for afternoon tea or perhaps an early-evening visit. Vancouver was not like Victoria, the home of Grandfather and Grandmother and their family, where all the married Chinese women, often pregnant, locked themselves away.

Mother quickly discovered a coterie of women who loved to gossip and, even more, to play mah-jong. Mother began to socialize with the wife of her boss at Kam Yen Jan, who was soon as good a friend as Dai Yee. Mrs David Lee, Leong Sim as she was called, looked as if she could be Mother's sister.

"Take some time for yourself," Leong Sim said, a mother of four and pregnant again. "I always go out whenever I can. Take in a few rounds of mah-jong. Bring Sonny along."

Our friendship with the Lee family was the result of the two women's love of mah-jong. During those social evenings, Garson, two years younger than me, came along with his mother, and I with mine. As we grew older, Garson and I ended up playing together with the other children, rough-housing behind the Pender Street alleyway apartments where the ladies often gathered. Leong Sim took to calling me Garson's *dai goh, big brother,* whenever we played together. If it was still daylight, Garson and I, and several other children, ran up and down Chinatown's streets, playing hide 'n' seek, or we played kick-the-can at the False Creek vacant lot, our unofficial playground beneath the huge six-storey tank that ominously proclaimed, in ten-foot letters: GAS THE MODERN FUEL. We jumped over rainbow-streaked oily puddles, breathed into our lungs the toxic smells of nearby refineries, and ran around piles of rusty metal junk. As Garson's *dai goh,* I was to keep an eye on him, while much older kids, in fact, watched over both of us.

If Mother wanted to gamble longer, I would go home by taxi with Leong Sim and Garson, and stay overnight at the Lees'. When we moved just one block east of them, Mother and Leong Sim became best friends, and I was a constant visitor, sharing meals with Garson's household. Mother never thought there was anything wrong with her taking me out gambling. Her friends, including Leong Sim, Fifth Aunty and Dai Yee, who brought along her son, King, did not seem to mind taking me home with them. She could stay out late and have a break from me as well. It made perfect sense.

Mother took to mah-jong and her mah-jong friends as happily as they took to her. Whenever Father was away, and only then, I was bundled up with every necessity, in case I went home with one of her friends, and Mother and I journeyed by taxi out for our long nights. The games were held at different houses, each family taking a turn at hosting. Leong Sim and the other women openly breastfed their youngest while briskly playing their game. There were also large curved woven baskets where sleepy babies might be rocked with one foot while their mothers went on clicking the game tiles into play. A few of the women also brought older children, counting on them to fall asleep on couches, divans, rocking chairs, and small mattresses placed on the floor. Soon, Mother hardly worried about me. I played with whoever was there, while she gambled and gossiped and ate the midnight meal with her friends. Mother fitted in perfectly. I did, too. I had all the playmates I wanted, and their toys to share. I fought sleep, but never succeeded in staying awake till the end of the mah-jong parties. In bright sunlight, I would struggle awake, already snuggled in my foldaway cot, staring up at our ceiling.

Mother grew to love the feel of the inch-high ivory-and-bone mah-jong tiles, the sensual *click* of the played pieces, the quick exchange of cash and chatter at the end of every round. She had a knack for the game, whose strategies were as satisfying as those of bridge, and she often won.

"Smart play," someone said as Mother turned over her trumping hand.

"No, no," Mother would quickly respond, afraid to tempt the gods. "Luck. Just luck." And she would tip the hostess with three or four coins from the winner's pot.

Stepping out, at Father's urging, Mother forgot the *bak kwei*, who tended to visit around midnight. A different kind of spirit had distracted her.

MOTHER ADJUSTED UNWILLINGLY to Father's long absences at sea. Each time he returned, she would wait up for him, however late his arrival. When thick fog or storms delayed him, she still waited up.

Mother knew she should be at home whenever Father came back and thought that a reasonable expectation.

But one day Father came home a day too soon. He arrived in the evening, carrying a stack of restaurant treats for Mother and me, and some extras—stale foodstuffs from the ship's pantry that the crew was allowed to buy cheaply or to take for free. Father must have opened the door with his key and shouted up the staircase. Seen the light at the end of the hall, glowing from the kitchen, which Mother always left on to mislead thieves. Shouted again. Listened. He may have assumed we were out for a little while and waited, thinking we would be home within twenty minutes or so. The night being cold, Father may well have turned to the bottle of whisky that sat in the oak cupboard, and poured himself a small glass to sip.

One or two hours dragged by. Mother and I were still not home. Father waited. And drank. And waited, pouring himself another shot.

When Tom's Taxi delivered Mother and me from her gaming place, it was 5 a.m. I could barely stand up as she set me down to reach into her purse for the house key.

The front door opened. Looking down the long, narrow hallway, we could see a light on.

Someone was sitting in the dining room. Through sleepy eyes, I recognized Father.

"So you're back," he said. There was a long pause. Then a glass exploded against the wall. The smell of alcohol filled the air.

"*You're drunk!*" Mother shouted.

A chair toppled over and Father staggered down the long

hallway towards us. Mother slammed the front door shut, turned, and ducked up the stairs, yanking me along. In seconds we were in the bedroom.

From the time when our house was home to roomers, there was a key-lock on the bedroom door, and a slot-lock above and below. In the seconds before Father reached the door, Mother had turned the brass knob, and pushed the two bolts shut. Father stepped back, then threw his weight against the door.

"Stop it! Stop it!" Mother cried out.

The voice of a demon howled back. Mother put her hands over my ears. She held me tightly, waiting for the door to collapse.

"*Damn you!*" Father shouted. "*Damn you!*"

I imagined a red-faced, horned creature forcing its voice through Father's mouth. I saw the muscles of a demon tearing through Father's legs and arms. The battering lasted for several minutes, and then there was silence.

"Not to worry," Mother said, looking at me sitting on the big bed, frightened and amazed. She slumped down beside me, as if she were being struck, and I imagined the door buckling and bending, like cartoon doors. But it held.

Father spewed out more expletives. Curses. Obscenities. Demon oaths. Mother rubbed my ears.

The banging stopped. We heard his breathing, a sound like a beast foaming, clawing, snorting. Then all was quiet, but for my crying. Perhaps Father heard this, and my sobs stopped him from going further.

We heard him stomping down the stairs. Mother rocked me, and we waited. We heard Father stumbling back into the dining room. Again, silence.

"You see," Mother said, "everything's fine—"

And then a volley of crashing reached our ears.

The unmistakable sound of smashing plates and exploding

glass rose from our dining room and began to shake the whole house. The racket lasted at least ten minutes. There were momentary silences when Father stopped to regain his energy, followed by the frenzy of another round of shattering china and glass.

"Not to worry," Mother kept saying to herself, as much as to me. "Not to worry."

Then there was a really long silence. We waited, barely breathing. Father's voice roared up the stairwell, "*Damn you!*"

"He's leaving," Mother said. "He's going to leave."

Father slammed the front door with such force that the glass in our second-storey windows rattled. Mother carried me over to the window. We saw Father's dark figure hurrying away into the night.

"Oh, Death." Mother sighed.

The *bak kwei*, I knew, had tricked Father, had driven him mad. Mother held me against the night. Father took the demon with him.

Exhausted, Mother and I fell asleep, leaning against each other.

---

LATE THE NEXT MORNING, Mother changed into her house clothes, put me in a shirt and itchy pants, and walked me downstairs. When we reached the end of the hallway, she picked me up in her arms. "Look, look at that mess," she said. I looked. Broken glass and china lay everywhere. Mother swallowed, as if she were choking back tears.

Mother stepped carefully into the blind-darkened dining room. I put my arms around her neck and looked where she gingerly stepped, her slippered feet pushing aside shattered porcelain and splintered glass. Carefully, she manoeuvred her way to the dining-room window. She lifted the blind all the way up.

Sunlight glittered about us, reflecting off piles of broken plates, knife-edged crystal fragments, and the dented silver tray. The remains of flowered teacups, two bone-china teapots, spouts and gilt handles broken off—everything Mother treasured lay on the floor, cracked or totally demolished. Mother held me securely and neither frowned nor winced. But I could feel her heart hardening against Father.

I looked up from the floor and surveyed the long shelves where the silver serving set, the rows of crystal glasses, the china plates and the flowered teacups once sat. Father must have used his hand to clear off shelf after shelf.

Mother stepped back, and I could see at last the lower shelf where Mother's treasured English cups once sat.

We both saw, round and full—intact—Piggy looking back. Fifth Aunty was right: I had the same *chee* as Father.

"Piggy," Mother said, "buy me some new dishes."

Mother went to the pantry and took out the Quaker Oats to make me breakfast. We could still use the everyday kitchen bowls. She filled a pan with water and turned on the gas ring.

"Call me when the water boils," she said, tying on her apron.

Mother picked up the empty sawdust bucket and walked over to the closet for the broom and a dustpan. When she began sweeping, I knitted my fingers together.

Piggy stood on the shelf unharmed, watching the brisk swing of the broom. The broken pieces of Mother's treasures tumbled together, like madly clicking tiles.

# Three

*At the opera*

THE YELLOW BACKDROP curtain of the Sing Kew Theatre shimmered in a sudden blaze of light. Speaking formal Cantonese, a plump man in a drab suit stood erect on stage and pleaded with the packed house to buy the new 1942 issues of the Republic of Free China and Dominion of Canada war bonds. I licked my fish-shaped caramel all-day sucker to the rhythm of his talking.

"Ally victory over our common enemies!" he said suddenly in English for the benefit of some white officials in the audience, then translated the statement into Chinese, raising his fingers in a Churchillian V. Fifth Aunty told me there was always someone who was appeasing these visiting officials during the opening ceremonies. They were often invited by Chinatown's politicians to stay a few minutes to witness the community's loyalty to the Crown.

Vancouver's Chinatown crowd politely applauded. Pinkish Chinese gold and mutton-coloured jade bracelets jangled on the slender wrists of Mother's companions. I grew restless at the speech-making and climbed onto Mother's lap.

My four-year-old mind wanted cartoons, like the Bugs Bunny ones I saw with *Dai Gung, Great Uncle*, who for the first time, last week, had taken me to the Lux movie house on Hastings Street. (Bugs Bunny was all I got to see; Mother told me I was too excitable and had to be taken out of the theatre, pants wet.) Finally, the man read aloud the names of all the performers, stiffly bowed and left the stage.

"*Eeeih-yah! Gum daw yan!,*" Mother said, in her Sze Yup dialect. "*So many people!*" Her lady friends on either side clucked their tongues in agreement. Mother reached over my shoulder and wiped my mouth of candy residue. One of the ladies ambushed my sticky fingers with her handkerchief.

As the front-of-house double doors opened to accommodate a last rush of ticket-holders, a draught of night air swept through the auditorium, bringing noxious chemical smells from the False Creek refineries a block away. Some Great Northern Railway trains coupled with an abrupt BANG, causing the three-storey Shanghai Alley building to vibrate. Most of the audience continued to chat, unconcerned; the only people disturbed by the noises and smells of *Tohng Yahn Gaai, China-People Street,* were tourists.

Mother held me tightly on her lap and leaned back against a

stiff wooden seat to let a young couple bump by us. The chattering audience began pointing to the rectangle of light and the billowing back curtain; people sighed with expectation, shook off their drenched raincoats, and sat down.

A foghorn bellowed once, twice, and the doors of the Sing Kew slammed shut. Stubborn latecomers were now directed through the side entry. The opera was to begin. The houselights dimmed. I wiggled forward onto Mother's boney knees. The brightly lit yellow curtains made me suddenly squint-eyed.

To the right of the stage—a stage bare except for a plain brown carpet; a small, rectangular table covered with a red cloth; and two plain wooden chairs—an eight-man orchestra began to play. The crowd applauded.

The rising notes of a dulcimer stilled the audience; the pliant notes of the two-stringed *hu chin* and the violin dispensed quivering half-melodies. Cymbals shivered; gongs and drumbeats throbbed; a pair of woodblocks clacked.

My all-day sucker slipped out of my hand. All at once, I felt my heart pounding to a rhythm outside of myself. I was thunderstruck. I clenched my four-year-old legs, tightened my candy-stained fists: I wanted to pee.

"*Hi-lah!*" Mother said to me in Toisanese. "*Hi-lah, look!*"

Balanced on the edge of her knees, feverishly swallowing the pungent air, I pushed forward, stretched my neck and *hi-lah*ed between the big heads and shoulders in front of us.

The door-sized side curtain parted. A burst of colour struck my eyes. In sequinned costumes of forest green and gold, jolting cobalt blue and fiery red, living myths swayed onto the stage, their swords slashing the air, their open ornate fans snapping.

Mother whispered into my ear who each was as, one by one, the performers made a few stylized movements to introduce their character, briefly sang their histories, and danced away before my amazed eyes: that's the *Hsiao-sheng*, the *Scholar-Prince*; there, the Princess with pretty eyes; now the grand King with his servants; last, with orchestral roars, the fierce South Wind General, his soldiers swirling behind him, tumbling like madmen. I could tumble, too. I could even stand at attention, like a soldier, arms stiffly by my side. Some of the older boys had taught me that. But these soldiers were different from the ones I saw walking on the streets of Vancouver.

Mesmerized by the tumbling warriors, I didn't care about the growing dampness on my pant leg, but Mother made a clucking noise to signal her disgust and lifted me off her knees. I stood beside her on the box provided for children, my knees bending and straightening as if I myself were majestically stomping about the stage.

A maternal hand pressed against the buttoned-up fly of my woollen pants.

"You just went ten minutes ago!"

Mother's Chinese words were pitched high above the clamorous music.

"I should chop you to death!"

"*Ngoh m'pee-pee!*" I said, afraid she would snatch me up and take me away from the magic. "*I not pee-pee!*"

"Stand still!" Mother's lipstick-sweet breath tickled my ear, her dialect as lush as the whining strings of the orchestra. "Look. Look at the warriors."

I stood on my tiptoes and lifted my head to peer between the adults in front of me. The strangers felt my fingers urgently pushing against them and, used to children in the theatre, shifted their shoulders to let me see better.

In my excitement, I took big breaths and caught in my nose the exhaled puffs of the men's Export or Bull Durham, the women's Black Cat or Sweet Caporal. The tobacco smell was seasoned by the aromas of salt-sweet savoury dumplings and roasted red or black melon seeds. Whenever hunger pangs hit me, I nudged Mother, or her lady friends on either side of us, and the smoky air was made sweeter by yellow-eyed egg tarts lifted up from B.C. Royal Café pastry boxes.

On the stage, poised at opposite ends, painted faces fierce in blood red and cobalt blue, the King and General made threatening gestures towards each other's kingdoms: fists shook; swords waved menacingly. The King uttered stylized shrieks that melded with the majestic singing of the bold young Prince. With hypnotic force, the General sang counterpoint. When the Prince left the stage, the King and the General broke into soliloquies of talk-patter, then dipped and darted at each other. With a clash of cymbals and drums, they both stormed away.

The audience roared their approval.

A Princess dashed onto the stage, waving her long white sleeves. Her eyebrows made an exaggerated arch above her crimson cheeks, and, I thought, she looked like Mother. She began to sing in shrill veering rhythm. I impatiently sucked my thumb and held my breath, my fish-shaped sucker now forgotten in the darkness at my feet.

"She's in love," Mother said.

The Princess sang on and on. For ever.

"Doesn't she stop?" I asked.

"Stand still," Mother said.

"She just keeps singing."

"*Hmmo cho! Be quiet!*" Mother gently tapped my head to get my attention. "She's supposed to sing. She's happy. Sit here."

I climbed back on to Mother's lap. I might have closed my eyes then; I might even have napped. Eventually her aria concluded and I sat up, sleepily rubbing my eyes. The prolonged applause was comforting: everyone else was just as relieved as I was that the lady had stopped singing. The man in front of us was even shouting "*Hou yeh, hou yeh! Excellent, excellent!*" Others cried out "*Ho-ho, ho-ho! Bravo, bravo!*"

The lovesick Princess bowed twice. I thought she was looking very sorry that she had wailed so long. One more bow and she scurried off stage with her maidservant. Everyone clapped to see them leave.

Next, the sound of drums stirred my interest. The King was returning from hunting, Mother explained. His elaborate headdress, made of long, exotic feathers, fluttered elegantly in the air, like antennae. His servants carried carcasses of deer and fowl across the stage. The royal court followed, their sequinned gowns and mirrored robes throwing coins of light into the audience.

---

IT WAS LATE SPRING, 1942, and the Sing Kew Theatre, a warehouse at 544 Shanghai Alley, played host nightly to a clamorous Chinatown crowd. For years, Mother went regularly with her friends to the Sing Kew, the Royal on Hastings, or the Yun Dong (Oriental) Theatre on Columbia Street; she thought nothing of taking me, even when I was only a few months old. Other mothers had their children with them, too, and newborns nursed indifferently at breasts wet with milk.

Tonight's fundraiser had been advertised for weeks, and featured all the Canton and Hong Kong professional touring actors stranded in North America by the war in China. Vancouver devotees also performed in these operas, talented men and women recruited from three clubs: the Sing Kew Dramatic Society, the Ching Won Society and the Jin Wah Sing Troupe.

Agile young men would volunteer to be soldiers, and lithe Lim Mark Yee, one of the stars, would coach them in the acrobatic art of sword- and spear-dancing. Even some of Mother's friends played bit parts, though she herself was too shy to volunteer. The theatre men were handsome, the women beautiful; aside from being shy, Mother never felt she was suitable.

Usually, the Sing Kew admitted toddlers and children free; adults paid from twenty-five cents to a dollar-fifty, depending on what time they entered the smoky theatre and which stars were singing that evening (one female star was said to earn as much as three hundred dollars a week, a small fortune). Every adult knew the opera stories by heart, so between shifts at work—or rounds of mah-jong or fan-tan—opera devotees could stop by for their favourite arias. Those who walked in after nine o'clock paid much less—an appealing option, given that a typical perform-ance began at seven and often lasted until midnight, long enough to test the endurance of the most dedicated fan.

Before the Chinatown crowds, Tam Bing Yuen played the clown; Kwei Ming Yeong and Sui Kwung Lung performed as warriors, lovers or kings; Gee Ding Heung and the lovely Mah Dang Soh . . . they all sang to ovations. (At eighty-two, Mother's younger friend, Betty Lee, could still recall for me the performances of the most famous stars, the handsome heroics of Kwei Ming Yeong and Gee Ding Heung, the exquisite singing of tiny Mah Dang Soh.)

Some nights, white people, such as city inspectors or Chinatown-friendly politicians, would be given free seating. They never stayed beyond an hour. With her lady friends, Mother always stayed until midnight.

From the beginning, I was enchanted. I fell in love with the dramatic colours, and the clowning, for I believed the whole opera was a clown show: didn't clowns paint their faces and jump about?

"Look, look," Mother said, pointing at the stage. "Buddha is laughing at Monkey."

I looked, only dimly aware that other eyes followed my every move. On either side of us, well-to-do lady friends rattled their new gold-coin bracelets from Birks, turned their amused heads to see how my eyes widened, how I kicked into the air—the same kick Buddha gave to naughty Monkey. When Buddha laughed, I laughed. When Monkey rubbed his bum in regret, I rubbed my bum in sympathy. The comic hijinks bewitched me.

At first, when the actors vaulted violently about the stage, and the orchestra produced an explosion of drumming and ringing gongs, I clung to Mother and peeked at the menacing antics through her enfolding arms, and used my fingers to plug my ears against the actors' yowling.

"First time at Sing Kew," Fifth Aunty told me years later, "you bunched up like a jack-in-the-box. But you keep looking."

As the evening performances and matinées paraded by me, these same ferocious faces quickly grew into familiar kings and warriors, into matchmaking clowns and an aberrant Monkey-King; I began to see—aided by Mother's simple narrations—that actual *continuing* stories were being played out.

One of the operas told the story of the Monkey-King who defied Buddha's warning not to eat the Peaches of Long Life. His adventures were often told to me by my Chinatown aunties and uncles.

"See the Monkey-King grab the Peaches of Long Life," Mother said, and I saw all of it, as if the stage were a living book.

As the orchestra at one side of the stage raised a clamour, my body rocked with a sensual pleasure, my fear for Monkey's safety flaming my cheeks. Monkey pushed against his long staff and pole-vaulted over Buddha's humble, rag-dressed buffoon. Clown was sent by Buddha to test the Monkey-King, to see if he would keep his promise to be a good monkey and not steal the forbidden peaches. I sat up. Monkey and Clown began to stalk each other, just like cousin Donald and I did when we played Catch You! on my birthday, in front of Aunty Freda's house.

Clown dove at Monkey and snatched away Monkey's long pole. With it, the round-faced fool poked and pointed at the ripe sacred fruit that hung from a branch way above their heads. The orchestra was silent, except for the woodblocks—and my heart—*knock-knocking* in unison. Would the Monkey-King be tempted?

Monkey shook his head, thinking hard. He stopped, looked out at the audience, skipped—winked at *me*—then suddenly hopped up like a spring onto the startled clown's shoulders.

Perched there like a tipsy bird, Monkey reached up, as if to spread his wings and fly. Instead, he came crashing down, a juicy peach clutched in each paw. Buddha's clown went tumbling backwards, raising puffs of dust from the stage carpet. Monkey, chortling and triumphant, ran off.

"Naughty Monkey!" Mother said. "*Hai m'hai ah!*"

"Silly Monkey!" I said. "*Hai! Yes!*" And Mother laughed. I laughed, too. Buddha's faithful servant could never have fooled me!

I very quickly caught on to the many characters' ritual gestures. Whenever a great king stroked his long black beard and pounded his chest, I knew there was trouble. Mother curled her fingers to my ear and whispered the story to me.

"That's the bad King," she said, pitting her Toisanese against the thundering drums and the squeal of strings. "He's jealous of the young scholar who loves the princess."

The Student-Prince ambled onto the stage, unaware that the jealous King was hiding behind trees. The handsome Prince, looking like my father, touched his forehead, then patted his heart, a heart clearly struck by love. Then he sang.

"The Prince sings too much," I complained. But Mother just held me tightly, rocking. By this point I had acquired a furious dislike of arias.

Still, I was left with some defences against the tedium. If tortured with an overlong aria, I could shut my ears with my palms, fight sleepiness and fervently hum, or even sing, my own songs. (Mother said I could do that, "if not too loud.")

I whisper-sang songs Aunty Freda played for me on her phonograph, songs like "Old MacDonald Had a Farm, EEE EYE, EEE-EYE, OHHH!" Sometimes I heard Mother sing, *oohh-ahhh, oohh-ahhlaah*, and I vowed to teach her the real words.

When the drums began, and the cymbals and gongs—*chang, chang, chang*—I stopped singing, and lifted my head and opened my eyes, my senses on alert.

If I turned my head in any direction, I could observe men, women and children eating and drinking. Whenever there was a lull at the Sing Kew—that is, when a third-level star was attempting to sing, or a local talent was apprenticing on stage—out came thermos cups of steaming tea. I loved the life that blossomed all over the auditorium, as if it were a busy village square. Those who were skilful enough used their front teeth to crack open tiny melon seeds, scattering the *quai gee* shells at their feet. Vendors offered small bags of dried apricots, dumplings and salted plums, and children ran up and down the aisles. Old men sometimes bowed their heads and spat neatly into round brass spittoons placed along the aisles.

A chattering kind of freedom filled the space, which Chinatown citizens treated more like an open-air teahouse than a formal theatre. In the traditional Canton and old village way, the Sing Kew was a place to "be home," as in back home in Old China—a place to pass the time, to meet friends, to gossip, and now and again to focus on the stage.

GUARDED BY TWO LOYAL servants, the Gentlewoman, played by Mah Dang Soh, stood ready to sing a challenging aria.

"Oh, those opera love stories just like *Wuthering Heights,*" one of Mother's oldest friends, Betty Lee, recently told me. The opera may have been *The Beauty on the Lake,* or the popular *Lay Toy Woo, The Romance at the Bridge.*

The star tilted her proud, confident head to one side. The audience stirred. I was mesmerized by the lengths of pure white silk cascading from the embroidered sleeves of her emerald-green dress. Her elegant hands rose like the wings of a swan, and the silk "water sleeves" swept backwards. She seemed to be brushing tears from her eyes. Mother told me the lady lived in exile, and was aching to see again her long-lost family, just like all of Chinatown was longing for their own families in faraway China.

"She's going to sing of her village," Chulip Sim told me in a more formal Chinese dialect. *"Hm'mo cho-lah. You be quiet now."*

*"Kay-dee. Stand up,"* Mother said. "You be her guard."

I stood up, ramrod-stiff like a soldier, at attention.

With long fingers now resting against her cheek, the actress began to pierce the air with her falsetto voice, and the audience—suddenly—responded with silence. We children knew we were not to run about, but to tiptoe, and not to utter even a whisper.

Listening to the sing-song evocation of Old China, the lyrics conjuring up images of a genteel country life and lost family, of the Gentlewoman's dream to be in her village home again, our elders and our parents sat transfixed; then, after a defiant vibrating note, which escaped wildly from her throat, and after a final sweep of her water sleeves, the words she sang turned into a call to arms—*Oh, no, never give up hope!*—and the actress stood frozen in a heroic pose. Brushing aside their own tears, the audience gave her a thunderous ovation.

"It's so Chinese to long for home," the elders said to each

other. Others said, "Oh, for the children to be still Chinese and go back to China!"

Her headdress shimmering with gemstones and pearls, the star bowed to the shouting audience. I bowed back.

---

IT WAS MANY YEARS before I understood that, although Mother always wore her bracelet of gold and her jade pendant, my parents were not as well off as many of their friends. I never thought of my parents as a working-class, no-citizenship family, despite the fact that they were each working long hours and earning only minimum wage. Whatever daily struggles my parents faced, the Cantonese opera at night bestowed upon me such a wealth of high drama, of myth, that I lacked for nothing in the ordinary world. The booming drums thrilled me. Mother half-shouted in my ear, "*Huang-Dai loy-lah! The great King comes!*" and gods and royalty sang before me.

Sometimes the thundering sounds and the imagined action were so beautiful that I nearly stopped breathing. I wanted to become what I saw before me: the General, the warriors, and the frightened guard who led the way to the prison.

"Here come South-Wind General's one hundred warriors and horses!" Mother's talk-story words blew into my ear, her Toisanese breathless. The plot was like *King Lear*. A good princess, not unlike the faithful Cordelia, was to be rescued.

"*Hi-lah!* The Princess can see their dust rising from the valley!" Mother held my hand and pointed to the action. "*Hi-lah! Hi-lah! See! See!* The General and his soldiers will rescue her!"

Two tasselled riding crops wielded by an emerald-costumed warrior guided invisible horses across the stage. In my mind's eye, I could see the steeds—their tall, sloped-back bodies, their crested manes and proud tails shaking in the valley wind, more splendid than any horses I saw in cowboy movies. The General came behind, shook his head at the herd and galloped forward on his splendid charger. He dismounted, raising one leg, then the other. Behind his jewelled headdress, two outstretched peacock plumes quivered in the air: the horses, the General knew, could climb no further. With an angry tilt of his head, South Wind General dismissed the horsemen: he and his footsoldiers would climb the steep slopes of the mountain—a chair and a table—left unguarded by the false King. Sound and fury thundered from the stage orchestra as they climbed, and the ordinary world vanished.

"*See, see!*"—I grabbed Mother's wrist—"*All the soldiers are climbing up!*"

I saw them, in their hundreds, just as Mother told me, though only six men in gold-braided maroon costumes stormed onto the stage. The front soldier scooted forward and swung a pole topped with long, scarlet pennants. The Sing Kew audience saw a whole regiment before them, every man climbing upwards. In minutes, two actors, arms linked, stood precariously atop a single chair, itself balanced on a pyramid of two wooden benches, the longer bottom bench sitting on two chairs. The two actors mimed reaching down to haul the South Wind General skyward. The four footsoldiers, each representing a garrison at least, moved their arms in unison as they scaled higher and higher into the glittering light of the mountain sun.

At last, they reached the summit. The two warriors somersaulted into the air and the chairs and two benches were quickly removed. The General, stroking his long beard, now stood on the table draped with a slate-grey cloth embroidered to look like clouds and rocks—the mountain's pinnacle. Teetering dangerously, he looked far below him, surveying the treacherous slopes he had conquered. He stepped back, and his feathered headdress shivered in the mountain winds.

I lifted my head higher to see more, to hear more. If I had first supposed the theatre was a strange dream, thought the tales unfamiliar, there came a moment when I no longer felt separated from the stage. Suddenly, nothing about the opera was foreign to me: I belonged. I could not make out the words spoken or sung on stage, but my mind could trace the stories like a magician tracing fire in the air.

The beautiful Princess was saved from the wicked King. The audience shouted their approval. But Mother told me she now had to pass a test to prove she was the real princess.

"She's going to perform a trick," Mother said.

The beautiful lady was offered a gold cup from an ebony tray held by a soldier. The soldier trembled with expectation: a stream of wine was poured until the cup was full. He carefully lowered the tray to the level of the royal lady's knees. Would the Princess know what to do? The only sound was the steady tap of a woodblock.

The beautiful lady turned away from the tray and slowly bent over backwards. Her spine arched, and her head dipped lower and lower, until, using only her teeth, she lifted the gold vessel off the tray. Still backward bent, she slowly tilted her head and tipped the wine down her throat. If she was the true princess, not a drop would be spilled. The audience held its breath; the woodblock beat a rhythm that matched her careful swallowing. Mother stopped me from talking.

The actress bent her head lower and lower, until she was almost doubled-over backwards. She unclenched her teeth, and the cup clicked back onto the tray, almost tipping over. The audience gasped. The servant lifted the tray. The General looked into the gold goblet. After a beat, he triumphantly turned the cup upside down to show the audience that every drop had vanished. The General now knew that she was the long-lost Princess he had loved when he was a young scholar. At last, they were reunited.

Mother and her lady friends wept and broke into applause. Now the General took the Princess by the hand and sang, his voice rousing and deep. Then he let her go, then grabbed his gilded belt, as if in anguish, and wept.

"Why is he crying?" I asked Mother. "Has he a tummy ache?"

"He's very happy," she said. "After all their struggles, the South Wind General is singing that they will now be blessed with good fortune. His tummy doesn't hurt. He cries for happy."

Unfortunately, he also sang for happy—sang and sang; then the Princess cried, tearing at her long hair and spinning about.

"She's happy, too," Mother told me. "She cry for happy."

Mother cried, too. Everyone was crying for happy.

It would be many years before I finally understood why every one of those melodramatic operas ended in happiness.

"They cry for happy," Mother had told me. But Mother lied. It was easier for her to deceive me, easier to weep in peace than to explain to a small child the dire outcome of the romantic tragedy on stage.

In fact, the beautiful Princess had just been told her poor father, the real King, believing her dead, had gone mad; and her lover, in despair, had committed suicide.

"They cry," Mother said, "they happy."

I remember sensing *something* was amiss; not knowing any better, I grew to dread happy endings. To this very day, if ever I wish for anything, I never wish for happiness.

"No, no, no, *no*," Fifth Aunty protested when I told her my memory is saturated with weeping. "You got it all wrong, Sonny.

In those days, Chinatown so damp. So many hankies because everyone has so many colds. Eyes watery. Bad flu! Always sniffing. Polite to use hankies, not sleeves!"

What I did not know for sure until I was almost seven was that Mother had oversimplified and recast all those opera stories; that many of these epic dramas ended tragically. Twists of fate, not luck, condemned heroines to suicide; drunken heroes were murdered by watchful villains.

I knew only Mother's versions of these stories, and so came to believe that the mythic forces of good eventually won out over evil; Luck always conquered Bad Fortune. Crossing my fingers, I told myself in a dozen different ways, "Good luck will be my life."

Whenever I worry about whether my good fortune will last, I think of those drowsy nights at the warehouse theatre on old Shanghai Alley. I hear again the encircling tales of my mother, her Toisanese rising above a cloud of sleep, each narrated episode a happy one. I never saw the same opera everyone else did.

I now understand that my perceptions in life grew out of the fables told to me by my mother. Her whispered narratives constructed within me a permanent barrier against pessimism, perhaps even against adversity.

If I turn my head at a certain angle, I can still see Mother crying, her perfumed hankie above me, her face streaked with tears. And, in some other sphere, I see Mother laughing like the Buddha, her spirit unyielding, her mythic lies flying between us like bright pennants.

# Four

*The Ladies'
Auxiliary*

THE WAR IN ASIA AND EUROPE hardly interested me, though it seemed to me that everyone in Chinatown talked incessantly of it. Mother was involved in fundraisers, selling war bonds and collecting money, and volunteered to join the teams of women armed with pins and ribboned labels who trooped outside of Chinatown on tag days. They stood, rattling their tin donation cans, on the busiest corners in downtown Vancouver—on *low fan gaai*, on *white-people streets*, such as on Granville, near the Hudson's Bay, or on the hectic corner near the Bon Ton Shop and the Capitol Theatre. Signs in some merchants' front windows boasted: WE HIRE WHITE LABOUR ONLY.

The bustling corners west along Hastings near Spencer's and Woodward's department stores were also covered. Mother was to take up a corner with one of the actresses new to the Sing Kew company. The woman, one of a half-dozen players who had come up from a troupe stranded in Seattle's Chinatown, had a lean, stern face.

"Bring Sonny, of course," the actress had said when Mother asked her if I might come along. We were just leaving the mezzanine floor at Ming Wo's hardware store, where volunteers gathered to pick up their donation cans and assignments. As Fifth Aunty tells this story, the slender lady looked at her ageing face in her compact mirror and then looked at us.

"You stand between your mother and me, Sonny. I'll play the granny."

Mother asked whether she had heard any more from her family in Canton. There were rumours, she replied. Her two grandsons might have survived. But with the Japanese occupying the city, it was too soon to know what had happened. There were only the Pathé newsreels and the pictures in LIFE, images of panicked refugees and devastation in the bombed-out cities of Shanghai and Canton, and the eyewitness accounts of atrocities reported in the Chinese newspapers.

"Just as bad as Nanking, Sonny," Fifth Aunty said. "The Japanese bayonet live people. Toss the children in the air!"

"We fight our own way," the actress said, letting me carry her tin can. She helped me to button up my coat. She put her arms around me.

"If my family gone," she said, "you remember me, won't you, Sonny?"

According to Fifth Aunty, everyone at the store laughed because my eyes widened and I nodded my head so eagerly. She showed Mother and me a picture of her China family, her grandsons.

"Yes, yes, I remember," Fifth Aunty said. "A picture of her grandsons, *twins*, five or six years old, just like you, standing in a garden beside their mother."

Neither Fifth Aunty nor I could remember if the two boys survived. I remember putting three coins in the empty collection can so that they would make a good loud rattle, loud enough maybe to be heard in China.

---

TWO OR THREE MEMBERS of the Women's Auxiliary of the China Salvation League of Vancouver covered each of Chinatown's busy corners, urging passers-by to surrender their coins:

"Small change for *Big Victory*, sir!"

Mother's and my job was to shake the tin can vigorously, taking turns, since we were both too tongue-tied to shout out *"Change for Victory!"* either in Chinese or in English. Mother hardly spoke English at all, and her Chinese habit of adding a last *ah*-vowel to any final word turned *Vic-tor-ree* into a plea for donations to the city of *Vic-tor-ree*-AHH!

"Never mind, Lilly," said the actress in impeccable Cantonese. "You and Sonny keep smiling."

Mother's job was to pin CHINA–CANADA VICTORY ribbons on bystanders; my job was to rattle the can. I also tried to shout the English words, but my voice definitely lacked volume. However, I was not entirely too shy to smile. There was a good reason to do that: the lady had promised me an ice-cream cone at the end of our stint.

If someone bent down to make a deposit, I stopped shaking the can, listening as the change *clinked* loudly at the bottom, and grinning as if it were falling into my own piggy bank at home. When Father stood with us for a few minutes one day, he noticed how I barely smiled, even looked disappointed, if folding money was pushed into the slot. I was like those Russian dogs trained to salivate at the sound of a bell: coins provoked a better response from me.

Evenings and weekends, the women of Chinatown folded bandages in church basements, packed first-aid kits in Tong Association halls, knitted endless socks and sweaters at socials, and boxed and shipped all these donated supplies to Kwong Ming Tong headquarters in the embattled homeland. For the war effort, everyone saved up balls of string and tinfoil, collected old pots and pans, bundled up newspapers, rendered lard and repatched old clothes.

There were no end of fundraisers, bake sales, church and school charity drives for the Red Cross, and the like. The grand Imperial Theatre was rented for performances of special operas depicting the war in China, with actors dressed up in copies of Chinese and Japanese military uniforms, uniforms as drab as Canadian ones, and having none of the flash and splendour I expected an opera costume to have. To my disappointment, when the Chinese soldiers began pursuing the fleeing Japanese, waving their olive-coloured sleeves instead of bright pennants, neither side seemed to be scaling a mountain, only a pyramid of chairs and benches.

I hated those modern shows. The acrobatics and the rifle fire kept me alert, but all the colourful sword-dances had disappeared, and the drama with them. Gone were the gem-encrusted robes, the spears and tridents. Gone, too, the quivering feathered headdresses, replaced by dumpy military hats. And these operas featured an oppressive number of arias.

Mercifully, these propaganda displays ended earlier than usual.

Mother would wake me up, and we would have tea with friends at the Mount Shasta. Then she would take me into the magical world of the Sing Kew, in a storage room on the second floor, adjoining the building's common residential area.

The room was packed full of old stage props. The swords and spears hung on the brick walls. The *real* opera costumes reflected the dim light like scattered fireflies. The broad-shouldered robes were draped over stout dummies or suspended on wires in the air, like ghosts. By comparison, the drab Chinese and Japanese military uniforms stood like a dead forest. There, in cleared spaces, tables were set up and mah-jong sets spilled out. Meanwhile, an oversized wok was used to stir-fry the *sui yah*, the *late-night meal*, for the actors and musicians, and the cook used to let me taste a bit of stir-fried chicken. I hated bok choy or any kind of greens. Tea was poured for all, though sometimes it was hot water or rice-gruel water instead.

Mother played mah-jong with the theatre people and the ladies of the Chinatown auxiliary. Someone always herded the children into groups and entertained us in a room with a dark carpet and large carved chairs. There were old metal trucks with warped wheels and stuffed dolls and toy guns and spinning tops to play with.

I preferred to play with the opera dolls, the puppet-like miniatures I discovered one evening in a small trunk behind some discarded scenery. The fierce-looking dolls, dressed in embroidered robes, gripped tiny swords and tridents or painted fans and wore jewelled headdresses. At first I was told not to play with them, but then someone tall, a man with a kind voice, showed me how to hold the heads of the dolls, as their necks were only stitched onto the costumes.

"Don't be rough with them," he said.

There were eight of them. I picked one up, held it in my hand, gently, gently. I believed at once that, when it was dark and everyone was asleep, the dolls in their majestic costumes came alive: stood up, bowed, and told elaborate tales in quivering small voices.

I soon discovered it was possible to prop them up with the stick stands in the trunk. I made opera music, pretending I could sing, and eventually attracted a crowd of adults to look at my "shows." Other children were allowed to watch me play with the opera dolls, but, when I asked them to join me, someone always came and said, "Only Sonny can play with these. You just watch."

Sometimes when Father came home from his seasonal sailings, I would play-act Cantonese opera for him. Aunty Freda gave me some old silk shirts whose long sleeves she slit and then restitched, so that I could swing my hands and have my own silk watersleeves cascade into the air. At first, Father was charmed.

Mother helped me set up pots and pans, and let me bang them with chopsticks and spatulas. I wore old hats and decorated them with lengths of ribbon and Mother's junk jewellery. Aunty Freda picked out multicoloured remnants from her sewing bags, and stitched and safety-pinned the pieces of silk and velvet brocade to the front and back of a flowery cotton shirt. Belted, the multilayered shirt looked, to me, like the splendid costume of the South Wind General.

To make myself fierce-looking, I slashed lipstick on my cheeks, rubbed rouge on my forehead and dipped into the stove for soot to outline my "beard." I ended up resembling a scruffy clown more than a warrior, and Uncle Wally's response was to dash into our hallway to stifle his laughter.

I didn't care. Serious theatre was not for everyone.

Father, however, no longer found my operas charming. He was angry with Mother.

"Why do you let Sonny have your lipstick?"

"I don't," Mother said. "He just takes it."

Father spoke of the notoriety that my costumed dramas, now performed publicly on our front porch and in front of our house, were bringing to our household. My cousin King had been seen running down Keefer, waving a toy sword that Third Uncle had bought for me. I ran ahead with a real red pennant tied to a bamboo pole taller than both of us, a pole given to me by one of the actors from the theatre.

"Now you can have your own army," the actor said, and showed me how to wave it so that its triple silk tails swirled like flames. Behind me, a hundred warriors would follow.

"Everyone's asking why a boy dresses up like that," Father complained. "Why do you let him behave like that?"

"I don't encourage it," Mother said.

Amused neighbours gathered. Mrs Wong applauded. Some grown-ups even threw me pennies and nickels; others walked away, shaking their heads.

Now and again, a friend or two banged on the pots and pans to accompany my screeching imitation of screeching arias. But often these friends, mostly my age, would be intimidated by the laughter of older boys and stop playing with me.

---

ONE DAY GUNG-GUNG left his Victoria family to visit with us for a week. (Grandmother refused to come with him.) He had come to Vancouver to see a doctor. The old man looked very tired and took a taxi everywhere, as he had trouble walking. Father told Third Uncle, "He has heart problems."

"Too much stress in Victoria," Third Uncle commented, and looked over at my big ears and said nothing more.

"He's going to move in with Freda," Mother said.

One afternoon, visiting with Aunty Freda, the old man witnessed one of my performances, and he said to Father in his formal Cantonese, his voice weakened by his mysterious illness, "What... what will become of such a boy?"

"Oh, leave him alone," Aunty Freda said. "He's just got a good imagination. Take your medicine."

"Mother spoils him," Father said. "Spoils him too much."

I went on playing. I liked Aunty Freda. I didn't care what Grandfather or Father had to say. As Gung-Gung sipped his bottled Chinese medicine, I wondered for a moment why he looked so ashen. He didn't look like the man who was always bossing me around, telling me when to talk and where to walk.

"Ah-Gung," Mother said, looking worried, "please take more medicine."

When Grandfather coughed and held his side, the bottle shaking in his hand, I felt that I could do anything I wanted to. Just because I wanted to. And as I did not worry about happiness, I didn't know then that I was happy.

# Five

*At the Pacific National Exhibition*

AFTER THE USUAL PLEAS for donations to the war effort had been shouted out over the squeaking microphone at the Sing Kew Theatre, a man in a suit stepped up to announce the Chinese and English names of enlisted men sitting in the audience.

"*Soldiers of Chinatown, receive our gratitude,*" the man shouted in formal Cantonese. After each name was called, a soldier stood up. My opera aunties would swerve their heads in unison.

"*Hai-lah! See!*" Chulip Sim nudged Mother with her elbow.

"There's the Lew boy! The other one *there*, Wong Sim's second son!"

The uniformed men looked shyly around, listening as their names rustled like autumn leaves through the hall. After the last soldier was introduced, the audience burst into applause. Mothers and girlfriends smiled and wiped their eyes.

"My oldest is talking of going to Burma," Leong Sim said, "maybe India." Mother held me tighter. "They need two-language soldiers who look oriental."

"Why?" Mother asked.

One of the men turned around in his seat and said, "Make good-looking Jap spies."

The soldiers sat down, their shapes like shadows around me. Unwanted and deemed undesirable before 1942, Chinatown's young men were now being sent to secret camps: for language training, to learn how to infiltrate enemy lines, to plant bombs and to deliver covert messages. They were to carry poison, in case suicide was the only option.

But little boys sitting on their mother's knees did not understand anything about the overseas battles or the desperate need the Allies had for spies. I did know that the war had placed limits on Chinatown celebrations, created inconvenient curfews for night society of the kind Mother enjoyed, and, most disappointingly, had banned the burning of firecrackers.

Any evidence I saw of the war on the streets of Vancouver was mundane: posters and uniforms. Mother would not stay to watch the propaganda films that were shown outdoors in the crowded alleyway between Hastings and Pender, off Columbia, the black-and-white images flashing across a taut cloth screen high above our heads. As she dragged me away, I glimpsed a vision of a panicked Shanghai street, heard the sound of planes and bombs, heard a Chinese voice speaking harshly, but saw nothing more.

"We visit Chulip Sim's," Mother said, pulling me away.

I thought war should have been like what I saw enacted in the Sing Kew Theatre: there should have been silk and swords, the sound of drums and cymbals, urging my dragging feet to step lively.

---

THE CANADIAN MILITARY uniforms were a disappointment, but I was impressed by the smart outfits worn by the Capitol or Beacon theatre ushers. Their braided-gold epaulets, perched on padded shoulders, appealed to me much more than the shine of brass buttons and the thud of heavy boots.

The military men who walked through Chinatown were mainly Caucasian sailors and soldiers, tall as giants. The city of Vancouver, with its crowded railway stations and packed harbours, was the last stop before soldiers and sailors shipped out; and the perfumed and powdered ladies from the back rooms of Gastown hotels and bars made Chinatown a favourite place to take shore leave. The military men and their dates elbowed each other and pointed at exotic displays of braised ducks in shop windows and wandered into Lucky Star Drugs for smokes. Once, while Mother was negotiating the price of a rare pair of stockings, I remember, a soldier pushed through the busy aisles of Kuo Kong Silk to outbid her.

By the winter of 1944, the curfews had been relaxed, and there were fewer air-raid exercises. The pages of war news posted on the walls of the *Chinese Times* building and stuck on the windows of the Kwok Min Tang Reading Room showed maps of Europe and Asia, where the Germans and the Japanese were retreating "like wounded dogs," the elders said; the men's talk across the tables of the Chinese Benevolent Association, even the sad letters from China, all spoke of oncoming peace, of an inevitable victory for the Allies.

Chinatown held its breath. Basement stocks of forbidden fireworks were unearthed from sand barrels, ready to be lit in celebration. Barbershops displayed more and more Union Jacks and Nationalist China flags. Chinatown was humming with expectation and jammed with tourists. The Japanese and Germans were everywhere being routed, beaten back. People were sniffing the air, waiting.

When noisier couples sauntered by us, Mother looked away, discomfited. She would clutch her purse tighter, and jerk me closer to her, so that I, too, stumbled. Thinking it was a game, I always laughed or jerked back. Mother's quick pull on my arm caused me a few times to fall, sprawling away from her. On the ground, I was the centre of street attention. Once, a soldier patted me on my head and lifted me up into the air. His lady, after she dusted my coat off, reached into her purse and handed me a shiny coin.

"New as a nickel," she said.

The soldier said, "You all right, Sonny Boy?"

I was staring, open-mouthed, astonished: the total stranger knew my English name. Mother forgot to tell me to say *"Doh jhay. Thank you."* But after that incident, Mother seemed less worried about the high-spirited strangers that crowded Chinatown.

"They seem so *kai doy*, so *rough*," Mother complained.

"Don't be silly," Chulip Sim said at the mah-jong table. "They're on our side." All the other ladies agreed.

I saluted some of the men who saluted me, and sometimes they gave me gum and candy. Then Mother made me stop because I was being spoiled.

To me, all of the outsiders looked perfectly ordinary, just part of the growing crowd of tourists who now ate at the affordable chop-suey houses. The round tables and high booths of the Yen Lock, the Chung King and the On Lock Yuen were nightly filled with as many white customers as Chinese.

Outsiders happily rediscovered the hand-made quality goods of Chinatown, buying inexpensive fitted shirts from Mr Wong's Modern Silk store near the corner of Main and Pender, or ordering jackets and pants ("Free pants!") to be made from pre-war bolts of cloth hoarded for years in Chinatown. At Pender and Carrall, popular Modernized Tailors, next to the Chinese Freemasons' Hall, blocked hats and made suits to measure.

And because they were featuring popular bands and local jazz singers nightly, the New W.K. and the Mandarin Garden Cabaret attracted exuberant, young crowds. Everyone wanted to swing and jive, to be part of the passing parade.

Up to the mid-1930s, Chinatown was an impoverished, undesirable place for tourists. The restaurants and tailor shops then were mostly empty of visitors, who came either for the New Year's fireworks or as part of a trouble-making gang. Perhaps Hollywood movies initiated the changing attitudes towards Chinatown. Films featuring Anna May Wong and Charlie Chan made Chinatown seem exotic and less frightening than the Fu Manchu opium-addict world of the silent era.

Chinatown was now seen as a friendly two-block exotic adventure, safe terrain in which to spend the extra wartime dollars pouring into West Coast port cities such as Vancouver.

---

WHILE THE TOURISTS were discovering Chinatown, I was discovering my own exotic landscape: East Hastings Street.

To me, not anything in Chinatown could prove as interesting as what I now worshipped: *c-o-w-b-o-y-s*. I thought that all the world's cowboys lived in the Hastings Street hotels. Nothing quickened my heart more than gawking at the rough, unshaven men who swerved out of barroom doors and loudly sang rude songs, swore openly, spat anywhere, and shouted at Mother, "Hey, good lookin'!"

Mother and her friends marched by these street corners, looking neither right nor left, the flowers in their bonnets bobbing with majestic indifference. As far as I knew, the ladies were never harmed; East Hastings was an everyday city nuisance that paralleled Pender Street, a gauntlet the ladies ran with cheek and courage.

"If any of those *kai doys*, those *louts*, try anything," Chulip Sim instructed my mother, "take your hatpin and use it. Like this."

She jabbed into the air to demonstrate. Long hatpins were perfect weapons. Chulip Sim had already taught Mother how to use a hatpin in dark movie houses, where the hands of strangers sometimes wandered onto a woman's lap.

"And like this," Chulip Sim said, jabbing downwards. "That stops them."

"I use my gun," I said, and fired a cap into the air. The *bang!* echoed loudly across the mezzanine of Ming Wo's. Mr Wong looked up sternly from his counter down below. His eyes were hard and piercing. Mother took my gun away and put it into her purse. Chulip Sim gave me a hard candy.

"Just walk quickly away, Choy Sim," Chulip Sim said to Mother. "Those *ngah-shee, cow turds,* too drunk to do any real damage."

"*Haihn fie-dee!*" Chulip Sim said. "*Walk quickly!*"

But these were the same street corners where I pulled back on Mother's hand, dragged my heels along the sidewalks and feigned an inability to keep up. My instinct was to take in everything cowboy-and-Indian that Mother avoided.

Walking that stretch of East Hastings Street, I had to be careful:

if I dug in my heels too much, scraping them, Mother would tuck her purse under her arm and scoop me up, huffing away. Sometimes I got a knock on the head with her knuckles. If we were walking with Chulip Sim, each of the women would suddenly take one of my arms and yank me along, double-quick. It was a fine art for me to slow Mother and Chulip Sim down. Just to catch a glimpse of the colourful, churlish cowboy crowd in front of the hotel *Men Only* entrances, I tried everything. I wanted to be a cowboy, too.

My trump card was the discovery that some of my "uncles"— the bachelor men of Chinatown—loved the Saturday-matinée double-feature cowboy movies at the Rex and Lux as much as any kid did. Tagging along with them, starting from the age of four, I got to see as many horse operas as opportunity would allow.

## Six

*Father (right)
and one of
my uncles*

T HE UNCLES I GOT TO know were descendants, not of the
first Chinese who came in the 1850s to pan for gold, but of
the Chinese who came during the railway and steamship days of
British Columbia. Chinatown called them "bachelor men."

After the "Last Spike" of 1885—the end of the Canadian Pacific
Railway contracts—the pioneer Chinese labourers' usefulness
ended. Instead of finding themselves returned to China, as many
had been promised, thousands of railway labourers, and some
women who worked as prostitutes, were betrayed and abandoned

in near-poverty. Left to fend for themselves in mountainside work camps and in ghost towns, hundreds travelled east to work in mines or to establish laundries and restaurants in the small towns and cities across Canada.

The majority of the men and women found their own way back from the Rockies to the ghetto Chinatowns of Vancouver and Victoria. Those who remained for whatever reason, often because they were too ashamed to leave, or were too poor or too sick, lived in Vancouver's slum tenements and shacks formerly occupied by Irish, Italian and Eastern European labourers along Water Street and Dupont–Pender.

When I was small, I remember seeing the last of these old men sitting on the steps of Chinatown, waiting to die, chatting and laughing at my toddling legs. Beneath street signs that read, in English: NO SPITTING, they spat out bad waters.

Of those unemployed men stranded in B.C., countless numbers died of malnutrition in Chinatown's rooming-houses; throughout the Depression, bodies were found in the makeshift shacks along False Creek. Suicide was not uncommon.

Those who returned to China by 1910 found that in the famine-struck villages of southern Kwangtung province a man could barely earn five cents a day—if he could find work, that is. In Canada, if there was work, Chinese men were being paid twenty-five cents a day. Before the 1923 Exclusion Act, other immigrants took the place of those returning to China. These men and women had to find work in Gold Mountain or their families would starve.

By the 1920s, the men were finding jobs in B.C. lumber camps and shingle mills, in the galleys of CPR steamships and in fishing camps. These men, like our kin-name uncles, Uncle Dai Kew, and Sam Gung, Third Uncle, all worked long hours and saved their money. The few women who came over took jobs as waitresses, slaved away in laundries, became the brides or concubines of wealthy merchants, served as house servants or worked as prostitutes.

The men and women spoke of the day when they would be reunited with their families. Tragically, the passing of the 1890s Chinese Head Tax, a tax raised from fifty dollars to five hundred dollars by 1904, had proved prohibitive for those who earned seasonal wages of twenty-five cents an hour. After Parliament's passing of the Exclusion Act of 1923, which forbade any Chinese from immigrating to Canada, except for a few merchants or scholars, Vancouver's Chinatown entered what historian David C. Lai has called "the withering stage." By 1934, the province of B.C. offered to pay one-way passage home for those Chinese wanting to go back to China, on condition that they never return to Canada.

In the ten years between 1931 and 1941, Chinatown's population was cut in half, to seven thousand. The racist Exclusion Act was made into law on July 1, a date my uncles and aunts always called "the Day of Shame."

———

MANY OF THE MEN remaining in Canada had to keep working in order to send their family remittances, becoming, in their isolation, "bachelor men." My family elders and uncles were among the last wave of Chinese immigrants from China. Until after the Second World War, no Chinese, even those born in Canada, like me, were given citizenship: I was a *Resident Alien*, forbidden to vote or to enter any profession, including law, teaching, medicine and engineering.

"Everything better after the war," Third Uncle used to say to my parents, like a mantra of hope.

Third Uncle's wife and son were in Hong Kong, living in a

third-floor room on the remittances that somehow managed to reach them despite the war. He had not seen them for seven years. It would be another ten before they would reunite. Resident Aliens or not, Third Uncle's generation dreamed of one day sending for their wives and children, who would all have enough to eat in Gold Mountain.

By the onset of the Second World War, the bones of the dead Chinese who never made it back to China—who died of old age, of despair, of ill-health—languished by the ton in the Bone House in Victoria at Foul Point (Harling Bay), or were tagged and wrapped in gunny sacks piled up in damp warehouses in Nanaimo and in Vancouver.

"Spirits," Fifth Aunty called them. "Spirits wait for the war to end. Wait to go back to family."

Chinatown residents were never sojourners by choice. If they were buried in Gold Mountain, their coffins were packed into Victoria's segregated grounds at Ross Bay or triple-buried in the rocky headland at Foul Point. In Vancouver, the dead were interred in poorly drained land reserved "For Chinese Only."

"Yes, yes, many go back," Fifth Aunty told me, thinking perhaps of her own father and mother's bones.

"Why?" I asked. "They're dead."

Fifth Aunty gave me a puzzled look. Tears welled up in her eyes. When she spoke, at last, I could barely hear her words.

"Bones long for respect," she said.

———

"WE ALL DO WHAT WE have to do," my uncles used to say, when I asked them why they stayed so long at the tea houses. "You just be good boy and obey your grandfather and your parents."

When they weren't labouring, many of the bachelor men

gambled, socialized, drank and fought, kept women or kept to themselves—did what men might do to keep their sexual and mental sanity, separated these five, ten, twenty years from their wives and children. With plenty of bachelor time on their hands between seasonal jobs, and haunted always by the family life they desperately missed, many became extensions of the families already established in Chinatown.

We shared meals with such men. The uncles would bring a pound of pork or some vegetables, sometimes a pound cake or tea cookies from the CPR galleys. Mother would be busy cooking in the kitchen, and Father would read his paper. I got to sit and listen to Old China histories, even watched a few weep over photos of distant families, of suddenly grown-up sons and daughters. Their Toisanese and other dialects sounded like music to me, instructional notes sung for my benefit.

"My boy smart as you, Sonny," I was told by one uncle. "You be sure to go to school. Be even smarter."

I have no doubt that many bachelor men would have been bitterly jealous of couples like Father and Mother who were safely settled in Vancouver. But a few of them must have felt that a surrogate-family life was better than no family life at all, and sought to balance the empty hours they faced in cell-like tenement rooms on outings with the children of working parents.

"You're going to have an adventure," Mother would announce. "You're going out today."

A tall man, who always seemed much older than Father or Mother, would be introduced to me. While Mother served tea and small pastries, I would shyly meet the new "uncle." I watched how familiarly he spoke to Father, listened as they chatted away about the war in China, the family, and, I suppose, about politics and the weather.

Finally, as if everyone had agreed upon this moment, Mother, looking at the clock, would say to me, "Are you ready to step out with Uncle?"

The very first time it happened, I was shocked to discover that she meant I was to leave the house with a stranger. Alone. Without her. Despite my concerted effort to cling to Mother, my arms were briskly threaded through my coat sleeves, and reluctantly I let the friendly giant take my hand.

"What shall we do today?" the stranger asked.

"See cowboys," I said.

By age five, I was a veteran, an opportunist.

———

HOW I ADDRESSED these "uncles" in Chinese depended upon their connection to Grandfather or to Father. One "uncle" I was instructed to address as *Ah-Sook*, another *Ah-Bak*, yet another *Ah-Gung*. Each term was a different form of *Uncle* or *Mister*, designating their age and relationship to Grandfather or Father.

Very quickly, I grew to welcome and look forward to those outings with my half-dozen uncles. No wonder. When I went out with an uncle, I got to see a picture show; often came home with lucky money in my pocket; was given a box of Cracker Jacks, and a new pressed-tin toy to play with once the box was empty.

Once home, I would earnestly tell Mother and Grandfather, if he was visiting us, about the latest cowboy flick I'd seen, which —Father recalled years later—I sometimes confused with Tarzan plots, cheerfully includng Tarzan's pet chimp in cowboy shoot-outs.

One day I proudly let Father know how I had loudly slurped up my first cherry float sitting at the counter at the B.C. Royal Café, and how everyone had turned to stare at me.

"Uncle drank a cup of tea," I reported, "but I had lots more to drink. My glass was taller."

Raised in the old peasant style, this uncle believed slurping was the way you took in a balance of *feng-shui*, of cooling wind with heated water. Slurping also showed others your appreciation of the beverage.

"Sonny, you shouldn't slurp!" Father said, after Uncle Slurp (as he came to be known) had taken his leave. "In Gold Mountain, it's rude for children to slurp."

Father shook his head. Working as a bellboy at the Empress Hotel, Father had studied the ladies and gentlemen of Victoria congregating at teatime; he had watched how the amber liquid slipped noiselessly from cup to mouth, and taught himself to sip his own tea and soup silently. From Father's stern look, I knew that, if I were to make a symphony of sucking through two straws, I had best be with Uncle Slurp. The habits of East and West all depended upon who you were with and what the circumstances were. And how, if you didn't tell Father anything, you could still get away with it.

But trying to get away with anything with Grandfather was another matter. If I forgot my good manners or called one of my uncles by the wrong appellation—that is, if I called a man much younger than Grandfather *Lao-Baak* instead of *Ah-Sook*—he would scold me.

"*Nay mo-no doi!*" the old man would say, tapping me on the head. "*You no-brain boy!*"

A *mo-no* was what the elders called a local-born like myself, someone raised in Gold Mountain who was thoughtless and mindless of the Old China traditions. A *mo-no* was Chinese and not-Chinese at the same time, someone doomed to be brainless. Gung-Gung tried his best to teach me everything, he told me, so that I wouldn't be *mo-no*.

Whenever he happened to take the overnight ferry from Victoria to stay with his oldest daughter, my Aunty Freda, or to stay with us, and he took me walking on his Chinatown rounds, there were strict lessons. Gung-Gung wouldn't let me speak out of turn when he was talking to others, or let me run ahead of him if he walked too slowly—that would be disrespectful—and I wasn't to ask for any treats unless they were offered to me. That was humility.

Grandfather wouldn't even take me to the movies, not once. The old man told me that sitting in the dark was unhealthy for children's eyes. His Chinese sounded sharp and authoritative.

"You should learn to read," he said. "Read Chinese. Look"—he pointed to a sign—"there's the word for *sun*—that's your name, *Way Sun!*"

On our strolls, Grandfather gave me one instruction after another. But there were compensations.

With Gung-Gung, I tasted, for the very first time, a small handful of rare Hong Kong crickets that had somehow made it through the wartime shipping embargos. The crunchy full-bodied insects had a nutty, deep-fried flavour. There were also the galvanized bins of dried apricots and withered honey-soaked plums that lined the crowded aisles of Kwong Man Sang, where I could point to whatever I wanted.

"Just a sample," Grandfather would say to the storekeeper.

We sauntered here and there, examining open crates of B.C. fruits and vegetables, squeezing peaches and holding up leafy greens. We looked over buckets of fighting crabs, and poked at sluggish, half-dead fish in crowded tanks. I peered through dingy Chinatown windows at wind-up acrobatic toys, and Grandfather looked at books.

But Grandfather tended to linger too long with the storekeepers to discuss politics and the war in China, while I tugged at his sleeves for us to leave. Then he would sternly remind me about my bad behaviour.

"You naughty boy?" the old man would say, shaking me by the shoulders and in a voice that commanded attention. "Naughty boys go right home to bed!"

In the end, under Gung-Gung's piercing eyes, I had to do whatever he wanted to do, walk wherever he wanted to walk. My lips tight with frustration, I was not sure I liked Grandfather.

———

I HAD MORE FUN WITH my uncles. The Saturday special matinées at the Rex—"Triple Cartoons! Double Features!"—lured me into the black-and-white world of cowpoke heroes and dastardly villains, a much simpler world than I had ever encountered at the Sing Kew. Hollywood horse operas, with their stampeding quadrupeds, their chiselled heroes who yodelled simple-minded songs and pulled the triggers of six-shooters that puffed out clouds of smoke, became my new fascination. And these fantasies hardly had anything to do with aria-whining girls, except those who needed to be rescued.

Through the mostly cowboy movies, and the few cowboy-and-Indian ones, I began to wish I did not look like a Chinese boy. Good and Evil became crayon strokes: Good Guys were handsome, and Bad Guys ugly. Good Guys, like Hopalong Cassidy or Roy Rogers, rode smart white or palomino horses, and Bad Guys rode stupid, dark-haired nags. Good-Guy horses could jump over wide canyons, chew loose the bindings on a fallen hero's wrists, and, with a blare of trumpets and a bounding leap, outrace all other horses in the known world.

And if the hero had to sing—admittedly a slight flaw in the proceedings—at least any boy could hum along with him; and any boy could wait a short two minutes for the singing to end and the adventure to resume. The cowboy operas were ideal; the plots happily predictable. No napping necessary, and no mothers or aunties needed to explain anything. And the Bad Guys—their singular virtue—*never* sang.

I wanted to be a cowboy. All the boys in Chinatown wanted to be cowboys. Woodward's, Kresge's, the Army and Navy, the Five and Dime, all the local merchants began to sell cowboy stuff. I wanted everything: smoking cap guns, Red Ryder rifles, Tonto knives, Roy Rogers six-shooters, Lash LaRue whips—and all the cowboy comics, the flip-book images of the Lone Ranger *hi-ho-Silver*ing; I coveted the sheriff's badges, embossed boots, Gene Autry hats, Hopalong Cassidy suspenders ... Even Chinatown general stores began carrying cowboy gum cards, displayed above the flags-of-the-world and the military-airplane cards.

You could never buy opera stuff. Never see the South Wind General's pennants on store counters, never pick up the head-dress with the quivering peacock feathers from any store display. The cowboy-and-Indian world was infinitely superior, because it was infinitely available.

Like most Chinatown boys, I wanted to ride in the saddle and shoot away at Bad Guys. I would be one of the Good Guys, of course—fair-haired, pale-skinned, grey-eyed, and tall in the saddle.

At the toy counters, there were even boy-sized guitars that could crank out tinny cowboy tunes. Man-sized guitars were hung on wires and displayed in the windows of the B.C. Collateral on Hastings. I stopped with Mother to gaze at them. She explained how these instruments once belonged to people who left them behind and took away a numbered tag and a few dollars.

I asked Mother why a cowboy would part with a real guitar.

"The cowboys need the dollars," she said, looking sad. "The dollars get spent."

Maybe the cowboys came into Vancouver, Mother explained, where they took jobs on the trains, or on ships like Father did. Money was important in the city. I knew that. Father was always away working for dollars. Dollars paid for food. More importantly, dollars paid for toys.

I thought of the cowboy's rocky terrain, where there were hardly any stores at all, just a saloon and lots of adventure. I began to dream of wide-open cattle ranges, shiny guitars and guns, and horses with embossed-leather saddles, just like the ones I saw at Exhibition Park. I wished we didn't live in a city surrounded by stupid ocean and useless mountains. I wished we lived in flat and barren cactus country.

Being a cowboy was easier than being a South Wind General. I needed only to urge Chulip Sim or Uncle Kew, or even Mother, to buy me the latest cap gun, a boy's holster and a cowboy hat, maybe even a belt with Indian beading. I had only to ride on our porch banister, and shoot at strangers daring to stare back at me. I quickly dropped my obsession with opera and raced into my new addiction.

It was all the fault of my Chinatown uncles. One after another, Third Uncle and Dai Bak and Uncle Dai Kew deepened my addiction to cowboy movies, for they delighted in the celluloid adventures, too. No one had to know much English to understand what was going on. Soon I refused to go to the Cantonese opera. Canyons and cactus and the bright stretches of the desert horizon captivated me, and made the table-and-chair landscape at the Cantonese opera laughable. The living dramas that had once stirred my imagination now seemed ridiculous. I would rather stay with my cousin King and his older sister, Lena, and play upstairs in the living quarters of the sausage factory, or be taken care of by the Jung sisters, or even be left at Leong Sim's house with the Lee sisters.

By the time Robin Hood came to town, it was hopeless. The South Wind General storming up a chair and table just couldn't compete with Robin storming up a real castle wall, arrows and spears zipping down upon his band of merry men. And when Tarzan and Cheetah rode on an elephant and scattered the gangs of Bad Guys, I was completely lost to the movies.

Soon, English words and phrases became more interesting for me to speak. More and more, English vowels marked the rhythms and sounds my Chinatown playmates and I responded to. Our multiple family Chinese dialects would soon become a language many of us would use only in an elementary way. Mother understood what I was losing; she resisted.

"You Chinese," she said firmly, in Toisanese. "You speak Chinese."

I had heard from some of the older boys how I might reply, in English.

"No!" I said. "I speak *Chinglish!*"

Mother's knuckles landed smartly on my head, punctuating my Chinglish vocabulary.

"Wait until I speak to your father!"

But Father said to her: "There's more than one war going on back home. You don't think we'll ever go back to Old China, do you?"

Mother looked at me and saw the victory in my eyes.

———

MOTHER WAS AT A DISADVANTAGE: she spoke only broken bits of English. And even in Chinatown, a world of English surrounded us. Mother could identify store-bought Canadian goods by the colour and design of packages—by the pictures of a kerchiefed black woman or a smiling Quaker man—or by the smell. If she encountered a problem, and we were by ourselves, she asked me to read aloud the words I knew, and the sounds I spoke she understood. I would recognize the first word as Aunty Freda taught me, and knew what the two o's in the next word meant.

"Chicken *Noooo*-dle," I said, handing her the can.

Mother began to depend upon me.

Father seemed to approve of my English vocabulary. He could speak enough English to work on the ships as Head Chef, supervising men who spoke only Chinese or only English, and he could read work orders, study recipes, write out stock inventories. At home, Father printed out menu words on lined CPR paper without making any spelling mistakes. As for me, I revelled in the new words I could now decipher.

My English world, however, centred around the boyish images of Hollywood. Nothing Chinese could save me. I saw cowboys everywhere. I collected cowboy comics. And when I chose a bedtime book, it was always an English-language book, and some of my babysitters even read them aloud to me. I pointed at words and saw how they meant something, and how certain letters, such as *a* or *o*, were vowel sounds. Then I repeated their sounds. I could not do that with Chinese characters, however much I stared at them.

Soon, Chinatown began to fade, like a ghost. I was turning into a banana: yellow on the outside and white on the inside.

Many nights, I dreamed I was sitting tall in the saddle, posed heroically on a rearing palomino, speaking English words I pronounced perfectly: my face glowing like moonlight, my eyes gunsmoke-grey, my cowboy hand waving a cowboy farewell—to silk, to jade, and, most of all, to boring arias.

## Seven

*Cowboy
ambitions*

**M**OTHER WAS NOT FAZED BY having a cowboy for a son. If she had any concerns about me, and of course she must have had a few, she seems to have mostly ignored them. At least, I don't remember many signs that I was troubling her.

Mother had been doing with me what I needed to do, that is, doing things mostly my way. Left by myself to play in my own make-believe cowboy world, I was as good as gold, though not always well mannered. Grandfather Choy King, who had his Second Wife and his own grown-up family in Victoria, helped Mother to instruct me whenever he visited with us.

I remember my father's father very well, a well-built man with white hair who babysat me when he visited us, and always told me stories. On and off, from the time I was a baby, he was a part of our household. When we moved to the wooden house with the banistered porch that sat directly next door to the Good Shepherd Mission at 636 Keefer, he moved in with us, having suffered a number of strokes. Both buildings still stand today, though the church is now a Vietnamese one and the old porch now creaks when you step on it.

Of course, as a child, I never questioned why Grandfather eventually came to live with us permanently: he was just a part of my universe when he was there.

My earliest memory of Grandfather involved my toilet training, Old China style. I said I wanted to peepee. This time, instead of Mother picking me up and sitting me on the enamelled potty, she turned me over to the old man. Grandfather took me to the toilet, pulled down my pants, and began to demonstrate.

"Stand like this. Now do what I do."

I did what he did, and to our shared delight, our yellow streams crossed each other's, like duelling swords.

"Shake it like this," he said. "Good, that's what a grown-up boy does."

I don't remember that I was startled by any obvious discrepancies in size and proportion. The lesson was so simply and naturally taught to me that, when I ran out into the kitchen to tell Mother, I knew I had passed some kind of test.

"I did it just like Gung-Gung," I said to Mother, using her Chinese kinship reference, which meant *father-in-law*.

I might have more properly called Grandfather Choy *Ah-Yeh*, or the more affectionate *Yeh-Yeh*—which would indicate that he was my father's father. I called Grandfather *Gung-Gung* because I had always heard Mother call him *Ah-Gung*. Father did not seem to mind, nor did Grandfather Choy. At any rate, after that lesson with Gung-Gung, Mother seemed pleased that her son could now, along with all the other young cowboys of Chinatown, shoot straight.

SOME LESSONS MOTHER hadn't counted on.

One day, shy, benevolent Uncle Dai Kew took me to my first Wednesday matinée at the Beacon, the vaudeville theatre next to the Army and Navy store. I had just turned four. The small man heard that there was going to be a juggling clown, a magician, a dog-and-pony act—all perfect for children.

"Take the whole family," another bachelor friend had urged him. But Mother knew he sent most of his money back to Sunwui, and only had enough money to treat himself and me, so we walked down to the theatre on Hastings Street.

I came home in the late afternoon feverish with amazement. I told the family about a stage-wide chorus line of pretty birds, each one swaying in rhythm to the music.

"They were really all these ladies dressed up with feathers," I continued. "They waved big feathered fans and moved *like this.*" I waggled my behind happily. "*Boom! Boom! Boom!*"

Mother's eyes widened.

I went on, encouraged by her clear interest in my story: "Then all their feathers fell off!"

"And then," Grandfather wondered aloud, "what happened?"

"Oh," I said. "Uncle Kew told me they were all going to go and take a bath."

"Yes?" Mother wavered.

"Just three did," I went on. "In a bubble bath." Mother sat down. "Each lady had two big balloons stuck *here* and *here*!"

Grandfather said, "It must have been very, very pretty."

"Yes," I said. "Lots and lots of soap bubbles!"

I threw up my hands just like the three ladies did in the big bathtub and pretended to wash myself.

Uncle Kew, who had mixed up the theatre schedule, smiled shyly. Finally, he said to Mother, "Very clean show."

A CHILD'S CLEANLINESS and diet were two of the worries of China-town parents. Mother found excuses to scrub me silly or keep me away from dirt. There was always talk of whose child was sick and with what symptoms, and all childhood maladies were traced back to the dampness in the air, or to imbalances in the diet, between "hot" and "cold" foods. The children of my day were vulnerable to whooping cough, polio, tuberculosis, German measles, scarlet fever, chicken pox . . . and a few more mysterious disorders, such as epilepsy. I had had my share of perplexing fevers, endured a bout of whooping cough, suffered through German measles and chicken pox—nothing unusual. On most counts, I had survived these ailments rather comfortably.

Whenever I was ill, Uncle Dai Kew and my other guardian uncles brought me endless treats. Butterhorns, egg tarts and sugar-crusted ladyfingers from the B.C. Royal Café; steamed pork buns, honeyed dried fruit, chewy red ginger—all were intended to increase my strength. And some uncles even sat beside me and told me stories of Old China, about when they were boys themselves, and how, like warriors, they or a best friend fought off demon convulsions. Sometimes, in the midst of a boiling fever, a family ghost appeared and told them they would get well. They gave my mother plenty of advice.

"Wrap a hot towel around the boy's neck," one of the uncles instructed Mother, when I had a temperature, and another advised, when my cheeks were burning, "Sonny needs ice water."

Politely, Mother listened to—and ignored—the uncles' advice about hot and cold winds, and quietly set aside their offerings of mysterious root herbs, mustard plasters and powdered medicines. Instead, she listened seriously to the advice of other mothers, such as Aunty Freda, Leong Sim, and Mrs Jung, or other aunties, such as Dai Yee.

---

THE UNCLES OF MY childhood who helped to watch over me had wives and sons and daughters of their own back in China, to whom they faithfully sent money. And, from famine-plagued, war-torn China, family letters came back, begging for more. When I was seventeen, my friend Philip Mau told me about such a letter from the 1940s, a letter the Chinese Benevolent Association had discovered in the death-grip of a suicide.

"Husband, if you cannot send us more money," the letter read, "shall I sell our daughter?"

Philip's father had told him the story, to remind him to appreciate Canada and to study harder at school.

Many of the men made a life that held back the flood tides of their anger and frustration; but, for a few, the relentless poverty and the monotony of their lives turned deadly.

"Do you remember Lum Jing Bak?" I heard Mother's mah-jong ladies ask each other at Duck Moh's second-floor Pender Street apartment.

"Yes, yes," Mother replied.

"Dead," another voice said above the washing of the mah-jong tiles. "Found him in Hogan's Alley."

A sad clucking of tongues. A moment of silence. Tiles would be piled into "walls" for the next round.

"How?" Leong Sim finally asked.

Duck Moh put a finger to her lips and looked around. Everyone stared at me and Garson.

"Go play in the parlour," Duck Moh commanded.

In the parlour, she kept a box of toys for us children to play with. Garson and I stumbled off, having been given a few nickels by our mothers for us to plug into Duck Moh's illegal slot machine. One time, alone in the parlour with the hostess, Garson hit the jackpot, and Duck Moh told him he had broken the machine and took all the nickels away.

---

WHEN I WAS WELL, most of the uncles enjoyed the first hour or so of my company. After that, they didn't always bother to answer my repeated questions or let me climb on their backs, or pretend to chase me down the street. They grunted discouragingly and turned away, preferring to sit down and read their Chinese newspaper or slurp their tea.

When I had exasperated Uncle Lam, he made me sit down and listen to more stories about good and bad children. I quickly grew tired of his stories—the good children always came to a good end, and the bad to a wicked end, which made me suspicious. After all, in real life things seemed otherwise. Like bad Mr Woon, for example, who drank all the time and beat his family, but never seemed to suffer. Or his two oldest boys, who stomped down the street, pushed all us smaller kids aside, took our playthings and threw them into the road.

"Oh, you just have to wait," Uncle Lam told me when I brought up the Woon family. "Bad endings will come to bad people."

"What about good endings for good people, like you?" I asked. I knew he was waiting for his wife and two children to join him in Canada.

"I'm patient," Uncle Lam said.

He had already been patient for thirteen years.

———

THE UNCLES AND I ATE lunch at Chinatown cafés such as the White House Chop Suey; on the way from one corner to the next, we lingered in stores where they displayed toys, and dropped into grocery stores where they sold paper-wrapped, dried and salted plums or red ginger. One of my favourite places was Kwong Man Sang; I liked to smell the dried shrimp in the glass-covered bins, inspect the packages of red coin-shaped sugar candies, watch the clerks push scoops into barrels and tip weighed measures of seeds and spices into paper cones, and hear them sing-song the prices and tabulate with demon speed the totals on the clicking beads of an abacus. I also liked any general stores that sold stationery, like Lucky Star Drugs or Sun Lee Tobacco, where Uncle might pick up a free pencil stub for me, or even buy me a new pencil and a Five-Cent Big Tablet of notepaper.

Uncle Dai Kew always looked at the window at the Yucho Chow Photo Studio on Main Street to see who had had their picture taken recently. He was saving his money to have his picture taken to send back to China. It was not the picture that would cost so much, it was the business suit he wanted to buy to be properly dressed for the photo. The backgrounds were always so modern, as if you were standing before the archway of a new bank building, and not one of the narrow and dark doorways of Chinatown. With a proper dark suit, one could appear physically filled out, look Gold Mountain prosperous, however little he might have.

At other times, with other uncles, after the *Movietone News*, three cartoons and a cowboy movie at the Rex or the Lux, I would sit at soda fountains and have Boston cream pie or ice cream, or both.

Father and Mother must have picked my uncles carefully and well.

Once Father found out from a friend that I had been selfish and demanding when I was with one of my uncles. Father came home that night and took away the Dinky car, the Three Pigs puzzle blocks, the Roy Rogers colouring book and the box of crayons I had been given that day, and locked them up in his trunk. Mother stood in the doorway and watched. I smelled whisky on Father's breath.

"You don't deserve to be given anything," he scolded. "I'm sending these toys to a good boy who lives in China."

Too bad for him, I thought, for I had snatched one of the puzzle blocks when Father wasn't looking. Being good did not mean you were going to get everything. I tried hard not to cry.

I could see that my parents, exhausted from their own labours and wanting some rare time to themselves, were grateful and happy that others might take an interest in me, but Father was always sensitive about how I behaved. I was not to shame him or Mother. As for Mother, she was mostly worried about my pants being clean ones, or long enough.

ON MY MANY OUTINGS with Third Uncle, who was a blood rela-
tive to us, what I hated most, what I fought against, was being
forced to wear extra layers of clothes, whatever the weather.
Then, the battle lines would be drawn. Mother would hold up in
front of me short pants or long trousers made of a heavy, coarse
material—the dreaded "pricklies": Irish tweed.

Irish tweed was a material that every Chinatown mother invested
in because it would, they reassured each other, keep out harmful
draughts. And the iron-like material seemed to outlast anything else.

"Hides the dirt," they said of the salt-and-pepper pattern. "Very
easy to mend; no matter white or black thread."

Irish tweed was sensible, I heard the women tell each other, an
investment. It was *hoa kim, very practical.* A good bargain. A buy.
In the long run, anything *hoa kim* saved you money, hid the dirt,
saved you washing and mending time. Worth the extra dollars.

The Irish tweed at that time was a stiff, coarse, sandpaper-like
fabric that scratched sensitive skin like mine. At the very idea of
being forced to wear the abhorred *pricklies,* my bony legs would
flinch, as if menaced by a million mosquitoes. Coarse wartime
wool sweaters were bad enough, but Irish tweed was the worst.
Mother never understood this. She always bought new itchy
clothes that I would, as she put it, "grow up to fit into"—that is,
one, two, even three, sizes too large. You could always tell who
was wearing new clothes: baggy bum, rolled-up sleeves, and
rolled-up cuffs were the hallmarks of a Chinatown kid's first-
season wardrobe. All the poorer Chinatown families followed this
rule. *Buy larger, save more.* It was a credo.

---

WITH THIRD UNCLE, MOTHER felt that wearing the very best
clothes was the rule. She always wanted to impress him, because

he would write back to family in China how we were doing in Gold Mountain. That meant my having to wear my *pricklies*.

Third Uncle himself always wore a Windsor-knotted tie with a starched white shirt. Over this, on warm days, he proudly wore a slightly frayed pinstriped jacket; on cooler days, he wore an equally frayed plain black suit, and, in winter, one of Irish tweed with a dark vest. A gold watch-chain hung elegantly from a small pocket. In summer, if it was too hot, he took off his jacket and exposed metal armbands that held his shirt sleeves at exactly the right length. His clothes were meticulously clean; his oxford shoes, bright. He told Mother that his kitchen assistants on the ship took pride in polishing them, making them as shiny and reflective as the ship captain's own pair. Third Uncle wore a simple Burmese-jade ring on his right hand. It gleamed like green fire. Something else shone—the seat of his pants, buffed with wear—and the pleats, like Father's, were razor-sharp. He wore a gentleman's hat, too, a pheasant feather sitting on the brim like a tiny butterfly's wing.

Unlike Father, who smelled of Yardley's lotion when he dressed up, Third Uncle could never quite get rid of the smell of flour and baked cookies that clung to him. Perhaps it was because he always brought with him bags of CPR tea biscuits, a tin of heavy pound cake, broken bread rolls and scones, all booty from his labours as Head Cook on the steamships. The stale bread and hard scones we would take to Lost Lagoon and tear up to throw to the ducks.

Third Uncle always took particular care not to spot or stain his clothes. For example, at the Hong Kong Café, when we sat down to share one of their popular deep-crust meat pies—a fist-sized creation sopped over with an oozing brown gravy and loads of mashed potatoes—Third Uncle always unfolded extra paper napkins to tuck over his shirt front. He handed me a couple.

"Do this," he said. And I jammed the corner of the napkins just beneath my neck and patted everything down.

"Stop scratching yourself," he ordered. I couldn't stop—it was the Irish tweed. But Third Uncle would not do anything until I ignored the itching.

Finally, with me sitting still at last, he would carefully slice into the pie, which burst open to display steaming thick cubes of beef, slippery carrots, green peas, and chunks of potato. A portion would be spooned onto a bread plate for me. Wary of a six-year-old's awkward ways with a fork, especially as the main meal was dripping with gravy, Third Uncle would lift up his own plate and shift one counter seat away from me. On the empty seat between us, he would place his fedora on top of my sweater or jacket. On top of the fedora, he would put down, tent-style, his *Chinese Times*.

"Bad news is useful for something," he would unfailingly say. And the waiter always laughed, hoping for his nickel tip. It was customary to tip if you split a dish with anyone, but otherwise no one felt obliged. I ate as much as I could, but always conscious of Father's instructions on how to use a fork properly, and always aware of Third Uncle's watchful eyes.

When Uncle indulged in a rare ice cream, he bent his head over the cone and licked away like a long-necked bird with eye-glasses perched on its beak, so that any drips would fall away from him. A few times his glasses would fall off, too. But that was the least of his worries. Third Uncle was an immaculate gentleman.

Other bachelor-men uncles struck me as less of a nuisance to be with. Others were less bossy, less mannerly, less careful, and, thus, more fun. Yet Third Uncle was always given top priority if he asked to spend his free day with me. When I complained, Mother said, "He's your father's direct and oldest relation."

Which meant, of course, that Third Uncle would be sending back to our China family his latest reports and conclusions about us.

As a child, I accepted without question that Third Uncle had priority in our family. He had, after all, lots of white hair, just as Grandfather had. He was a man in his late forties, but, to me, ancient.

I was always warned to be on my best behaviour. Third Uncle had complained that I was stubborn, like Father.

"Respect Third Uncle," Mother said. "Do what he says. Otherwise, you come home and Father teach you respect."

Father could stare at me harshly, look disappointed, shout my name, bang his fist down on the kitchen table, and I would crumble. He never once hit me, but his theatrics were enough to cause my lips to quiver, tears to fall.

I could understand respect. No one, not even Father, had to teach me *that*. All the children of Chinatown had absorbed the Confucian respect for elders. You especially respected those who were older than your own father or mother.

To Third Uncle, day off was a time to show the world that you were well employed. No matter how you might have sweated and wiped your brow the rest of the time, to dress well and appear well off was to keep to a standard set by the merchants and leaders of Chinatown. Many of the steady-working men of Chinatown, Father included, dressed in Sunday-best suits whether their day off fell on Sunday or not. It became the rule.

My once- or twice-a-month outings with Third Uncle may have been a trip to the Stanley Park Zoo, a walk along English Bay, or a leisurely stroll through Chinatown. Mother did not care where we went as long as I dressed respectably.

"You dress up," Mother commanded. "You don't want to let people think you have *mo li, no manners.*"

Of course, I know now that *mo li* meant much more than "no manners." It meant having no *Confucian* manners. Being *mo li* branded someone as having no sense of the Right Way or Right Behaviour—the *Tao*. Having *mo li*, you were marked as someone ignorant and crude; in short, you were someone destined to fail in life, fated to become life's fool. A loser. A bum.

I would rather wear torn overalls, scuffed boots and a cowboy hat than my Sunday best. But my protests meant nothing to Mother. Even if the day was definitely too hot for any normal boy to be putting on tweed pants and a starched shirt over an undershirt, as long as I was dressing to go out with Third Uncle, I had to submit. I was a boy destined to die of heat exhaustion.

———

I WAS A STRONG-WILLED child, as quick as Father to set off temperamental fireworks. On a second's notice, I could lie flat on the floor, screaming, gasping for air, hands flailing, feet kicking, and, as quickly, I could hold back my last sniffles and be absolutely, peacefully, absorbed in whatever I had decided to do. I ruled and lived by the Spoiled Child's Credo: Let me do what I want to do—*or else!*

Mother was desperate for peace. She came home exhausted from her daily work at the Chinese sausage factory, too weary to battle my tantrums, and she barely set any limits on my behaviour, except to demand that I be polite and remember to say *please* and *thank you.* Most everyone else who took care of me during Mother's work shifts eventually discovered what she had come to accept: if Sonny was left alone to amuse himself with a few toys, he was mostly quiet. It was an introverted child's perfect paradise; except, of course, when I didn't get my way.

Fifth Aunty tells me Mother was both cowed by my strong-willed nature and trapped by her fatigued desire to avoid any fussing and fidgeting with a five-year-old.

"You weren't a bad boy, Sonny," Aunty Freda tells me. "Just a stubborn one."

By the time I was born, Mother was thirty-eight and Father, forty-two. They carried within themselves the ominous stories of Chinatown children who had succumbed to whooping cough, measles, deadly consumption, pneumonia... or who had stopped breathing from no known cause at all. Almost every family Mother and Father knew had lost one, two, or even three children, often before the child reached age four.

Some Chinatown children, as I later discovered, were barely tolerated, sexually abused, beaten, even starved. Of these sad victims—the children who were traded, "adopted," or bought with cash to be raised as family servants; the unwanted girl-children; and the children of parents who were themselves beaten or abused as children, and who then repeated the same oppressions upon their own flesh—the darkest personal histories have rarely been recorded. Fifth Aunty did whisper a few tales to me, of her neighbour's two-year-old son who died of starvation, of the niece who would not let her uncle come near her and finally killed herself...

"Oh, plenty reason to kill yourself in those days," Fifth Aunty said, then threw her head back and broke into laughter. "Plenty, too, to make you go cuck-oo!"

When I mentioned how I resented Father being away so often when I was a child, she slapped my arm.

"Your poor father away! Why not?! Everyone *work, work, work*— or starve to death! Go crazy with working! All the good your mother and father do for you! They never hurt you once—no one ever hurt you!"

Fifth Aunty looked like she would throw her cup of tea at me.

"No, no, no," I protested, "don't be upset, Aunty! I'm just saying I understand all that now."

"Ahh, of course!" Aunty put her cup down, clucked her tea-moistened tongue. "Slow learner!"

FIFTH AUNTY WAS RIGHT.

In fact, I can recall only three incidents that gave me night-mares. These were part of the misadventure of growing up, slightly traumatic events when, ironically, the disciplined child might have unwittingly taught the adults a lesson—except that things went very wrong.

The first time I was terrorized was at the David Lee household. The two Lee sisters had been taking care of me and their toddling baby brother in the dining-room that afternoon. Their mother, Leong Sim, and my mother were out visiting a neighbour. Two-year-old Garson fell asleep, exhausted, and was put into his portable crib. I was four, disdainful of naps.

When our two mothers came home, Lil and Shirley cheerfully left me. I protested, but Mother ignored me. I needed company and decided to wake up Garson. I tugged at his pillow. He stirred. I pulled at his blanket. Mother told me to stop.

"You're his *dai goh*, Sonny," Leong Sim said. "You're his *big brother*."

I pushed against the crib, rocking it. Mother came for me, her eyes narrowed with fury. I threw myself flat on the floor, kicking and screaming.

Well-meaning Leong Sim—who truly cared about me—decided to scare me into good behaviour with a smelly, mum-mified black bear paw. Eventually to be boiled and used for medicinal purposes, the gnarled, tuft-jointed body part—three times the size of a large man's hand—now served a more omi-nous purpose. In the Lee house, everyone was aware of the deformed bear extremity that hid waiting in the pantry, waiting to crawl out to scare bad children into good behaviour. Leong Sim had used this trick on all her children, even on two-year-old

Garson. But he was fast asleep when I, his *"big brother,"* started to behave badly.

Leong Sim got up and went into her kitchen pantry and came back with a sinister-looking parcel. Sheets of butcher paper fell to the floor like crumpled wings. Leong Sim suddenly floated a flattened, yellowish paw in front of my defiant four-year-old face.

"The demon *bearrRRRR* is going to get you!" she cried.

When I could make out the dark tufts of hair, the menacing claws, coming towards me, I jumped away from Garson's crib and darted under the dining-room table. I screamed and kicked with unstoppable terror, and clutched at the table base, refusing to let go.

Finally, both Leong Sim and Mother ended up on their knees, begging me to come out from under the ten-seater table. From his crib, Garson started to cry, which inspired me to double my volume. The two mothers both reached down; one unclenched my fingers while the other attempted to drag me out by the shoulders. With Garson now sitting up and screaming as well, his fists hitting the air, and with me kicking away, Leong Sim and Mother looked overwhelmed. Pulling me out at last, the two women began to hyperventilate.

Leong Sim lifted Garson up, opened her blouse, and put him to her breast. Eyes wide with gratification, Garson immediately calmed down. The bear paw was nowhere to be seen.

After about five minutes, when I had recovered, I was given honey water to drink and promised a double-scooped ice-cream cone if I would only stop gasping and promise to be a good boy. I gulped back tears and tried my best. Pressed against Mother, I could hear her heart pounding.

"Don't stop breathing," Leong Sim told her. "Keep breathing."

THE SECOND TIME THINGS went wrong, we had been invited to Choy-Gut Moh's for dinner. We were to visit our bloodline cousin's Winter's Hotel, a rooming hotel near the docks in Gastown managed by old Choy-Gut Moh and her family.

I was about four years old. We were having dinner with our cousins when trouble exploded. During the afternoon at home, while I played with my toys, my parents had been shouting at each other. Doors were slammed. That evening, as I sat at Choy-Gut Moh's steaming dish-laden table, the all-day tensions that had boiled over between Mother and Father irked me and I grew restless.

Mother may have let me skip my nap that day. Whatever the reason, I was short-circuiting; I could not stop whining or kicking my feet against the table leg. The dishes shook. Unfamiliar spicy greens, odd meat concoctions, and a creamy soup confounded me; I nagged for familiar foods. The chicken pieces were a raw, slippery pink, which was the degree of doneness our hosts believed to be ideal for fowl. I remember old Choy-Gut Moh lifted a translucent wing onto my plate, but I could not eat it. Mother was not touching her chicken piece, either. Father sat simmering.

"What do you want?" Choy-Gut Moh finally asked me in her nicest Toisanese. "I get you whatever you want, Sonny."

"*Ngoh fan kay,*" I said. "*I go home.*"

With Mother having to save face, and Father having lost his temper, I was yanked from my chair and hastily told we were leaving.

Outside the Winter's Hotel, I refused to walk. Father snatched me up and flagged down a taxi. I bit my lip. Mother took me from him and I began to cry.

When we arrived home, Father, shaking with fury, tossed me into our cluttered hall closet and slammed the door. In the black well of the closet, I threw myself frantically against the door, and pushed with all my might. With Father leaning on the other side, the door wouldn't budge. I rammed the inside door knob with my head and fell whimpering, huddling, crying out for Mother. The bump was hard enough to open a gash in my head. When I licked my lips, I tasted salty tears mingled with the odd flavour of iron.

After a few minutes, Father opened the door. He and Mother nearly collapsed when they saw my bloodied face. Like a Chinese orchestra, their wailing and my sobbing see-sawed back and forth, accompanied by Father's yanking me out of the closet amid the clatter of broom handles and knocked-over storage bins. He dropped me into Mother's open arms and ran into the kitchen to wet a cloth with water. I shook my head, scattering the blood. Mother's dress was ruined.

Finally, Father calmed himself down, turned off the tap, then came back and gingerly wiped my forehead with his damp handkerchief. He expertly gauged the wound on my head. It was a deep scratch, but not a long one. He sighed and got up off his knees.

By the time I stopped crying, Mother had carried me over to a chair beside the dining-room table. My fingers felt the two small bandages and the cotton batting Father had arranged over my forehead, then accepted a glass of cold milk from our icebox and a cookie from the pantry. No one said a word.

With his tie unknotted, Father sat, collapsed, across from us, his legs sprawled out. He poured out a shot of Hennessy, lifted the thick-bottomed glass and threw back his head. Mother closed her eyes, as if she were praying with each sip of her dark tea. The clock on our mantel chimed the half-hour. No one promised me ice cream, but I promised aloud to be a good boy.

For years thereafter, the Bear Paw and the Shut Closet clung to my worst childhood nightmares. I would wake up sweating and find Mother standing over me, lifting me up.

"Indigestion," Mother explained. Only after Mother hugged me and held me against her warmth, slowly rocking my damp body, would I finally calm down. Then she and Father, if he was home, would turn on the light and stay with me until I eventually drifted back to sleep. If Father tried to come too near me, I pushed him away. I never thought that I would ever push Mother away.

———

IN THE FALL OF 1944, when I was getting used to being five years old, a third fearful experience overtook me. Without any warning or preparation, I was separated from Mother and left among strangers in what seemed to me to be a House of Death.

It was all Mother's fault. She didn't like the idea of being away from me or leaving me with strangers. She preferred to have me close by her, banging on the kitchen pots and pans, swinging wooden swords at phantom warriors, or shooting toy guns at bad cowboys and Indians. In fact, after Mother helped me to throw flannel sheets over chairs and tables, I would crawl into caves of yellowish light and play Make Believe for hours while she busied herself with cooking or cleaning.

Inside those hallowed tunnels, like the matinée magician at the Empress Theatre, who asked himself which hat he should reach into, I sang and talked, outlined plans, and even argued over them:

". . . hide in the cave and wait for the Indians to come."
"No, don't do that."
" . . . climb up onto the chair and shoot at the robbers."
"No, it's Tarzan's tree house!"

I had a rousing vocal William Tell Overture down pat, climaxing with drum rolls on Mother's stock pot. And when I played Tarzan and jumped from chair to chair, bellowing out a hearty Tarzan yell, the parlour windows rattled. Sometimes I sang my version of cowboy songs, sitting on the porch banister, half-inventing with my voice the plunking sounds of a guitar.

"Way Sun should join the kindergarten," Fifth Aunty said.

Mother told Aunty that she was—we were—doing fine. I overheard Mother tell old Choy-Gut Moh and her other friends over the mah-jong table how she couldn't bear the thought of my being left at the mercy of total strangers.

"Way Sun's not a baby," Third Uncle said. "What about school later on?"

"Of course, Way Sun's got to start somewhere," Father agreed. "He's old enough."

Since summer, there had been pressures put on Mother to let me join the kindergarten class held at the United Church Chinese Mission at 447 Dunlevy, at the corner of East Pender, just a block north of Keefer, where we lived. Other children of the same age were already attending.

Fifth Aunty remarked to Mother it wasn't too healthy for a boy to spend so much time by himself, talking to himself under blankets, shooting caps, and yodelling so miserably.

"Sonny should go," Father said. "He should play more with other children."

It was the third week of September, and the Chinese Mission classes started after Labour Day.

Father asked, "Has Way Sun registered yet?"

Mother ignored the question and recited a list of groceries Father was to pick up in Chinatown.

Aunty Freda and Grandfather had lunch with us one weekday,

and, after noticing how I had been home all day, Grandfather said, "A boy can't get enough schooling."

"Sonny will like kindergarten," Aunty Freda said.

But I wasn't sure what everyone was talking about. Being an only child, I was aware only of the big kids' Strathcona School a block away from our house. Mother, however, heard from her shopping and mah-jong friends, too.

"Sonny should have started kindergarten by now, Choy Sim," Mrs Lim said to Mother. "You should have more time to do other things. Clean up the house."

"Catch up on sleep," Betty Lee said.

Finally, Fifth Aunty offered to sign the church papers for Mother. She checked off "Christian" on the registration form and read out to Mother what she had neatly printed in block letters nearby: "PROTESTANT." That, Fifth Aunty explained to Mother and me, was what we were on paper. This was strange to me: we had always been *Chinese*-something before. It was also strange because neither Mother nor I could ever have pronounced the multisyllable word giving us our new paper identity.

"If anyone asks about religion, you and Sonny just say *'Church!'*," Fifth Aunty said. "And, Choy Sim, be sure to pay them the monthly fee."

With everyone pestering her to send me off to kindergarten, Mother's resistance finally shut down. One day she claimed she needed to clean the parlour and kitchen, and I could help her. We put the dented utensils back into the pantry, and packed the stick swords, the toy guns and the old sheets in boxes, which Father carried to the basement. The limits of my opportunity to be left alone to amuse myself had been reached.

# Eight

*Graduation day,*
*Chinese Mission*
*Kindergarten*

ON A BRIGHT SEPTEMBER morning, Mother woke me up, scrubbed me clean in our large galvanized basin, made me dry myself and dress in my best short pants and cowboy suspenders. I thought one of my Chinatown uncles was coming to take me out. My hair was parted in the middle, daubed with Father's brilliantine and brushed down flat on both sides.

I ate my porridge. Drank my milk. No uncle arrived.

"After you take this," Mother said, "you're going someplace."

Under my nose rose the brown-bottled smell of Fisherman's Cod Liver Oil, an oozing *guck* mixed with honey.

"Open up," Mother said. "Get it over with quickly."

The taste of sweet grease coated my tongue. I twisted my face, choked, gagged, pretended I was going to throw up. I hated the stuff.

"Stop it," Mother said. "Don't you want to grow up tall and strong?"

I made another face.

"Face get stuck," Mother exclaimed. "Then who will marry you!"

She adjusted my suspenders, then said what she always said: "Have to get you new pants soon."

Still no uncle showed up; not even one of the favourite aunties arrived. Instead, Mother changed into her best flower-print dress, put on her below-the-knee russet coat and picked up her best going-out purse. Together, we walked out of the house into the morning light. A chilly wind, smelling of fresh mountain snow, blew against us, lifting up my chocolate-brown corduroy jacket.

"Where we go?" I asked in English. Mother could speak only a few words in English, and only if she had to. She stayed mysteriously silent, then lightly brushed her cheek against mine, leaving behind the flowery scent of Florida Water. I said, in Chinese, "Why we rushing?"

Mother said. "*Kint-ter-gart-ten.* School."

I had no idea what she was talking about. School, I knew, was for those giant kids who threw balls at wooden bats and carried books in school bags or satchels. School was not for small kids like me. My older playmate Tommy Cheong told me that, before I could go to Strathcona, I had to grow at least another four or five inches, like him. When he first saw my foldaway cot, he looked seriously worried for me.

"You can't grow any taller if you sleep in a rinky-dinky bed like that," he warned me. "You'll cramp up."

That made perfect sense to me. Mother was always getting me bigger shoes so my feet would grow into them, and larger-size clothes, too.

"I want a bigger bed," I said, out of the blue. Mother ignored me.

We turned the corner on Keefer, walked north along Dunlevy and crossed Pender East. Mother stopped in front of the basement entrance of the United Church Chinese Mission. Bits of glass pressed into the grey stucco walls of the church building sparked in the sunlight. To our right, a criss-crossed slat fence blocked off a parcel of lawn. Mother took a deep breath.

I thought we would walk past the place, as we had always done before. My mind, for the moment, was focused on how I could get a bigger bed. When I tugged at her arm, Mother refused to move.

The chilly, late-September wind rattled some papers in the corner formed by the meeting of two impassive walls; a whirl of trapped dust and grit rose into the air. My mind buzzed with secrets. *Lots of ghosts in churches,* Uncle Gee had told me. *Ghosts with wings.* Mother took another deep breath. She pulled me towards a darkly painted door. Our footsteps echoed.

Now it was my turn to take a deep breath. I tried to hold Mother back, but it was too late; we slipped through a thickly panelled door that opened soundlessly.

Walking by this church many times with my uncles and aunts, I had observed boxes of dead people being carried up its steep steps. As a wooden box went by us, my uncles always took their hats off, while my aunts hushed me up. Then, if there was a Chinese person standing near us, my uncles or aunts would ask in a dramatic whisper, "*Who* this time?"

I had witnessed lots of boxes enter the churches around Chinatown, but I'd never seen a single one leave.

Once inside, Mother and I stood before a long hallway, with a small office to the right of us. The place smelled of old books and repellent lye soap. I peered through a partially opened doorway, on the other side of the hallway, into a large room: children—*dead children*—were sitting in two semicircles, awkwardly clapping hands to the rhythm of an unseen piano.

I glimpsed a long table at the end of the hall, in front of a set of water taps, and saw a huge metal sink that a child's body could neatly slip into. I guessed dead bodies were placed on that long table after they had been washed in the sink.

A white-haired ghost lady came out of the office to greet us. She smiled and spoke a strange Chinese dialect with Mother. A dead dialect, I guessed. She called out, in English, "Mrs Montgomery!" and a tall, dark-haired ghost lady suddenly emerged from the big room. Some of the dead children turned their heads to see what was going on.

I gripped Mother's hand.

"Go with the nice lady," Mother said in Toisanese. She thanked the older lady with the broad smile, a Mrs Car-car, or so I thought Mother had called her. A shadow crossed over me. The tall Mrs Montgomery had a broad white face, the face of a *bak kwei*.

I clung to Mother's coat. The dead children were now singing a song. I looked between the two white ghosts and could not find one mother, or even a father, there. Only children.

I remembered from my uncles' stories that dead people's bodies felt cold as ice.

"All dead things go cold," Dai Bak told me.

"Yes, yes, dead chickens go into iceboxes," Uncle Dai Kew said, "and dead people go into churches."

"*And the naughty children who die,*" Dai Bak warned me when I was misbehaving one day, "*are always taken away from their mothers and fathers.*"

THE CHINATOWN CHURCHES were where The Dead went. I knew that. I was not fooled by the white-haired lady's pleasant chatter with Mother. The tall lady, Mrs Montgomery, reached for my hand again. Her fingertips felt cold, like ice. I snatched my hand from hers and held on to Mother's fingers with all my might.

I stared wide-eyed at the dark, wainscotted hallway, the sombre walls of a giant coffin. I took a deep breath. The church smelled of disinfectant, the kind used at the Chinese sausage factory.

I tugged at Mother to pick me up and take me away, but I could not speak. The two fair-skinned ghosts had taken away my voice.

"I'm Mrs McCargar, Sonny," the old, white-haired ghost said. She touched the top of my head. "This is the boy we've been expecting, Mrs Montgomery. This is Sonny Choy."

"Come with me, Sonny Choy," the tall, younger lady ghost said. "You'll see your mother at lunchtime."

She smiled to try and fool me into letting go of Mother's hand. I began to cry and gripped even harder. She winced.

"Oh my, oh my." Mrs Montgomery shook her head gently. "*Ooooohhh*-my."

The old ghost looked disappointed and said in a resolute formal Cantonese, "You better leave, Mrs Choy. We'll take care of Sonny."

Mrs McCargar doggedly unclenched my fingers from Mother's hand, and Mother quickly scrambled out the door, hiding her eyes.

"She'll be back," Mrs Montgomery said.

I was too shocked to speak. Mother had run out on me: I was... *dead*... in the hallway of a strange neighbourhood church. As *dead* as a chicken in an icebox.

The two ghost-ladies each took one of my hands, then gripped my elbows and dragged me backwards, heels scraping the floor, into the big room, where all the other dead children silently watched us.

I resisted, pulled back, struggled in the women's clutches with all my might, but it was no use. They were two grown-up ghosts, and I was one dead child. I didn't have a chance.

Mrs McCargar left the room. I twisted my head around to see if Mother was gone. Instead, the old-lady ghost smiled back at me, her wide grey eyes shiny with tears, her hair a glowing halo. I turned my head and saw large drawings crayoned on butcher paper and tacked up on the walls: pictures of ghost-children with big balloon heads, large empty circles where they once had eyes. And some of the elongated bodies had wings jutting out where arms used to be. The piano stopped playing. *Dead piano.* I put my hands to my ears, collapsed on the floor, and screamed.

"Leave him alone for now," a voice said from the hallway. "Mrs Choy won't be back until noon."

I kicked and flailed and pounded my fists on the cold, unfeeling floor. Then the piano began again. The lifeless children turned their heads away from me and began a rhythmic clapping. Next, they stood up and did London Bridge. Then Patty-Cake. Then they sang another song, about a teapot, *short and stout.*

Even when I lifted my head from the crook of my arm, no one paid any attention to me. I was an exhausted, dripping-nosed mess. As I peeked out through a triangle of light, I thought of the long table at the end of the hall on which my body would soon lie.

"Playtime," the Chinese lady at the piano announced.

Boys and girls broke up into groups and some sat down at child-size tables covered with colourful books of all kinds; other kids sprawled on the floor with toys. Toys and books and games were everywhere.

"Do you want to play?" a voice said to me.

It was a boy's voice. I wiped my nose with my sleeve and turned my head. A boy in short pants sat down on the floor beside me. He had a box of wooden picture blocks. Spilling them near my head, he held up one of the blocks. I could make out a square of cartoon colours.

"You have to make a picture out of this," the boy said.

I had blocks just like that at home. The Three Little Pigs. The Three Bears. Little Jack Horner. Aunty Freda and Fifth Aunty had told me all the stories, over and over again. I lifted my head. The block the boy held up had what looked like a cowboy hat on one side.

"You can go first," the boy said. "My name's Larry." His tone was matter-of-fact. "You're Sonny."

I sat up and took the block. Then I rubbed my eyes and began to search for its match.

"Welcome to Chinese Mission Kindergarten, Sonny Choy," said the Chinese lady from her piano seat. "I'm Miss Lowe."

She held a tissue to my nose. I blew: my cowboy picture needed only one more block to finish. *There.* A lone wrangler sat on his horse, looking out at a desert sun.

The boy named Larry was now busy with another set of blocks he had taken from a shelf beside me. City pictures. Fire trucks. A toy store. We switched blocks, so that human and animal heads and feet were mismatched. A horse ended up with a pig's head. A lopped-off fireman sat on the back of a cow. We began to laugh.

"Do this," I said, and began to build a wall using both sets of blocks.

My new friend Larry put the last block on top. The structure was perilously tall. A little girl stomped by and the castle wall fell down, but I didn't care. I was distracted by another set of blocks sitting on the shelf near me. Larry and I could build an even higher one, and watch it come tumbling down, too. The Chinese lady at the piano suddenly struck a tinkling tune, then a rumbling one.

It was "clean-up" time.

"Hurry. It's story time," Larry said. "Put everything in the right boxes."

Mrs Montgomery clapped her hands and told us to get into our places. I followed Larry and we joined a semicircle seated around a felt-covered board. The first story was about an ugly duckling. A cut-out felt duck was stuck onto the board. "*Quack, quack,*" the duck said. At the end of the story, like magic, the ugly duck turned into a beautiful swan with outspread wings. A sad story turned out to be a happy one. I leaned back.

In the silence, I heard the North Shore wind rattling the windows above our heads. Dead leaves stirred and chattered beneath the panes. Ghosts were trying to get in. But I hardly noticed. Mrs Montgomery picked out some other felt cut-outs from a discreetly covered carton: *Another story!*

The second story was about a little boy named Daniel. Three lion-shapes in Mrs Montgomery's hand *grrrow*led menacingly onto the felt board. The lions turned out to be harmless, because, at the last second, just as the lions were opening up their massive jaws to gobble up the boy, a ghost with wings came down from Heaven.

"*An angel!*" Larry said aloud.

"Yes, an angel came down from Heaven," Mrs Montgomery said, and her eyes lit up. "Heaven, as you know boys and girls, is a beautiful place high, high up in the sky."

The tall woman serenely looked up and raised her hands into the air.

"God is everywhere, children, and he heard Daniel's prayers and sent an angel down from the sky."

Mrs Montgomery's hands slowly lowered, moving delicately like angel wings; then, her quick fingers pulled shut the hungry lion's jaws. Having saved Daniel from the savage beasts, the angel flew back up into the air, to Heaven, high above all our heads, higher than the sky itself.

"Let us all close our eyes, children," Miss Lowe said. "Let us pray: 'Our Father, who art in Heaven...'"

Fifth Aunty had told me that there were helpful ghosts called "angels." They flapped their wings and sat on clouds way up in the sky, and at Christmas stood on the very top of evergreen trees in Woodward's store windows.

I was surprised to learn that the Christian God could be every-where, too. At the sausage factory, the war-like Kitchen God, who was Chinese, surveyed his kingdom from the wall above the stove in the third-floor scullery; the Warrior God stayed trapped in the stained placard, until, with burning incense and a flaring match, Mr Wing torched the poster. Around the New Year, in a spiral of smoke and flames, the Kitchen God was set free.

Mrs Lowe clapped her hands for attention. She read aloud the words of a song we were to sing. Mrs Montgomery repeated the words slowly. The piano rang out. We sang:

"*Gee-sus luv mee, yet I no, four dee by-bull till mee sew . . .*"

I was having so much fun that, by lunchtime, when Mother came back to get me, I forgot that I had been dead.

———

"YOU WERE A GOOD BOY?" Mother took me to the back of the hall to talk to me. The other children were rushing about, grabbing their coats. I didn't feel like talking to Mother.

When Mother finished tucking my shirt into the back of my

pants, her arms tightened around me for a hug. I stepped out of her reach.

"See you tomorrow morning, Sonny Choy," Mrs Montgomery called out to me above the laughter of other children greeting their mothers and fathers, uncles and aunts.

I said nothing. I was busy wondering how high and wide a castle wall *ten* sets of picture blocks would build.

Mother held up my jacket. I jabbed my hands through the sleeves, pushed away from her, and made my way through the chattering crowd. As Mother struggled into her coat, her purse entrapping her arm, I saw my chance: I dashed out onto the sidewalk and started running south on Dunlevy. The fresh air felt exhilarating. I filled my lungs, laughing at the sky; my feet kicked fallen chestnuts into the air.

Without looking left or right, I darted across Pender Street. Cars honked. Brakes screeched. There was shouting. I kept running, tinny children's voices fading behind my back.

Half a block along Dunlevy, I stopped to catch my breath and looked back at the church. Mrs Montgomery was frantically pointing me out.

I didn't care if there was going to be a spanking when I got home. I didn't care how hard the spanking would be. I ran and ran.

With my arms outstretched, both palms out, the brisk, nostril-burning wind ballooned the arms of my brown jacket. The sensation of floating, soaring, overwhelmed me. I pushed my feet harder and harder against the sidewalk, faster and faster; my lungs felt as if they would burst with fire.

Turning the corner and racing up Keefer Street, I caught sight of Mother's coat flapping, she, a separate, airborne creature; while I—before the gods whose names Mother shouted with surprising vigour—flew higher and higher, twisting into the boundless sky.

## Nine

*With Mah-ma*

THE WORLD WAS AT WAR, but here, enrolled in the Vancouver Chinese Mission Church, read to and cared for, I hardly
knew what any of that meant.

When rain clouds passed across the mid-morning sun, sending
spears of light and shadow across our classroom, tossed smocks
became hunchbacks, and hanging coats gargoyles; on the highest
shelves, blue-eyed dolls and brown bears shifted their heads, eyes
turning. Lights were rarely switched on, due to wartime conserva-
tion. But no child minded. We were all intensely focused on the

cadence of Mrs Montgomery's reading aloud or the jaunty movements of Miss Lowe's piano fingers.

The stories we were told and the songs we sang together, of
the Good Jesus who loved us, and of the love of God and his
angels, made our spines contract, tingle; we shifted with skittish
glee. In our homes, we walked by grinning fat Buddhas, stared
back at the fierce God of Prosperity; we touched bald-headed
Longevity and rubbed his Peach of Long Life; our mothers said
prayers to Kwan-Yin, the Goddess of Mercy, who stood upon a
porcelain-white lotus flower. Our families burnt incense, bowed
three times, and, through fragrant haze, spoke directly to ancestral portraits; in our Tong Association halls, before life-size
bronze and gilt deities, our elders lit thick, red candles, bowed
and chanted prayers older than sorrow. This pantheon of spirits
didn't seem strange or foreign. No stranger than the Holy Ghost
or the Jesus who was born in a manger and died on a cross, and
who came back to life again. Ghost-talk was everyday Chinatown
talk. Spirits were everywhere.

Most of the gods, it seemed to me, were on our side. The Sunday school and kindergarten stories, the stories the elders told
me of the Monkey-King, or of the wily Fox Lady, or of Heavenly
Hosts, the tales told to me by Leong Sim and Fifth Aunty, occupied my mind as naturally as did the Cantonese opera stories
Mother whispered to me over and over again.

---

I GOT USED TO attending school, and was soon permitted, even
encouraged by Mrs McCargar, the kindergarten principal, to lug
home a couple of oversized, about-to-be-discarded children's
books, happily plundered from the nursery section. The soft covered books with the rows and rows of Chinese ideograms that the

elders read had never attracted me, nor did the thick textbooks pored over by my studious babysitters. Not until Mrs Montgomery opened those oversized picture-and-word volumes did I realize how much books could mean to me.

The kindergarten assortment was gratifying. When I got my hands on those books, stored upstairs in the church annex, everything about them fascinated me: their foot-and-a-half height and their heft; the stink of their pages, like mothy church dust; the nut-brown smudges smelling of soy sauce, and sometimes of spilt milk, soured by time. The books were mostly second and third hand, bequeathed to the United Church by congregations from as far away as Toronto. The volumes were destined for overseas English classes as soon as the war was over and the missionaries returned again to China to save pagan souls.

"We will go back," many of them told us in Sunday-school class.

After one of the Sunday-school classes I occasionally attended in the annex, Mrs McCargar noticed me in the almost deserted hallway, picking through a pile of torn covers and mauled pages destined to be picked up for the wartime paper drive. For some reason, Mother was late. I was among the last three or four children waiting to leave, but I was happily scavenging, lifting up bundles of printed matter to see what treasures might lay below—perhaps colourful pictures to tear out, or maybe even some comics.

"Don't touch those, Sonny," she said firmly.

I stood up, but sheepishly poked at the sagging pile with my shoe.

Her sharp eyes studied me for a moment. She called me over to the doorway. I stood at the entrance to a large office and looked inside at the stack of marked boxes of books. Mrs McCargar reached into one of the open boxes sitting beside a roll-top desk, pulled out two volumes and brought them over to me.

"These are yours to keep, Sonny Choy," she said.

I put my hand out.

Their covers were rich with promise, the corners dented, but the books felt solid, like a pirate's plunder. The first book cover showed little pigs dressed up in blue and white and red outfits, dancing around a brick house; the other, a smiling, chocolate-brown boy wearing a red jacket and short blue pants, carrying a green umbrella. From behind a jungle of trees, a tawny tiger hungrily stalked him. I stared hard.

"The little boy's name," Mrs McCargar said, "is Little Black Sambo."

Without hesitation, I told Mrs McCargar I knew the name of the other book. *The Three Little Pigs.*

"I can read that one," I said, meaning that I could retell the story from the pictures and, therefore, "read" the story. I put that one down and quickly flipped through the more intriguing volume.

I was unsettled: the second hardcover book had solid paragraphs of words on nearly every page. When there was just one large picture to give me any clues, how would I figure out that many words? How would I read the story to Mother?

I was truly stuck. A dark-skinned, broad-faced boy, looking the same size as me, stalked by tigers—how would I learn his story? I clutched the two books, leaned against the wall and sank onto my haunches. In the filtered light of the church hall, with the large *Three Little Pigs* on my lap serving as my desk, I opened the first book. Pages splashed with jungle colours enticed my eyes. There was a striped tiger wearing purple shoes on his ears . . . a tiger hungrily eyeing a little boy carrying a plateful of pancakes. . . .

When Mother finally arrived to get me, she spoke with Mrs McCargar. Lost in my speculations, I barely noticed them. I was trying to figure out why one particular tiger was wearing a red coat, and another blue pants. All at once, Mother's purse tapped heavily on my head. She made me stand up straight and say *Thank you* to Mrs McCargar, made me say it *twice*, as if the white lady were deaf. Being busy with my own deliberations, I suppose I might have just whispered. For sure, I resented Mother's rudeness.

Mother shook her head, embarrassed. To her, thinking was being lazy. I was *mo gay-sing* boy, a *witless* boy. I didn't care; I had a mystery to solve. Walking steadily home in step with Mother, my head pounding, I kept the books clutched in my arms like stolen booty.

Alone in my own room, I shut the door. Faintly, I could still hear Mother downstairs talking to Aunty Freda about Grandfather. The old man was supposed to come to dinner, but something had gone wrong. At Aunty Freda and Uncle Wally's house, Grandfather had fallen down for the third time.

"We'll have the dinner next week," Mother said, "Is he taking his ... ?"

From their voices, I knew it was all worry talk. I didn't care. Mother would call me down for lunch soon. I pitched myself onto the child-sized sofa Aunty Freda had made for me by covering an orange crate with padded blue oilcloth patterned with nursery-rhyme characters such as Humpty-Dumpty and Little Boy Blue. Then I slowly opened the mystery book, starting from the back.

On the last page, a ring of tigers chased each other around a tree trunk. On the back of the same last page, all the tigers seemed to have turned into a yellow pudding. Black Sambo and a big dark lady were beaming.

Because Mother was always bothersome about my toys and those kindergarten books, always asking me to pick them up or take them out of the kitchen, it never occurred to me to ask her for help. Of course, I could have gone right downstairs and asked

Aunty Freda to read the tiger book to me, or even asked one of
the older girls, Kate or Betty Jung, or my favourite sitter, Lena,
from upstairs at the sausage factory. I could have asked the Lee
sisters, Lil or Shirley. But I didn't want to ask anyone.

That afternoon, savouring the mystery, I slipped the tiger book
away in a box of toys. I would come back to it.

---

SOON AFTER MRS MCCARGAR gave me those two books, I was
allowed to borrow books for the whole weekend from a low shelf
of children's books in the church annex. Those of us who wanted
a book to take home promised Mrs Montgomery and Miss Lowe,
the piano player, that we would wash our hands before reading it
and keep it from falling into the dirt. One of the mothers entered
our names and the titles of the books we borrowed in a large
ledger. It made me feel important that someone would actually
spell my name out loud and write it down in a book, though I
wasn't sure why.

From the first time my eyes soaked up the vivid pages displayed to us on Mrs Montgomery's knee, the oversized illustrations spread open like Aladdin's magic carpet, I was drawn to
love books. Whether in the basement classroom or upstairs in
the Sunday-school room, Mrs Montgomery and the volunteer
ladies who read to us planted in me a lifelong infatuation. No
doubt, books enriched me, but I began to enrich them, too.
This connection evolved in ways no single-minded Anglo-
Saxon publisher—at least one in business in 1945—could ever
have imagined.

Long before I could read, printed words began to intrigue me.
I looked and looked at my Black Sambo book. Then, I fell into a
habit of studying other books. I desperately wanted to decipher

the tiny chunk of print sequestered behind their title pages: what did all those tiny numbers and letters mean? My Dick Tracy eyes noted similarities in those blocks of type, sometimes located beside bold numbers or a dark line of Roman consonants and vowels. The old-fashioned books, those with pictures of Victorian children, used Latin or Gothic lettering. In short, every book's copyright notice became a profound mystery for me.

Neither Mrs Montgomery nor Miss Lowe, whose fingers on the piano keys brightly "read" the black dots on her music books, ever seemed to read aloud to us those diminutive, isolated words. Mother couldn't help me. In fact, I felt that no one could. You had to solve a riddle by yourself or the answer didn't count. Everyone knew that.

Mrs Montgomery's and Miss Lowe's casual disregard of these mysterious blocks of print caused me to think of the recipes-for-use that were always expertly brushed in Chinese characters onto parcels of medicinal roots and dried creature parts. Whenever my bachelor-uncles or aunties decided they needed to balance the hot–cold, wind–water or *feng-shui* condition of their health, I would march along with them to visit one of the Chinatown herbalists.

In these stores, the air was always dry, and the smells sharp and pungent. Dried, encrusted black creatures sat in boxes under the glass counters; tea packages and brittle seahorses lay tumbled over ginseng roots and medicinal leaves. Even with so many things to look at, the best part was to hear the odd way the man behind the counter spoke of hot and cold winds, of pulse beats and the shade of dots on the tongue; he asked about the quality of stools, the colour of urine, whether one ate this or that. The herbalist would sigh, nod his head, adjust his glasses.

"You're feeling some heat under your chest, are you not?"

My aunts or uncles would inevitably confirm the symptoms the herbalist seemed to have intuited.

After carefully studying the client's tongue and eyes, and after feeling the pulse along the patient's wrists, the glassy-eyed man behind the counter would turn away and gather the necessary ingredients from half-a-dozen of the wooden drawers lined up along one wall, all the way up to the ceiling. He climbed up on a ladder to reach some of them. Fifth Aunty would sometimes flinch at this. The higher up the drawer, she told me, the rarer and the more expensive the prescription.

These elements the herbalist would wrap up in a neat envelope folded of newsprint. Then the herbalist would toss lozenge-sized pieces of wrapped candy into the package to help the medicine go down. I always got a few of these treats.

As I chewed on the red-coloured candy, sugarcane sweetness bursting onto my tongue, the herbalist would dip his brush into a jar of red ink and dance it across the front of the medicinal parcel. Calligraphy dashed onto the packet like windblown grass. This scripted writing was surely part of the cure, mysterious to me, and unspoken.

In the same way, the Roman letters on the copyright notices were also mysterious, also unspoken. Turning to them, book after book, I stared hard at each one, recognized a few letters from the Roman numerals. Said them aloud.

There was a *C*, an *X*, and a *V*.

The temptation to ask a grown-up what the letters meant was strong, but I resisted. The pleasure of guessing, of seeking my own solution, excited my mind.

I knew *C* was part of my name. Aunty Freda and the Lee sisters had taught me to spell *C-H-O-Y*. As for the upside-down arrow head, everyone knew soldiers made the "V" sign by holding up two fingers. It stood for "Victory," of winning battles over bad people like the Japanese or Germans.

I was breaking down the secret code, just like some of the

older boys did with their Dick Tracy Detective Kits. I stared at the *X*. That was easy. On handwritten letters, Big Sister Lena at the Chinese sausage factory had taught me *X*'s and *O*'s stood for "kisses and hugs."

In seconds, my heart pounded with recognition: the Roman numerals were a sacred script, a script only I had come to decipher, to recognize, and perhaps no one else understood, except in secret.

I quickly felt it wasn't necessary to ask about the other letters. Instead, I suspected the diminutive letters and numbers must together form a spell, an *abracadabra*. Tight-lipped, I kept this knowledge to myself. Shut my eyes. Rubbed my index finger over the numbers. *For luck.*

I sighed with giddy pleasure.

Words in certain books, I knew, like Mrs Montgomery's bible, should never be neglected. God put the words and the stories into the bible, we were told. The church people told us everything in the black book was sacred, and my books had come from a church. The secret codes of books were a test of those who truly understood the Holy Ghost.

I longed to read.

Some of the girls and boys in my class who had older brothers and sisters could read a lot of the words in the books, but I didn't always envy them. There were those who saw only paper and coloured ink, those who thought words were just words; those who tore or folded the corners of the pages, who saw no life in books at all.

My picture books were living things, like my rubber Gumby or my Cracker Jack prizes with pressed-tin faces, my rag doll and lead soldiers, my tanks and planes—each illustrated pig and tiger quickening into life the instant I, and everyone else in the house, fell asleep.

Sometimes, rubbing my finger over the tiny copyright print on the back of the title pages, I closed my eyes and made a wish. I never told anyone what I wished for. You were allowed *one* wish and, like the one made on a birthday, it was not to be told.

I stroked my fingers over the Roman numerals, imagining my deepest wishes coming true. I wished for a pony to ride and to keep for myself in our backyard, and I wished for a cowboy outfit, just like the one from the Eaton's catalogue that I told Aunty Freda about. She inserted one of her rag trimmings to mark the page. All this was *one* wish, I reasoned, because it all had to do with my desire to be a cowboy.

"What are you mumbling?" Father asked, shaking his *Chinese Times*. He looked across the dining-room table at me.

"Nothing," I said, and stood the book up on the table.

Crossing my fingers so Mother's back would not break, I turned the page over and sneakily, slyly, brushed the Roman numerals one more time.

This covert ritual, my rubbing copyrights, had been adapted from my observing the behaviour of people at Chinatown cele-brations. At New Year's and moon festivals, at births and wed-dings, families ordered crimson sheets filled with auspicious words such as "Double Happiness," "Great Prosperity" and "Long Life." Red, black and gold calligraphic banners and scrolls cheer-fully decorated doors and hallway entrances. People seemed to touch them for good luck; a few traced the elegant bird-like strokes, admiring the brushwork. One day, Tommy Cheong, age seven, taught me how to get my share of good luck.

"Do this," he said. "Don't tell anyone."

He wet his baby finger with spit, and I thought he was going to hold his finger up and make a wish. That's what all the big kids did, besides sometimes crossing their heart and hoping to die. Instead, Tommy reached out and rubbed the corner of a Good

Fortune greeting until the vegetable dye came off and his finger tip seemed smeared with blood.

I wet my baby finger with spit but had to jump a little to reach the corner of one that Tommy pointed out. After three swipes, Tommy whispered to me, "If you get some of the red colour to come off the paper, then you be ten times luckier than any one else."

No one was supposed to see you doing it, not if you really wanted to have the luck. Otherwise, Tommy warned me, however much you tried again, you lost your chance for getting ten times the luck. I knew "ten times" meant "more and more." It was good to have more and more luck.

My first try didn't count, he said, because he was just showing me the secret. He got a tea-wet napkin and wiped my baby finger clean. Now I could do it.

I waited until almost everyone was busy in the other rooms, and the hall was practically empty. I picked one of the banners just beyond my reach, a complex one with more words than the two-character ones, imagining that these challenges would increase the luck. I bent my knees, slobbered over my baby finger, and took my stance beneath it: *Jump up! Daub the corner! One! Two! Three!*

On the third stroke, my fingertip came down red with fortune. I showed one of Mother's lady friends my fingertip and proudly pointed to the sheet in the hall behind her that I had just jumped up and smeared three times. I explained how I was going to have ten times everything I touched. She turned to look at the sign and burst out laughing. Mother asked what was so funny.

"*Aiiii-yah,*" Mother said. "You touched that one?" She walked away, shaking her head.

I asked another lady what the Chinese words meant. She said it was an old-time blessing for the bride. I proudly showed her the red tip of my baby finger. The lady raised her eyebrow, looked down at me sympathetically; I sensed she didn't understand how lucky I was.

The sign had read: *May you birth eight sons.*

That night in bed, I closed my eyes, wet the tip of my right forefinger, held it in the air—and, with all my might, I wished my eight sons away.

# Ten

*The birthday boy*

I WAS ALWAYS MAKING wishes. I wished we would leave the *bak kwei* house. And we did.

Just one month after my sixth birthday, on a spring day, we moved to a new place, to a house next door to the Good Shepherd Mission at 630 Keefer Street, three blocks east of the house that Father decided was causing too much trouble. Being next door to a Christian church, he and Dai Yee reasoned, this new place would be a better house for us. Mother worked hard during the move, and I kept out of her way as much as possible. Father promised me a reward if I behaved.

I told Mother that Tommy Cheong had a bed with real brass trimmings, and he was at least a head taller than me. I wanted a bed as big as his. Crossing my fingers, I wished for a bed that would let me grow as tall and as big as Tommy Cheong.

"If you're a good boy..." Mother said.

A few days after we moved in, my reward arrived in a delivery truck from Woodward's.

"Choy?" the driver asked at our door. He towered over me. Mother looked up at him and nodded. She put an X on a piece of paper, and then the giant delivery man lifted up some planks and boards and a boxspring mattress, everything tied together, and, at Mother's insistence, took them upstairs. She gave him twenty-five cents.

"That's your new bed, kid," said the man, flicking the coin in the air.

I stood at the doorway of my bedroom, stared at the now folded-away child's cot that had been my bed.

"Aunty Freda helped me pick this new one out," Mother said, "just for you."

I looked at the headboard. It was padded with an orange-colour quilted material. The mattress had a flower pattern, just like the mattress on Mother and Father's bed. I was impressed. The planks and mattress, even unassembled, were almost twice as big as my cot.

That evening, after Father came home and put it together, I jumped into my new twin bed and let Mother cover me up with freshly ironed flannel sheets and blankets. I stretched myself out on the sumptuous mattress and lifted my head to see where the tops of my feet popped up.

"Now you have plenty of room to grow," Mother said. She patted the large space between the bottom of my feet and the end of the bed.

"Grow as tall as you want to," Father said. "You can get a job and earn some money."

I laughed. I would soon be as tall as Tommy Cheong.

Mother got me a wooden crate and showed me how I could fill it with toys and push it under the bed, a real hideaway. The first night, I half-dropped to the side of the bed and put my hand way under, my palm patting the rough side of the crate to make sure it was there.

I sank my head into the plush, deep pillow, and with a big yawn stretched out my arms and legs. Bare fingers and bare toes touched nothing but flannel. Outside my window, the moon and the stars were caught in the V between two roofs. I would grow as tall as Tommy Cheong. Maybe even taller than the delivery man himself. Taller than the stars and moon. I crossed my heart and wet my finger and waved it above my head, whirling wishes into the night.

———

MRS MONTGOMERY WET her index finger to turn the pages of books. At the piano, Miss Lowe did, too. I knew the moistened finger helped to turn the pages one at a time, but I had no doubt that Mrs Montgomery already understood what I had discovered: the gesture brought good fortune. Of course, she never gave this secret away. Not only I, but other children began to turn the pages with a dampened finger, too. I thought we all were secretly learning the same magical gesture. Of course, no one said anything about its meaning. You were not supposed to.

During storytime at school, I made every effort to sit closest to

Mrs Montgomery, where I could see and capture the names of
words that her fingers pointed to. Borrowing the same book, like
a parrot I could point to the words and "read" them aloud.

Then, I began to read by myself.

One of my favourite borrowed books, which I took out as
many times as I could, told the story of a cackling Mother Hen
who clucked around and around to ask all the barnyard animals
to help her make bread. Mrs Montgomery often read this book to
us, as we all shouted for her to read it: everyone liked to make the
barnyard-animal noises.

I read this book to Mother; or rather, from those borrowed
picture-pages, slowly . . . confidently . . . I *gong-wah, talked-picture.*

Mother sat on the sofa. I pulled up a chair a few feet away, my
feet resting on the second rung. I sat with the oversized book
opened on my lap, my head over the volume, tilted like Mrs
Montgomery's.

Some of the English words printed beside the illustrations
were simple enough for me to decipher. I now only had to
remember the shape or *look* of the whole word. "HEN," "PIG,"
and "OH, OH, OH!" for example, were all easy enough for me to
*point-and-say.* I could guess from the pictures what was meant by
the other words, and would confidently babble out my rendering
in a mixed vocabulary of English–Chinese—what Aunty Freda
and local-borns called "Chinglish."

I turned the oversized pages carefully, as Mrs Montgomery
would, shifting the book carefully on my knees to show Mother
the pictures, and with operatic confidence, "read" aloud to her,
confidently pointing to each word as I went along.

"*Gee*-Piggy *gong-wah,* oink! oink!" I half-sang, half-said, in
broken Toisanese and fragmented English. "*Ngoh m'help you-
ahh!* No! No!"

Mother listened thoughtfully, now and then tucking in her chin to suppress a sudden fit of strange coughing. She covered her mouth with a hanky or the towel she was using to dry her hair. Mother told me to ignore her and go on with my reading.

Of course, it was damp in our house. She coughed often when I read to her.

The book bounced precariously on my knee. Mother learned to shake her head sadly when I asked her, just as Mrs Montgomery asked us in class, "Did the other animals help?"

I wagged my head in unison with Mother, *No, no, no,* wet my finger and turned the page.

Not one animal, not even Miss Goose, would help Mrs Hen with the chores of gathering the grain for the cookout. Finally, when the toasty-brown loaf came out of the outdoor oven, Mrs Hen told all the barnyard animals, and especially Miss Goose, her fateful decision.

"*Nay m'help me!*"

I made cackling hen sounds.

Mother went into a fit of coughing.

My cackling did not sound as good as Mrs Montgomery's, but Mother only said, between raising and lowering her handkerchief, "Go—go on with the story." The damp was really getting to her. Mother settled her coughing and I went on.

"No-way help-*ahhh! Ngoh-gah* chicks and me, three, four, five..." I held up the correct number of fingers and recounted in Chinese, "*Sam, say, hmm*—we *hack* ALL the bread-*ahh!*"

By the last page, which I knew by heart, I would look at Mother, throw both my hands in the air like Mrs Montgomery, announce: "Mother Hen and the chicks ate ALL of it!" and, as the book cascaded to the floor, shout out the climax:

"*Ev-verry lit-tle bit!*"

By about my sixth reading, I realized that the five yellow-fluffed chicks had not done any work. Not one thing. Yet they were given bread to eat.

Back in class, I asked Miss Lowe about this. She said that the baby chicks were just too young to help their mother. Mrs Montgomery said they probably did help just by staying out of Mother Hen's way.

"All good children are rewarded," Miss Lowe emphasized with a few piano notes, "if they just stay out of the way when their mother is working."

Miss Lowe was right.

———

I ALWAYS WANTED TO help Mother and Aunty Freda with their work. But they usually told me to go and play, *thank you*. Aunty Freda sat me by a small table and let me finish a jigsaw puzzle or let me play records on the player. I sang to myself while she did some important sewing. She was always sewing or warming bottles of milk for baby Trudy.

Most times, at our new house, Mother was too finicky about her own housework for me to help her, what with my holding the dustpan tipped up too high or too low, or my dropping Father's wastepaper basket, or my waiting for a really good breeze before I banged the long-handled feather duster all over the side of the porch. I liked the cloud the duster made when I thumped the thing on the porch posts or, using the handle, raked the railings like a giant ratchet.

"*Stop that noise*," Mother shouted.

Motes of dust rose and scattered sunlit specks around me; the breeze blew swoops of dust through our loosely hinged screen door. It would swing open and Mother would take over. With a look of disgust, she always snatched the duster away from me and banged it in a no-fun manner along the outside of the porch.

Mother rarely did housework without moving like a demon, faster than me—faster than anyone. Whenever she started any serious housework, dusting and mopping and polishing in every room, I guessed that Father would be home the next day.

But once, in the spring of my kindergarten year, Mother cleaned the house every single day for a week and Father still didn't show up. That was unusual. With her long flowered apron tied tightly around her waist, Mother chased me and swatted me with the duster because I could not get out of her way fast enough. Father finally came home the following weekend. He and Mother spent a whole morning and afternoon shuffling trunks around in our upstairs storage room, taking away boxes of junk they wouldn't let me play with. Next, they both went downstairs and moved around our parlour furniture.

That same spring weekend, when I came home from Stanley Park with Third Uncle, Father said, "Today, I want you to play quietly."

He pointed upstairs. Mother took Third Uncle's coat and they went into the kitchen and sat down. Third Uncle quietly lit his pipe and Mother patiently filled the kettle. Father lifted up his chair and set it down gently beside Third Uncle. Everyone seemed to be tiptoeing about and whispering to each other.

"Grandfather is sleeping upstairs," Father said.

"Why?" I asked.

"He's been very sick, that's why," Mother said. "He just came back from the big hospital."

# Eleven

*Gung-Gung's last photograph*

GRANDFATHER'S VOICE HAD been very scratchy the last time he had dinner at our house, three weeks ago. He didn't look well then. His chopsticks could not grasp anything, and his eyes were half-shut. Finally, Mother discreetly placed a fork beside his plate. Silently, with no one saying anything, and even with Third Uncle pretending not to see, the old man picked it up. Mother quickly offered me some more soup.

But it was Grandfather's voice that really caught my attention; it stays in my memory even today. Without any warning, he

coughed and spoke in a harsh, gasping tone, as if he were out
of breath.

"*Feed Way Sun!*" he barked, as if we were all deaf, in Toisanese.
"*The boy too, TOO bony!*"

Mother jumped, looked very nervous. She put down her rice
bowl, and lifted her chopsticks to pick out a piece of chicken for
me. Father bit his bottom lip, to stop himself from saying anything. The old man's rough-sounding voice reminded me of the
Big Bad Wolf: growling, testy, could huff and puff our house
down. It was the voice both Father and Mother had heard often,
fifteen years ago, when they both lived in Victoria and witnessed
the verbal warfare between Grandfather and Stepgrandmother.
But I had only known the old man's voice to be soft. If he raised
his voice it was to call out a name or to make a point. Mother
lifted a piece of white meat onto my plate.

"I'm going to grow up really, really strong," I said. "Miss Lowe
at Sunday school said I'm..."

The chicken required some extra chewing.

"... I'm going to be——"

"Drinking your soup," Mother said, and ladled some more
strength-building broth into my bowl.

---

AFTER DINNER AND AFTER swallowing his medicinal tea, Grandfather returned to speaking as he always had, the gruffness gone
and unexplained. I asked him why I looked different from most
of the boys playing in MacLean Park.

"Way Sun," he said, "*nay-hei tong-yung—you're Chinese.*"

He raised his head from his Chinese book and delivered the
lesson in his proud tone of voice. He spoke firmly, as if thousands
of years of cultural history stood behind him.

"*Chinese are always different from all the peoples of the world,*" Father said, picking up his newspaper.

Father's words in Toisanese were spoken without arrogance or apology—simply spoken, and simply heard: I absorbed another lesson. Even as a *mo-no*, someone who would one day lose almost all his first language and live for more than two-thirds his life away from Vancouver's Chinatown, I always would be, and still am, as Grandfather said, *tong-yung—Chinese*.

"No matter how far you go," Grandfather Choy said to me, "you will come back to your own people..."

"*Gee gai yun,*" Mother said, finishing the old man's thought.

I looked into the hall mirror, studied my skin tone, hair colour, the shape of my skull.

"*Our own people,*" Mother had said.

I belonged.

---

GRANDFATHER WAS UPSTAIRS, resting. Mother was saying that he would need a room upstairs. My room was mentioned. I could hardly believe my ears. I was going to have to sleep on the fold-away cot again. That was impossible. Perhaps I heard it wrong. There was Mother and Father's room ... There was the storage room... *Whose room?*

I slipped behind Father and went upstairs to see for myself. There Grandfather was, stretched out on the twin bed that Mother just a few weeks ago promised was to be all my own. My heart sank. I wanted to drag Gung-Gung off my bed and shove him under it.

The old man lay on his side, a languid, grey-sweatered, half-sheeted mound. His cheeks were hollowed, his skin sallow. He laboured for breath, and his half-opened mouth produced a rasping sound that was not like Father's snoring.

Grandfather was sixty-eight, but looked much older and weaker than anyone else I loved. I did not know his health was failing then; I just felt annoyed and uneasy at his occupying my domain. My new mattress sagged with his weight, and one of his stockinged feet stuck out at one side. I thought I should point out to him that he was lying on my new bed, but Mother's hissing voice caught me by surprise and told me to get downstairs.

A pitiless hand gripped my shoulder and turned me around to face the staircase. I stomped down the steps. Mother knuckled my head. I held back my tears.

———

WHEN I EXPLAINED TO Grandfather how I needed a big, BIG bed so that I could grow up faster and faster, he looked at me very puzzled.

"You grow too fast already," he said. He patted me on the head. "You feel taller today, Way Sun."

I barely heard the *Sun* part of my Chinese name. The old man's breathing was heavy again, as if he wanted to snore but couldn't.

Mother had spoken to me for days about how I needed to care for him, as he was not too well. She said he was old and needed help in everything he did now. I was to help, too.

Grandfather looked very well to me. First of all, he was very tall. Anyone as tall as Father looked good and healthy to me. And he always dressed in his suit, even with no special reason. Mother carefully combed Grandfather's hair because he kept dropping the comb.

"I can't see the mirror," he said. "Eyes are going."

"No, no," Mother said. "The mirror's not too clean."

Mother picked up the brush and did my hair. She licked her fingers and pushed down a cowlick. She always used spit.

"Remember what I told you," she said, and turned my head to the side to look in her hand mirror. The glass was perfectly clear and clean. She held it higher. "You're taller today. Look."

I wasn't fooled. But Mother had warned me not to mention anything more about the old man taking over my bedroom and sleeping in my big bed. Mother said he could have anything he wanted because he was my father's father. He was my grandfather, too. I was to be patient.

"Take Gung-Gung for a walk around the block," Mother said, wiping her hands on her apron. "A walk will stretch both your legs."

When Gung-Gung and I stepped out of the house, Mother told me to take the old man's hand. She took his other arm and walked us down the steps. He stared at each step very carefully. I hopped down, but kept time so that Grandfather's hand wouldn't slip out of my grip. At our front gate, Mother instructed me to walk to the corner, turn down for a half-block more, and then come back, and never, ever, ever to cross the street. I was in charge.

———

OUR WALK THE FIRST day after lunch went very well. It felt strange for me to tug at Grandfather, to hurry him, a grown man, but he cooperated. Gung-Gung had always been like Third Uncle, who always decided the pace, who was always the boss. When I slowed down, the old man slowed down. People walking by said hello to us, and even stopped to talk to Grandfather.

The third day, things did not turn out as well. Grandfather insisted on wearing his best suit to take his daily walk. That was the suit Aunty Freda and Uncle Wally got him, the one she refitted for him when he lost so much weight. Grandfather, like Father, always liked good clothes.

Mother said the morning rain had made the streets slippery. She tried to help him straighten his shirt collar. Grandfather shook off her hand, tending to it himself. The old man insisted on going out.

"Look at all that sunshine," he said, pushing his arms into his best suit jacket.

I took Grandfather's hand and he seemed to walk proudly down the steps. The sun was shining brightly, sharpening every shadow in the bushes and trees along our street.

We walked almost to the corner of Princess, then the old man stepped out onto the rain-wet cobbled road. I remembered what Mother had told me and pulled him back, but he yanked hard. He was mad. He said some Chinese swear words.

"Gung-Gung," I said. "Mommy said *no crossing the street! M'mo gor-gai!*"

Grabbing him with both hands, I tugged harder. Gung-Gung's eyes widened, as if he couldn't understand what a mere boy was doing, trying to haul him back. I wasn't sure myself. But Mother had told me in her firm, no-nonsense voice when she put on my rain jacket: "*Don't cross the street.*" The stern way she said it came back to me. I jumped onto the sidewalk and yanked twice as hard. The old man stumbled, then picked up his feet in an exaggerated way and stepped back up onto the sidewalk, like the clown-man Charlie Chaplin at the Rex. I was surprised.

*A boy proved to be stronger than a grown-up.* The universe seemed to have gone awry. It was Gung-Gung who always pulled *me* back when we went for walks in Chinatown. *Was I supposed to obey Mommy or let Gung-Gung have his way?* My head was spinning. *Did I win or did I lose? Was I a bad and wicked* mo-no *boy?*

In the midst of my confusion, the old man attempted to speak, but managed only a gurgling sound. The patchy shadows thrown down by a giant Douglas fir across the street made the wet cobblestones seem to move. Gung-Gung's eyes looked glassy, empty. I wanted to say I was sorry, but I wasn't sure about what.

I gripped Grandfather's hand tighter, afraid to let loose my hold on his fingers, not letting go, but wanting to. As the wind blew, the wavering patches of shadow and sunlight on the road made me dizzy.

Grandfather closed his eyes, and his shoulders sagged. When I looked up, he stared down at me, his head like a giant's against the blue sky. His white hair scattered in the afternoon breeze.

"Mommy's calling me," I said. "We have to go home."

He tried to tell me something, but his voice went funny. Tears came into his eyes; he stood still for a long, long moment. From behind a chain-linked fence, at Strathcona School, two boys stood looking at us. One of them was Tommy Cheong. I was just going to shout for Tommy to help me. But help me with what? I wasn't sure.

Suddenly, with his free hand, Grandfather patted my head.

"Go... home," he said, at last. "*Fan ... kay-lah. We ... go home.*"

When we reached our house, the Chinese man with the white collar from the Good Shepherd Mission next door saw us and helped Grandfather up the front steps. Mother opened the door.

Because Mother looked so stricken, I told her right away that Gung-Gung had tried to cross the street.

"It's a *feng-sup* day," Mother said to Grandfather, in Toisanese, "A *wet-tempered* day, a dangerous day for catching colds."

I stood back a few steps, while Mother and the Good Shepherd man helped Grandfather slowly up the flight of stairs to my bedroom.

"You take good care of your *yeh-yeh*," the man said, using the reference to show that he knew the old man was my father's father.

"He's my *gung-gung*," I said, proudly.

Mother was helping Gung-Gung to take off his jacket. The old man lay in bed all that day and night.

No one said I did anything wrong.

---

WHEN GRANDFATHER DIDN'T come downstairs for supper, I asked Mother what was wrong.

"He's been sick," Mother said. "Remember that time you went to the hospital?"

I had awakened one day when I had just turned four and couldn't move or speak. It was my tonsils. I remember being carried in my father's arms into a taxi, and then being awake in a white room with a doctor poking at me. Next thing, I was home, taking all kinds of medicine, feeling sore in my throat. When I was strong enough to refuse the awful-tasting medicine and the bowls of rice gruel, Mother asked me what I would like. Sensing that this was a rare opportunity, I ordered fried steak and buttered corn and lots of red Jell-O.

"When will Gung-Gung get better?"

Mother said nothing, except to ask me what I wanted for supper. Father was away at work and she didn't feel like making a big dinner just for herself. There was *jook* still to make, a kind of nourishing porridge Mother would boil for Gung-Gung, using leftover rice and a mix of salty pork and soup broth.

"When will Father come home?"

"Soon," Mother said. "Very soon."

"When will I get my bed back?"

Every night I had to go into my room and look at the old man and say I hoped he would have a nice sleep. Grandfather always patted my head and said, "Thank you. G'night, Way Sun." Sometimes he could barely raise his hand and would just touch my shoulder, but I always heard his *G'night*, and my Chinese name, however softly he whispered it.

———

THE NEXT FEW DAYS I wandered in and out of my bedroom, tip-toeing as best I could. Taking off my *tat-tat hi*, my *slip-on slippers*, I put on an extra pair of socks so I could move about noiselessly. Gung-Gung sometimes half-opened his eyes, but he didn't seem to see me at all. I was very quiet. Mother let me take out some books and toys to play with. Later that week, Grandfather sometimes sat up, his eyes opened, staring at the steaming *jook* Mother held beneath his chin. One day after lunch, I slipped into the room and he was awake.

"Way Sun," he said. He looked thinner, his face drawn, but his voice was clear, strong. "I want you to read to me. Your mother says you can read books."

I got out the books I had, including the new ones I had borrowed from Sunday school, and put them down on his chest so he could peer at them.

"That one," he said, gently.

I pulled out one of the Bible-story comics. It was the one about the boy in the den of lions. Daniel. I turned to the first page and showed the old man the first panel of pictures.

"Here's the young boy, Daniel," I began. "He's going to fight bad people but he has to be strong first."

There were pictures I couldn't quite make out. The Daniel boy stood before someone like a king—he wore a crown—and there were soldiers. They were talking.

"Daniel *wah* the *whang-dai* King, '*Ngoh m'pai lao foo* tigers!'" I read, pointing to the words in the cartoon balloons. "*I not scared of tigers!*" If there were more printed words than my own spoken words conveyed, my pointing finger danced quickly across them. In fact, the faces of the cartoon characters made it easy for me to read the stories my own way, in perfect Chinglish. Grandfather looked pleased, even cheerful. We finished Daniel's story when the blond-haired angel, his dove wings glowing, put out his hand and stilled the roaring beasts. I thought of pancakes. I thought of Black Sambo.

"Read this one to me," Grandfather said, and picked up one of my favourites. With great alacrity, using my very best Chinglish, I read *The Three Little Pigs.*

Every day, right after I had my lunch, I went upstairs to read to the old man. Gung-Gung was turning out to be a perfect companion. That was what Mrs Mongomery called it when you had a best friend. Miss Lowe told us that person was a *ho pan yueh.*

Gung-Gung always paid attention. He asked me about kindergarten and what I was going to wear on the last-day ceremony.

"You'll be going to Grade One in September," he said.

"I know," I said. "Aunty Freda told me I passed kindergarten."

Grandfather got well enough that we had our walks again—*little* walks, just halfway to the corner of Princess and Keefer and back. Before we stepped out, Gung-Gung would insist on looking fresh and clean. Because the old man had grown weaker, his shaving involved the whole family.

Mother brought up a pan of hot water and his shaving mirror, and Grandfather lathered himself. Father honed the long blade of the razor on a leather strap. I never let my face brush up against Gung-Gung's unshaven cheeks, even when we read together. The sandpaper stubble made me itchy. After he finished with the razor, however, I got to test the old man's face for smoothness by rubbing my cheek over his. Then he would pat himself with Yardley cologne, and shake a few drops in my waiting palm for me to slap on my own face: the potion felt cool and fresh, like ice, and made me laugh.

In June, because he couldn't possibly walk as far as the Chinese Mission Church on Dunlevy, five blocks away, I got to show Grandfather my big graduation picture and point out my other best friends, my *ho pan yueh*, Larry and Nancy. All of us kids are dressed like grown-up graduates, in freshly laundered choir gowns. Our heads are topped with stiff mortarboards, an example of the Mission's earnest effort during those war years to lend dignity and significance to every transient event. There stand our three smiling guardians: firmly in-charge Mrs McCargar; tall, dramatic Mrs Isabelle Montgomery; and petite, cheerful Miss Lowe.

I imagine the photographer's words had been loudly and sternly barked out in Chinese. Each child looks frozen with solemnity—eyes front—like soldiers. No child is smiling. Except one.

I am standing in the back row, second from the right, the only child breaking ranks, grinning indecorously. Mother ended up misplacing this graduation photo, perhaps believing that her son had spoiled the picture.

———

DURING JULY AND THE beginning of August, we had visitors almost every other day. They only stayed a little while, always wishing to shake the old man's hand before they left. We had baskets of fruit, pots of flowers, some candies, and even some boxes of nuts. Visitors gave me money, too, in lucky *lei-see* envelopes.

When we were alone, after a long rest, Grandfather and I started reading the storybooks aloud together, like a team. As my finger pointed at the words, I would start reading first and he would finish my sentences. Sometimes the old man started first, tapping with his finger, and I finished his sentences. We alternated turning the page. I always held up the books. I didn't mind. It was serious work.

In the summer after kindergarten, Grandfather sometimes had me sit on the bed close to him, so he could see the picture books I was reading to him. I didn't mind. He helped me out sometimes with the telling.

"Swan," he told me. Then I had to repeat the Chinese word for *swan* back to him. We were reading *The Ugly Duckling*. Grandfather said he knew the story; he even knew the Chinese name for the author. That was puzzling. Everyone at Sunday school said God wrote all the stories.

Once, Father came by. We didn't notice how long he had been standing at the doorway. Maybe he was thinking how Grandfather had once read books with him, but Father never mentioned this. Once Father told Mother how Grandfather always shouted at him when he was little himself, how Father had to work every day, helping Grandfather with chores. Father had come to help the old man down the stairs for supper. The doctor told my parents the effort to walk would be good for Grandfather.

It was very slow going. I helped, steadying Grandfather's elbow and pretending we were on a mountain, just like Grandfather suggested. He had climbed mountains himself, when he was a boy in China, and when he was a young man on his first adventure from California to British Columbia.

"Maybe you can find a book about mountains," he said.

Grandfather always encouraged me to read more and more. By this time, with a little help from Aunty Freda, I had figured out most of the Black Sambo book. I told Grandfather how the tigers were greedy for pancakes, and wanted the shirt and pants Little Black Sambo was wearing. How hard his mother had worked to make the clothes and the pancakes. In the next picture, a tiger was holding up the boy's umbrella with his tail.

"Who made the umbrella?" Grandfather asked.

I hadn't thought of that. Mothers could not make umbrellas. Did fathers?

"Pick another book," I said.

All that time with Grandfather, though I looked, I never found a mountain book.

---

THE ONE TIME GRANDFATHER left our house that August, he had his picture taken in his best suit. He is standing by himself in a park, holding himself straight. It was something the old man insisted on doing. When he came home, Grandfather almost had to be carried up the stairs and into bed. Mother and Aunty Freda were both in the way, so I couldn't even steady Gung-Gung's elbow.

After that trip to the park, Gung-Gung was soon too tired to go outside any more, but sometimes I helped him walk to the toilet down the hall.

Father said that I was not to tire out Gung-Gung. But, in fact, the old man was tiring me out. Sitting too long with Gung-Gung, my bum hurt. I even sat on one of his pillows, but that didn't help much. The truth was, I wanted to go out and play.

"Play here," Grandfather said. "I don't mind."

I didn't at first, not until I invented a game that we could play around the bed—*my* bed.

"You take this soldier," I instructed Grandfather. "I'll pretend to be hiding down here."

I ducked below his line of sight, almost to the floor.

"Try shooting me when I pop up," I said.

I popped up. Grandfather aimed the soldier and shot away.

"Missed!" I said. I ducked and popped up again. Grandfather made a *bang-bang* sound.

"Missed!"

Mother walked in and said, "Gung-Gung's your *ho pan yueh!*"

"*Perfect companion!*" I said, in perfect English.

Grandfather patted my head.

———

ONE DAY, IN THE middle of playing Goldilocks, Mother walked into the room. Baby Bear was about to complain, "Someone was sleeping in *my* bed."

"That's enough," she said. "Grandfather's very tired."

I had been so involved with being Baby Bear that I had not noticed Grandfather had slumped over, fast asleep. His breathing was louder than usual; his head jerked a little.

"Leave the room quietly," Mother said. "Don't make a sound. Tell your Father to come upstairs. You go out and play at Tommy's. Go on. I'll phone Tommy's mother. You can stay there for supper, too."

That was a treat. I rushed into the kitchen to tell Father to go upstairs. He dropped the *Chinese Times* and walked swiftly past me. Then I ran out of the house and down the block to Tommy's house.

Afterwards, Tommy's mother carried me home in her arms. It was very, very late, and through my sleepiness, as she lifted me out of Mrs Cheong's arms, I heard Mother tell her that Gung-Gung was not coming home.

"I want my bed," I said, and Mother carried me upstairs and tucked me in. The sheets were fresh. The pillow was my very own, with cowboys on the edge of the case. As I stretched out and closed my eyes, I heard Grandfather's familiar voice rising from the grey depth of my sleepiness: *G'night, Way Sun.*

I think it was Father who kissed my forehead. The kiss was rough, like sandpaper. Mother, I am sure, patted my head.

———

ON AUGUST 14, JAPAN agreed to surrender, and on that night, and all the next day and night, Chinatown went mad with celebrations. Mother took me down to watch the parade of soldiers. As we drew nearer to Main and Pender, we could see crowds and crowds of people. Everyone was smiling and laughing and singing songs. All the Tong Associations had their orchestra of drums and cymbals banging away in front of their entrances. Firecrackers were being raised in long, woven strings, to hang from balconies way above the crowd, waiting to be lit. The Chinese flag and the Union Jack were flying in the hundreds, big and small, red, white and blue banners hanging from balconies and over doorways. Homemade "V for Victory" signs of all sizes were displayed in the windows of rooming hotels and tied to cars that honked and shook as they drove by, with cheering young men and women standing on their running-boards. Mother picked me up, and people tapped me merrily on the head and even grabbed Mother for a kiss. She laughed and used me as a barrier to keep people away from her face. We were giddy with the noise and excitement.

Past Columbia Street, people wearing party hats blew paper horns and spun wooden rattles, happily banging on all the store and restaurant windows. The opera-company actors were climbing onto flatbed trucks. Their costumes glittered in the daylight. People inside the shops, with their clerking jackets and café uniforms and aprons, waved to everyone and merrily banged back. No one minded. In various Chinese dialects and English accents, in European languages I couldn't then identify, I heard roaring—and above all the mixed and joyful tongues, the final English words: "The war's over! The war's over!" Mother saw some friends and they joined forces to work their way through Chinatown.

Exhausted, Mother finally put me down, told me to hang on. One of her lady friends took a turn carrying me, and we pushed our way towards Ming Wo's, just before Carrall Street. More drums and crashing cymbals deafened our ears. A dragon with glowing eyes tossed its fiery head above us, a creature five times as long and more sinuous than the trio of dancing lions paying their homage. Outside the ring of frolicking beasts, children and grown-ups lined up, clapping wildly to the sound of drums and cymbals. Kung Fu swordsmen and tumbling warriors leaped through hoops and somersaulted over spears.

Up and down Pender Street, lit firecrackers were tossed into the air, bursting into clouds of bitter sulphur and erupting above our heads like gunfire. Fragments of red paper littered the air, their edges burning, and swirled in the eddying wind. The black and gold lions and the huge dragon jumped into the air, expelling fire and smoke. Mother shielded my eyes and pushed harder against the tidal surge of celebrants. I swallowed the gunpowdered air; with my palms, grabbed at flakes of floating ash; and felt mothwings dissolving.

Mother met up with her friends and they dusted off their coats before banging on the large door of Ming Wo's hardware store to be let in. Helena Wong laughed as she opened the door. Everyone hurried upstairs and found places on the crowded balcony of the building and waved to the crowds running up and down Pender Street, glad voices shouting good wishes back and forth. Someone carried me to the edge of the balcony and let me look down at the street below.

"Never forget this day, Sonny," the man's voice said, in Chinese.

---

THE RIVER OF PEOPLE frightened me at first, then exhilarated me. People shook their "V"-sign fists at us and were laughing and crying and singing, all of them together. I had dreamed my opera stories of glory and victory, had imagined at least a hundred times these banners and glittering pennants, but had never seen such happiness.

Suddenly, on a signal, young men in green and red jackets, and gold and black pants—some from the Dart Coon Club, the Chinese Students' Athletic Society, the Wing Sang boys—began tossing chains of firecrackers into the air and dancing as the explosions sparked all around them. The air was sharp with the stench of gunpower and the sweet smell of beer, cloudy with fingers of smoke and pierced by fireworks. Uniformed men and women were crying, waving their handkerchiefs and flags, and wiping their eyes.

Looking down towards Columbia Street, I could see through the thick, milling crowd a troupe of actors in brilliant Chinese opera costumes standing on flatbed floats, their arms waving—animate jewels slowly moving up Pender Street. It seemed as if ten thousand drums and cymbals, ten thousand gongs and tooting horns and ringing bells, filled the vibrant air.

---

A FEW DAYS AFTER THE victory celebrations, Mother said, "We're going to the hospital to see Grandfather."

She pushed my arms through my summer jacket. I looked up at Father.

"Gung-Gung's not coming home yet?"

"No," Father said. "You say goodbye to Gung-Gung at the hospital."

In the taxi, Father gave me some books wrapped in brown paper and tied with string; my fingers felt two books sliding against each other. Mother said I should look at them later. The taxi stopped in front of the Vancouver General Hospital, and we went to the basement area, where all the sick and dying Chinese were housed. A disinfectant smell pinched my nose. A nurse pointed the way. The large room was crowded with rows and rows of patients, heads barely moving, sunk into white pillows.

Grandfather lay in a small cot-like bed against the wall. A white curtain was half-drawn around him.

"The boy's here," Father said to Gung-Gung, in Toisanese.

Mother pulled me closer to the bed. I clutched the parcel against my chest.

"*Ngoh yuh sun shee, Gung-Gung,*" I said. "*I have new books.*"

Father lifted me up to sit next to Grandfather's grey head.

"I'm going to Grade One next week, Gung-Gung."

I held on tightly to my new books. Grandfather turned his head to try and see them.

"Gung-Gung," I said, and he smiled. I could see his white hair needed brushing. The old man seemed to take his time. He moved his head on the pillow, took a deep breath; his voice was clear:

"You be good boy, Way Sun."

"I will," I said. There was no use showing him my new books. Grandfather's eyes were cloudy, just like the eyes of the blind man on Hastings Street. Another deep breath.

"You be good boy for Mommy and Daddy."

He tried to pull his arm up to reach me, but his breathing went strange. Then his arm collapsed.

No one had to tell me what I had already sensed. Grandfather was not coming home. Quietly, Father slipped the books away from my hands. I sat still.

"G'night, Way Sun," Grandfather finally said.

I looked up at Mother, at Father—*Didn't Gung-Gung know it was still afternoon?*

Mother's arms reached out to take me away. I said, "Bye-bye, Gung-Gung."

I knew what I would do. I bent down and gave Gung-Gung a quick kiss on the head. Then, carefully, I slipped from my place to take Mother's cool hand. Together, in a small waiting room, we waited for Father to join us.

"Can I look at my books?"

Mother nodded. She opened the package for me and handed me the books. Her eyes were wet. It was cold and damp in the waiting room. I opened one of the books. It had pictures of mountains.

———

GRANDFATHER DIED THAT evening. And five days later, on August 25, 1945, Choy King, age sixty-eight and wearing his best suit, was buried in the grounds designated "For Chinese Only" at Ocean View Cemetery.

# Part Two

## Twelve

*Choy King*

GRANDFATHER'S LARGE FORMAL portrait had been re-framed in anticipation of his funeral, and a broad black ribbon sat neatly tied at the top, black ends trailing down the sides. The picture had been placed on a table in the parlour. Smoky sticks of incense stuck in pots of sand burned all day before Grandfather's unsmiling face. Calligraphy painted on white paper was hung on the wall. People visited us in the parlour and spoke in whispers. The men took off their fedoras or bowler hats, held them in their hands, and bowed three times before Grandfather's picture.

When Aunty Freda visited, I overheard the family discuss what Grandfather should wear, whether Father had picked the right coffin, what foods might be served afterwards. Mother and Freda bought new dresses and picked out new hats and gloves for themselves. Fifth Aunty came and offered her advice. But so much of what they talked about, I could not understand.

"Why not some quotations?"

"Oh, he was so particular," Mother said. "He didn't think much of any religion."

"It's polite to have *something*," Fifth Aunty said. "Some of the guests will expect that."

"The funeral director said they could take care of all that."

"All right," Father said. "A little religion won't hurt any of us."

---

IN THE DAYS AFTER Grandfather's death, an intense sadness pervaded our house. Visiting older men, my Victoria uncles, even Father—all walked about with their heads bowed; the hushed movements of Mother and the shuffling aunties made me wary not to bring attention to myself. Even when Mother dressed me in my new dark suit and pushed my legs through real wool pants, I understood not to make any fuss.

At night, when all the visitors had left, Father sat by himself in the parlour, sipping at a glass of whisky, watching the incense drift in spirals towards the ceiling.

The day of the funeral, the stately pace shifted: everything moved swiftly. After Aunty Freda pinned soft black armbands on everyone's sleeves, dark cars drove us to the Armstrong & Company Funeral Home on Dunlevy Street. A few neighbours gathered on their porches or stood by their gates to watch us leave.

In our car, Father held the large framed portrait of Grandfather on his knees; I sat on Mother's lap. At the funeral home, he handed the picture to a white man, who whispered something; Father nodded. We were taken to a side entrance and shown into a small room.

The room smelled sweetly of fresh evergreen and perfume. Organ music played. Everyone spoke in whispers, then fell silent. In a row of padded chairs, Mother and my aunts sat down, and Father and my uncles stood behind them. A slatted screen, draped with ivory curtains, shielded us from the rest of the guests, who were seated in neat rows and staring straight ahead. One of my uncles lifted me up so I could see above the ladies' new black hats. I wondered where the organist sat, if the instrument being played had large, carved pedals and long pipes like the one at the Chinese Mission Church. But this music seemed to come from nowhere.

At the front of the room, a man was lifting up Grandfather's picture onto a stand. Beside the stand sat the long, polished box, draped with wreaths and garlands.

"That's where your grandfather's sleeping," my uncle said.

I knew that was not true. Grandfather was not sleeping; he was gone. *Gone*, but still here in that box. It was puzzling.

When the service was over, men and women dressed in black outfits, and some in plain everyday clothes, stood and walked along the rows of seats and moved slowly towards the front. Men and women, singly and in pairs, stood a moment before the box; looked in; bowed once, twice, three times; then walked sadly away.

When all the people had bowed and left our view, we stepped out from the screened area and sombrely entered the large, cream-coloured room. Before rows and rows of empty seats and between clusters of flower arrangements, we stood before the box that held Gung-Gung. I couldn't see much, except the handles. I tiptoed. Nothing.

Standing over the box, a man wearing a white robe intoned some words and pointed upwards with both hands. I looked up. There was nothing but a high ceiling.

Uncle Len and Aunty Daisy stood next to us, and so did Aunty Freda and Uncle Wally. Aunty Mary held my hand. I did not recognize all the other family members, though they had greeted me. Someone lifted me up briefly so I could look into the coffin and see Grandfather sleeping. The smell of pine oil tickled my nose. I brushed back my hair to see better; my eyes blinked.

Gung-Gung's head looked smaller against the satin pillow of the big box. His eyes were closed, sunken, his skin waxy; his cheeks looked rough yet shiny, his hair perfectly combed back. I listened for his breathing, watched to see his chest rise. There was no sound. No movement. Nothing. As I was let down, I caught a glimpse of the old man's clasped hands resting so still over his dark suit. One after another, uncles and aunts bowed their heads and stepped aside. Father reached over and touched Grandfather's stiff-sleeved arm. Mother bowed three times.

As the lid was lifted up to cover Grandfather, women's hankies went up and down, which made me think of the draughty Sing Kew Opera House. Some of the men opened up their pocket handkerchiefs and blew their noses and wiped their eyes. The crying grew louder when two strangers in dark suits, using their gloved hands, turned the screws on the coffin lid.

Mother reached down and wiped my cheeks.

As the coffin lid clamped down, I knew Grandfather would never again read books with me. Never again would Father or Mother—Aunty Freda or anyone—ever hear Gung-Gung and me sing-talking together, my cheeks ballooned out like the Big Bad

Wolf, with one growling voice: I HUFF-foo! I PUFF-foo! I BLOW nay-gah *house* DOWN!

Father put on his hat and took my hand. Mother and the rest of the family trailed behind us. Turning around, I glimpsed some men lifting the polished box into the air.

Afterwards, home at last from Ocean View Cemetery, there was food and chatting and standing about. Even though it was sunny, Mother had instructed me, on this sad day, not to play outside or get my new clothes dirty. That would be disrespectful, she warned. After everyone left, I could change into play clothes and stay quietly in my room. Maybe read my books or draw pictures. Everyone looked so solemn, especially Father, I knew to be on my best behaviour. Or else.

Despite Mother's instructions to the contrary, I stepped outside. On the porch, I could still reach out my hand and remember Grandfather taking it and our going down the steps together for a short walk. Shutting my eyes, I tried hard to imagine what "sleeping forever" would be like. It was useless. There would only be darkness and quiet and nothing, and knowing it was so.

Neighbours drifted over to say hello to me.

"What happened to your grandfather?" one of them asked softly.

It was the stooped-back old man with the cane, a man in his eighties, who often walked by our house on his way to the corner store at Princess and Keefer. When I was in the front yard as he passed by, the limping veteran of the shingle mills always reached into his sweater pocket, said hello, and presented me with a paper-wrapped, three-for-a-penny candy. He did this for all the children along his walk. Some of the older kids called him, affectionately, *Lao Tong, Old Candy*. Now he lifted his cane and gently touched the black armband pinned around my jacket sleeve.

"Your grandfather gone?" he asked.

Through his rimmed glasses, Lao Tong glanced once more at my black armband and peered kindly at me.

"*Aaaiiiyaah!* Your poor grandfather's gone?" he repeated.

I felt pressured to give an answer. I was not exactly sure what to say about Grandfather, but a familiar phrase came into my head that I had heard some of my uncles use over and over again in their talk-business. It made sense for me to say it, too, like a grown-up. Lao Tong seemed very patient with me.

"*Gung-gung sung fohr!*" I said, finally. "*Grandfather shipped out!*"

The old man's pupils widened, his wrinkled cheeks puffed out, puffed in. They twitched. He couldn't seem to stop himself, couldn't hold back—he burst out laughing. When he recovered, after hacking up some spittle, he tapped me on the shoulder with his bamboo stick.

"*Nay mh-pah?*" he said, smiling. "*You not afraid?*"

"No," I said, not exactly sure what I was supposed to be afraid of. The old guy tilted his head and broke into another smile. The lenses of his glasses and his gold-capped teeth shone in the sunlight.

"*Me,* too," he said, in Toisanese. "Very soon *sung fohr!*"

Uncle Wally had stepped out and overheard our conversation. He told this episode to Father, Third Uncle, Fifth Aunty, and then to Mother. No one ever bothered to correct what I had said about Grandfather. When I was much older, and attending other funerals, no one let me forget it, either.

But something else happened in that brief conversation I had with Lao Tong on the day of Grandfather's funeral.

I expected the usual treat, so felt very disappointed when the old guy with the walking cane forgot to give me a candy. I nearly asked him for one—I was always hankering for a sweet—but

resisted because, as Father taught me, that would be rude. Chinatown boys and girls were supposed to wait politely and, if you
were patient, the good would happen.

The next time I heard the old guy's cane tapping by, I ran out
into the front yard. Lao Tong grinned broadly at me. Maybe he
could see from my moist lick of my lips that I wanted to ask him
something.

"Hold out both your hands," he said. "Make a cup."

He pressed a brimming man's handful of paper-wrapped hard
candies into my cupped hands. I could see right away, there were
round chocolate toffees among the penny candies. Unfortunately,
Mother happened to step out at just that moment, and made me
give back at least a fistful of candies and say *Doi jhay, thank you,*
three times. Mother told the old man I was just a greedy little
boy; he shouldn't waste his money on me.

Bowing his head below Mother's vision, Lao Tong accepted
some of the candies Mother pushed back into his palm. My lips
bent down with disappointment until I caught the twinkle in the
old guy's eyes. He *harrumph*ed, tapped his cane, then winked at
me. We were conspirators.

I would be patient, I thought. The good would happen again.

A few weeks later, near the end of September, the old man
with the cane, who lived in the basement of the rooming hotel a
block down from us, ended his own life. It was the talk of the
neighbourhood. He had at last been unable to leave his tiny room
and decided to lay down on the floor and open the gas jets of his
small kitchen oven.

"The whole building could have blown up," someone said to
Mother. "Luckily everyone was at work and all the kids were in
school."

"But he must have known his cousin was dropping off groceries at three that afternoon," another said.

"Of course." Mother nodded. "He must have timed the whole thing."

I like to think that Lao Tong had remembered his encounters with a confused and greedy little boy; that perhaps he even smiled; at the very least, that, as he sank into unconsciousness, he was unafraid.

Now he, like Grandfather, had only just shipped out.

# Thirteen

*Father, James Bay Hotel*

B Y THE BEGINNING OF September, all Grandfather's things had been packed and put away, and I was snugly back in my own room, my carton of toys and books now grown to a total of two full crates.

Street lights shone again at night, and cars zipped up and down our streets, their headlights stripped of tape. The nine o'clock gun boomed every evening from Stanley Park. Ships and trains brought home uniformed men and women to raucous cheering at the docks and at the railway stations. Chinatown stores brimmed with new goods, and foods and herbs that had once been rationed or scarce now filled the shelves and packed Chinatown's outdoor stands. Fresh fruits and vegetables coloured the sidewalk displays; chunks of pink pork and red beef rested on butcher blocks to be sliced and weighed. Dried lizards and sea-horses, mandrake and ginseng roots, powdered tiger bone, and bear spleens and the appendages of other wild animals fell abundantly into the herbalists' hand-held scales.

Everyone in Chinatown was finding more and more work. With orders from as far away as Hawaii, business at the Chinese sausage factory boomed; Mother's shares in Kam Yen Jan increased in value, and since Grandfather was gone now, she went back to work as a meat cutter and sausage stuffer. Aunty Freda was no longer mending or refitting old clothes; there were more and more orders for new styles, and demand grew for her fine tailoring as women at the mah-jong tables showed each other the latest pages torn from *Vogue* and *Simplicity* pattern books. Meanwhile, the shipyards were busy with exports in lumber and wheat, and Third Uncle recommended more cousins and friends to his CPR contacts. Father worked longer hours to feed hungry crews, and Mother began to worry openly about the long periods of time he spent away from us.

If Father was away from Mother and me for extended stints, it was not only because of his work schedule. I sensed things were wrong between them when Father sulked and silently packed his things, and walked out the door without saying goodbye to Mother or me.

"Your father was always away," Shirley Lee reminded me many years later. "We hardly knew him, though all the women in Chinatown noticed him. Toy Choy was very handsome."

That seems to have been the problem. Mother heard rumours

about Father's temptations, how the waitresses at Chinatown tea houses fancied him, how he had looked a little too long at this pretty acquaintance or traded endearments with Miss So-and-So. Father, for his part, resented Mother's frequent mah-jong outings and disapproved of her habit of keeping me up until the early hours of the morning. But Mother lived her social life as usual, taking me along with her as if she did not take his complaints too seriously. Father was rarely home.

---

FATHER NEVER SHOPPED with me for my clothes or shoes; it was always Aunty Freda or Mother who took me to the stores.

At Woodward's shoe department, while Mother and I waited for the clerk to bring me a better-fitting pair of Buster Browns, a tall, gangly boy paused by us. He stared at Mother until she looked up. Without any warning, he pulled back the corners of his eyes and made gibberish sounds. Mother stood up, ready to swing her purse. Laughing, the boy ran away.

"You think my eyes slant that much?" Mother asked me. "Do yours?"

I looked at us both in the store mirror. I was not sure how to answer Mother. I knew some Chinese people had eyes that slanted much more than ours, but why would a boy make fun of that? The clerk came back with a new pair of shoes.

"These should fit the young fellow," the man said, cheerfully.

They did. I walked over and stepped up onto the wooden cabinet of the X-ray machine. As I fitted my feet into the bottom slot, the man showed me how to see my own toes moving inside the viewer. I flexed my toes, felt them bump against the stiff leather uppers. The machine hummed. Shadowy toe bones moved. Mother peered through the scope, too.

"He's got room to grow," the man said. "Look at the outline of the shoe."

Mother took a deep breath. I wiggled my toes.

"We buy," she said.

Halfway home, my new shoes squeaking, as some children my age pushed past us I wondered if there was a machine that could tell how much our eyes slanted. Deep in thought, I did not notice the colour of the sky or the immensity of the North Shore mountains.

———

THAT VERY FIRST DAY at "real school" for my Grade One enrolment, Mother carried my birth certificate with her, and Aunty Freda sat down at a desk and filled in the official form. I stared down at my shiny new shoes. Mother still had on her black armband from Grandfather's funeral when we stopped in front of a student monitor in the hallway of the school and were directed to my Grade One classroom.

Miss P.M. Barber's classroom was in the north-east wing of the Strathcona complex. I remember sitting quietly during one of our first lessons.

"A is for 'Apple,'" Miss Barber said, in a strong, musical voice, and we repeated: "*A is for 'Apple.'*"

What I liked best was the green felt board the tall woman used, like the one in kindergarten, and how, at the end of every day, Miss Barber opened a book and read to us. She handled every book as if it were precious, holding the pages before us as she read *upside down!*

She always wore a bright red blazer, her chestnut hair neatly pulled back. Miss Barber was the prettiest teacher in the world, and I thought everything was going well. But that first term my report card noted that I needed to pay more attention, to talk less, to learn more. After Uncle Wally translated the bad news, Mother gave me a spanking.

"What would Grandfather think of you?" Father said.

For the rest of the term, I looked at Miss Barber with great uncertainty, and my uncertainty must have calmed me down: I wanted to please Gung-Gung and Miss Barber. At the end of the year I was promoted to Grade Two.

That July, feeling like a big boy having finished with Grade One, I began to take a stand against "the pricklies," against wearing anything made of Irish tweed.

"Stop scratching," Mother ordered.

Since those coarse pants were my best pair, it became a struggle for Mother to get me ready for my excursions with finicky Third Uncle.

"Don't you want to see the bears?" Mother would say, slapping away my hands and holding my legs still. "Don't you want to feed the ducks at Lost Lagoon?"

Or, as she did say this time, since reasons related to Third Uncle's sense of pride failed to sway me, "I hear there's a castle-building contest at English Bay. Imagine, building a castle!"

"A Robin Hood castle?"

I stopped scratching.

"Yes, Sonny." Mother knew she had me. "Castles made of sand."

"You mean, dirt?"

"Yes," Mother said. "Dirt."

Mother had been letting me get dusty and messy lately, since she couldn't stop my independent excursions to the school playground to play marbles or swing chestnut conkers, after which I came home as grimy as any of my friends. Leong Sim told Mother that a bit of dirt was good for a growing boy. "Toughens their guts," she told Mother.

"Castles made of sand," Mother repeated.

I couldn't imagine how that was possible. Castles were made of stone and brick, of thick pillars and huge wooden planks that knights on horses rumbled across. A castle made of sand?

"They're small castles," Mother explained.

For the moment, I was holding still. My imagination often tranquillized me. Mother smiled and, taking advantage of my daydreaming, quickly pushed my legs through the itchy pants and buttoned up my shirt and fastened my suspenders. Mother kept talking.

"The very top of the castles won't be any higher than the top of your head."

"Just like the Santa Claus windows?"

At Christmas, Aunty Freda always took me to tour the store windows along Hastings Street and at Spencer's. Always, there was a North Pole castle the height of a seven-year-old. It was a castle with red-and-white turrets.

I thought about the patches of bare ground in our backyard, the small heaps of dirt piled around the tomato plants, the rich loam thickly spread between the stringed rows of pea stalks. Sand was just like dirt. If I went to English Bay, I could see how to build my own castle.

When I greeted him with great excitement at the front door, Third Uncle said, "Don't scratch."

———

BY THE TIME Third Uncle and I got off the streetcar and walked down to English Bay, the sculptors were almost all finished their work. It was a cloudy mid-afternoon, but the sun broke through often enough that it made all the sculptures suddenly gleam with texture. Sea creatures rose from the shoreline, mermaids and dragons and fantasy beasts; there was a line of castles beyond these. From my seven-year-old's vantage point, the sculptures were impressive, breathtaking. I began to imagine myself creating something, too. Then the brittle, Toisan accents of my guardian broke into my daydreaming.

"They won't last," Third Uncle said, which I thought was a stick-in-the-mud thing for him to say. "Nothing lasts."

Nearer the incoming tide, groups of older children and adults were creating smaller versions of seascapes and castles by filling wooden boxes, tin buckets and open-ended cans with wet sand. Fists and palms banged on the box and bucket bottoms. Perfect rectangles of sand slipped out. From the tin cans, perfect cylinders.

"Don't get your feet wet," Third Uncle warned, pulling me back. He sniffed the threatening air. "The dampness can make you sick."

Two men and a woman were going around, giving instructions and encouragement. I listened, watched, too shy to participate. Like me, hardly anyone noticed that the sky had darkened.

"*Jul lot-sui.*" Third Uncle said. "*Rain soon.*"

The air was moist. On my tongue I could taste the iodine-smell of English Bay. Between the bare legs of adults, their feet carelessly sunk into dangerous wetness, I saw mounds of sand being carved and shaped into seahorses, crabs, lobsters, and turtles with deep-grooved backs. The sun broke through. Their shadows waned and deepened in the sunshine, then disappeared, bringing the sand creatures to life.

"I want to do that," I said to Third Uncle, meaning that I was going to go home and do that in our backyard.

"Only grown-ups do that," he said. "Too dirty for children."

"How come those kids over there are doing that?"

"They're not like you, all dressed up," Third Uncle said. "They don't know better."

One of the castles nearest the water's edge was particularly splendid, and I imagined my tin soldiers climbing those walls, my tanks pushed along those paths; my miniature cowboy horses and Indians scouting about—all of them, tanks and horses included, fighting their usual mixed-up war. There were moats for careless horses to drown in, and little pathways that no tank could navigate. My staring caught Third Uncle's attention.

"Step away from that water," he commanded.

At seven, I was old enough to know that I was never going to go out again with Third Uncle. He was never much fun, a spoilsport. He surveyed the happy scene and saw the coming of doom.

"In a couple of hours, the tide or the rain will wash everything away."

People in swimming suits dashed by us to run down the slope and jump into the water twenty feet away, but I hardly noticed them. I was busy studying how toy shovelfuls of wet sand took shape between slapping hands, how scooped palms of water were splashed onto dry patches, how fistfuls of dark silt adhered to slopes and curves and were carefully recarved with spoons, how creature-eyes were poked with thin sticks, and sagging castle walls were reformed with fragments of wood pulled across their sagging base.

When we got home, I ran into the house and changed into my play clothes as fast as I could. But just as I dashed into the kitchen ready to build my palace in our backyard, the rain began to fall in torrents.

I pulled aside the curtains and pressed my face against our kitchen window. I saw fortifications rising from a dark, glistening patch of earth between the fence and the woodpile. As the rain turned our backyard into promising mud, every detail of my dream castle grew more and more vivid. With an odd thrill, I knew it was the same downpour that must be sending the English Bay crowds scurrying for cover.

———

I THINK IT RAINED FOR TWO WEEKS.

Every night at bedtime, I told Mother how my castle would look exactly like the one I saw in the Robin Hood movie, a building even more handsome than the best one I saw at English Bay. When he was home for two days, I told Father, too.

One day I awoke to sunshine. After I ate all my porridge and willingly swallowed a spoonful of cod liver oil, Mother let me go out to play in the backyard. First, she put me into a pair of my oldest, ill-fitting, unmended pants and buttoned me up in an old shirt she had been intending to tear up for house-cleaning rags.

I gathered the castle-sculpting tools I had been saving, day after day, for this moment—a pair of chopsticks, a variety of blade-like wooden staves pulled off an orange crate, a collection of wooden cigar boxes, a bent fork and a spoon, an empty Campbell's Soup tin that Father had opened at both ends and hammered away at to blunt the sharp edges.

Outside, I knelt down around a swampy mud hole between our back fence and the woodshed. Scooping up the wet black earth with the empty soup tin, I started to make round mud forms that would stand up on their own. I had no idea there would be any difficulties. I thought all wet ground—loam, silt, beach sand, mud—was pliant and amenable to a boy's dream. My fingers were alive with the swish and slosh of thick, sucking mud as I pressed handfuls of the fragrant muck into cigar-box moulds. Out slurped five rectangular blocks to be textured with fingers and sticks and fork tines. The slabs were too soggy yet to be shifted or raised, but, with the sun beaming its heat down, I could wait. I was flushed with confidence.

I remembered the lady at the beach telling one boy how, in half an hour, he could lift with a plank a single roof-like slab and slide it off in one piece wherever he wanted.

My first idea was to put five or six soup-tin cylinders on top of each other, to build castle towers from which my toy Indians could rain down their arrows upon tanks and horses. But no more than two round clumps would stand on top of each other. A third cylinder would send the bottom two slumping down in slow motion. It was frustrating. No matter how careful I was, no matter how gently I banged to guide the cylinder of mud into place, the bottom two would gradually sag, split open, collapse.

Everything went wrong.

I tried to move one of the "walls." It, too, split, cracked, fell apart. Maybe everything was too wet. I waited. I tried again. Split. I waited more minutes. Crack. Collapse.

Mother came out and jammed a straw hat on my head. She looked at the mess around me and said nothing. I lost track of time.

When Mother called out to me from the kitchen window, I was nearly in tears and called back to her to come out. I wanted her to explain why my castle was not working out, why things fell apart. But she only stood behind the screen door and kept calling me to come in. I refused to move. She called me five times, banged the back door loudly, then finally stepped out onto the porch, waving the business end of a bamboo flyswatter menacingly in the air.

As I was brushing off my dirty knees on the sun porch, suppressing the tears of frustration that were ready to pour out, Mother commanded me to wash off my hands at the sink. I was expecting her to rap my head with her knuckles for not coming in right away. Instead, she knelt down and tugged off my muddy shoes, matter-of-factly wiped the single tear that happened to slip down my cheek, and let me walk to the sink. She was even smiling.

"Hurry," she said, as I climbed on the stool to reach the tap water. "I want you to see something special." She briskly brushed the back of my pants and took me into the dining room. I bit my lip. Third Uncle peered back at me through his rimmed glasses.

"How do you like it?" he said, pointing to the oak dining table. I turned my head.

There, on a cardboard platter in the middle of our dining table, stood a frosted box-shaped cake. Rising from the decorated cake, four towers made of joined-together cupcakes anchored the corners; thin red lines of icing outlined the shape of bricks. Half-broken tea biscuits formed turrets.

"Well," Mother said, "what do you say to Uncle?"

I thought of my perfect castle, the one that lay in sodden ruins in the backyard. I stared hard at the cake. Abruptly, before I realized what was happening, I turned around and ran into the kitchen, pushed my feet into my shoes, and slammed the screen door after me. At a safe distance, I shouted into the house, "I HATE IT!" and dashed down the back-porch steps.

As I stood crying beside the broken shapes and decaying forms of my own unmade castle, I could hear the two talking away. Then there was a long silence.

When the screen door squeaked open, I looked up. In the noon sun, thin, white, peppery-haired Third Uncle was coming towards me. I knew I deserved the worst punishment, but I didn't care anymore. And I wasn't going to say sorry to anybody. I pulled my straw hat down my brow. Though he had never done so, Third Uncle could hit me with all his might; Mother probably gave him permission. He stepped into the wet backyard and strode firmly forward, his polished shoes squishing with each step as bad waters seeped into them.

"Stop crying and do what I say," he said. "See those grass cuttings by the fence?"

Third Uncle's hand gripped the top of my hat and steered my head left. I nodded.

"Take a handful of that and mix it with the mud."

I was so astonished, I dashed to grab two fistfuls and threw everything in the muck.

"Mix it well," the dry voice said. "Now get some more cuttings."

As I added more cuttings, and mixed and mixed the mud, I could see how, gradually, the mixture thickened and became more gluey, how everything began to stick and stay together.

"Back in Old China," Third Uncle said, lighting up his pipe, "we boys had the job of making bricks like this."

I was shocked to hear that Third Uncle had been a boy once. In his day-off best suit, he looked impossibly too grown up, too old, to have ever been a boy.

"Now," he said finally, tobacco smoke streaming from his nostrils. "Do what you were doing. I'm going to have tea and a piece of cake with your mother."

He strode back up the stairs and the screen door shut behind him.

I filled the five cigar boxes with the mixture and slapped out perfect rectangular shapes that did not crack nor split. The Campbell's Soup tin turned out one cylinder of muck after another, and three stood firmly on top of each other. No collapsing. By one o'clock, my castle was finished and drying in the bright sunshine. I was covered in dirt and grass cuttings. I stepped back.

Even as a seven-year-old, I could not fool myself into thinking that the crude structure I had finally built was better-looking than the sugar-frosted one sitting on our oak table. In fact, it wasn't even close. Nor did my creation bear any resemblance to the one I had for days and days dreamed of building, no more resemblance than a scrawled crayon drawing would look like a real painting.

When Mother came out to bring me in for my late lunch, she told me Third Uncle had gone back to his ship.

"Next time he comes," she said, in firecracker Toisanese, "you apologize or I—*cham say nay!*—chop you to death with the cleaver!"

Mother paused a moment. She looked down at the squat, boxy thing with its fork-tonged scribbles, its four disproportionate cylinders. She shook her head and said nothing.

She could chop me to death with a cleaver all she wanted: I loved my humble castle.

# Fourteen

*Ready for school*

I N GRADE TWO, MY NEW teacher was Miss McLeod. She had a
calm, sweet manner, and a voice that barely rose above a whisper. She did not impress me at first. She was a stout but naturally
dainty woman with steel-grey hair. Unlike Miss Barber, who wore
impressive red jackets, Miss McLeod wore delicate lacey shirts
topped by a grey or blue sweater. Elegantly rimmed glasses
perched on her nose, and if anyone was inattentive, the slim nose
wrinkled with disapproval. We children sat quietly in her class and
strained to hear her barely audible voice call out our names to

recite or read. Some of the girls began whispering like Miss McLeod, as if we were sitting in the light of cathedral windows.

One day, after all the other students had left the elementary building, I remained behind and huddled in panic, afraid to leave. Three bullies, headed by an older Italian boy, had vowed to beat me up after school. Closing her classroom door, Miss McLeod caught sight of a frightened boy standing alone at the end of the hallway. I could hear footsteps treading quietly behind me, the voice soft and familiar.

"What's wrong... ?"

I started to cry.

Miss McLeod's sweetly tranquil murmuring made me feel how even more hopeless my situation was. It was no use crying, of course, because that only proved the bullies were right. Some of the delivery men at Kam Yen Jan used to tell us boys that sissies needed to be beaten up. *Toughens you up!* they said, sometimes staring at me and punching hard fists into the air like Joe Louis.

From the sleeve of her cloud-grey sweater, Miss McLeod pulled forth a neatly folded tissue. In class, she was always wiping our noses. She bent down, dabbed my stained cheeks, and spoke in such a hushed voice that I stopped sniffing to make out her words.

"Sonny... tell me... what's wrong?"

She turned the door handle, began to push, but I stopped her. Through the partly opened door, I shakily pointed my finger.

"Miss McLeod," I gasped, as if the saintly lady could not possibly understand, "they're going to kill me!"

Peering through the doorway, Miss McLeod could see the gang of three killers waiting for me across the street. Two of the ruffians were punching each other for practice; the third roughneck blew out a cloud of cigarette smoke, made obscene grabs at his own crotch, and began kicking at his lackeys.

Miss McLeod's gentle face hardened. She took in a deep breath and stepped out before me. To my amazement, as she threw back her shoulders, she grew taller, bigger, more formidable. She lifted her hands and cupped her mouth, and when she turned away, her elbows angled back at me like wings. Suddenly, a military voice boomed like a cannon and yelled across the street,

"YOU BOYS GO HOME!"

Three blustering boys turned to see a stout woman stepping out the door, coming at them like a small tank.

"NOW!!!" Miss McLeod bellowed.

This time her voice was so loud, it rattled the windows of the row houses on Princess Street and echoed back. One of the boys hollered "*Jiggers!*" Each boy tore away in a different direction. I watched the tawny Italian boy disappear down the alleyway.

Miss McLeod adjusted her sun-reflecting glasses, dabbed at her throat with a fresh tissue, and nodded her head. Her cheeks were flushed and her eyes glowing; a thick vein throbbed above her temple. She gave me a gentle push and watched me walk safely across Princess Street.

For whatever reason, those three older boys never troubled me again.

---

THE SUMMER OF 1946, we moved across the road to 625 Keefer Street. Grandfather had left my parents some money, and combined with my parents' savings and a mortgage from the bank, it allowed us to move to a gingerbread-trimmed house. It had four bedrooms on the second floor, and ample room downstairs. Standing high above the street, the house was reached by climbing a first set of eight stone steps, then a second flight of wooden steps, to a large covered porch.

When we moved in, Father said I could take the farthest bedroom, beside the bathroom. He and Mother took the large front bedroom. The other two rooms were used to store Grandfather's trunks and family baggage.

I liked everything about the house, since it was twice as big as the one we had rented next to the Good Shepherd Mission. Now we had a front yard with a holly tree in the middle and a spacious backyard, with a tall maple that spread its shade over our neighbour's back garden. Next door lived an old lady named Mrs Joe, and her three foster children: Phoebe, Freddy and Henry.

Along that one block lived families by the name of Chomyshak, Splett, Bezzasso, Kelly, Anaka, Benastick, Minichiello, Parker, Wakaluk and Morrison. Between and among them lived Chinese families named Woo, Cheong, Soon, Joe, Chow, and Wong. Missing were Japanese names, since, after Pearl Harbor, all Japanese families had been forced out of Vancouver.

Mother had told Dai Yee that our new house had no ghosts, and Aunty expressed relief to hear it. However, each time one of our Caucasian neighbours went by, Mother would say in crisp Toisanese, "There goes the *fay bak-kwei* or the *goh bak-kwei*," meaning "the *fat white ghost* or the *tall white ghost*."

One day, one of the white ghosts overheard Mother as we were climbing up our steps carrying groceries.

"Hey, Missy China-lady," he said huffily, "don't call me a goddamn *kwei!* I'm no goddamned ghost!"

Mother quickly hurried into the house. After that, there was no more ghost-talk from her, at least not where a white ghost might overhear.

The summer passed uneventfully. We settled easily into the new house, though Father seemed to stay away from us for longer and longer periods. One day he brought me home a bell-glassed Lady of Fatima, a souvenir from a cross-country car trip he had taken with friends to Quebec. The chalk-white Lady inside the glass bell was eight inches tall and shone in the dark.

"To keep you safe from harm," Father said.

That night, as I carried the sleek object into the dark of my bedroom, its eerie light glowing, Mother whispered to me, "Now *that's* a *bak-kwei* for sure."

The next day I showed off the Lady to Phoebe and her brothers. Lydia Chomyshak walked by and decided then and there to teach me how to cross myself before the Holy Virgin and make wishes. Like Santa Claus, Lydia told me, the Lady would know whenever I was bad or good.

"Don't pray in Chinese," Lydia warned. "She wouldn't understand you."

"So?"

"So you won't get your wish," Lydia said, her eyes rolling at my stupidity.

"So?"

Exasperated, Lydia narrowed her eyes. "She'll jump out and strangle you."

From that same night on, I decided to let Mother display the Lady in the bell jar on the parlour mantel.

The week before Grade Three started, I decided to test the Lady. Alone in the parlour, I knelt before the mantel and, using my best English, prayed for a nice teacher. Not someone called Miss Doyle—who Shirley and Lil Lee had warned me was the toughest teacher alive—but a teacher like Miss Schooley or Miss Farrington, the ones everyone loved. *Amen.*

As she stood in the dark above my bowed head, just as Lydia had instructed me I prayed to the Lady of Fatima for three nights straight. Three was a lucky number.

MOTHER, LEONG SIM, Dai Yee and Lew Sim—all our mothers—
were gossiping over afternoon tea at Garson's house, and we were
allowed to play together on the sidewalk; so we four boys—Garson, King, Weiner Lew, and I—ran outside into the sun. I was
seven that year, the second-oldest of the four of us. A neighbourhood boy, Francey Franchini, came over and joined us. Rowdy
and high-spirited, the five of us immediately raced into a game
Francey had made up: whoever was "it" could sprint up or down
the street, and the others had to follow. The first one to touch a
spot the leader touched was the "winner." No one was to run into
the road, and the leader could dash between neighbouring
houses or up and down sidewalk steps but not into front or back
gardens. The one who was first to slap his hand on the exact spot
became the next leader. Ties didn't count.

We were giddy with the summer air, tearing up and down the
street, shouting and laughing, grabbing wooden rails and hopping up stairs, dashing down the tiny alleys between the row
houses and buildings along Keefer Street. I slapped my hand
down hard and took over King's third turn.

Taking my turn as leader, I zigzagged down the street, half
running up stairs, then jumping back down to the sidewalk,
and finally slapping my hand hard onto the cement wall of the
OK Rooms Hotel.

"Goal!" I said.

The others ran crashing into each other to slap the same spot.

Stepping quickly aside, I had to see who was first to hit the
mark. The smallest guy, Garson, pushed his hand through a gap
created by the other three boys and beat out King, Francey, and
Weiner.

"Garson first!" I said.

But no one gave up. Grubby hands kept flying up to hit the
bare-brick spot Garson had just slapped. He half-landed outside

the huddle of bodies that were now falling over each other, dragging me down as well. Laughing and wrestling each other, the five of us tumbled from the small patch of grass in front of the OK Rooms onto the sun-warmed sidewalk. Francey gave out a cowboy yodel, and Weiner Lew pushed him down; my cousin King started to climb over my back. I ended up tripping Garson deeper into a pile of arms and legs and bobbing heads. Like perfume, the smell of starchy shirts and crushed grass rose from the heat of our boys' bodies.

In the midst of our silliness, huge hands lifted Garson away from us. We were all aghast to see the bottom of his soles rising into the air, headed towards the blue and cloudless sky. Garson struggled at first, then recognized the man who was lifting him up and threw back his head to ride out the adventure.

Pushing aside King's arm and someone else's cuffed ankle, I recognized the new boarder from Mui Goo's house, the young, strong-armed shingle-mill labourer we were taught to address as Sum Sook. His muscled arms straightened out, and Garson rose higher into the air. One arm dropped down, and Garson's small body arched precariously over the giant's large palm. Garson screamed with giddy alarm.

With a swinging motion, Sum Sook flip-tossed Garson into the air so high up that Garson began to fall feet first. Faster than we could see what was happening, Sum Sook triumphantly stood up. High above us, Garson suddenly sat, giddily, legs astride his broad shoulders. Sum Sook knelt down and Garson hopped off, his small face flushed.

"Holy cow!" Francey said.

One after another we stood up. Who would be next?

"Sum Sook!" I said. "My turn!"

I was a head taller than Garson, heavier, limbs and back less flexible. None of that mattered to Sum Sook. His eyes reflected a stubborn fire. With one swinging motion, large hands scooped me up, lifting me off the ground. I went flying up, up, up. The world suddenly spun around me, sky and ground, ground and sky. I was being tossed and turned and tossed... My heart raced with fright. I wanted to laugh, to cry, to scream. I screamed.

Then, before I knew it, my body thumped down and I was astride the big man's shoulders, hands gripping his head, then slipping down so my fingers knitted together beneath his rough chin.

I brushed his jaw with my palms as if he were sculpture. The big man hardly noticed. He was talking to the boys about playing another game. He shifted and my body jogged against him. Then a warmth rose from my groin and began to spread, tingling, down my legs and up my spine. For a few seconds, the pleasure was almost unbearable. Someone called out my name, but I could not answer. All at once, another jog, and Sum Sook's angled trim body sunk down towards the ground and my feet touched the sidewalk. I began to slide off his wide shoulders. What was odd—what he must have noticed at last—was how I could not seem to unknit my fingers to let go of him. I felt dizzy, disoriented, every part of my body spinning.

"Hey, hey," a heavy voice said. "Are you OK, Sonny?"

"Move!" Weiner said. "It's my turn."

I stepped back, dazed. At my side, as I stepped back, the tips of my fingers remembered the rough, sandpapered feel of Sum Sook's jaw. One after another the boys took their turn with Sum Sook. He was tireless, fun-loving, our innocent big brother. But the force of something beyond my boy's universe had slipped between Sum Sook and myself. No one else noticed. Not even Sum Sook. I held my breath.

"Who wants another turn?" the big man asked, flexing his arm muscles.

I said nothing. I had had enough.

Someone else, perhaps it was my cousin King, went swinging into the air. I stood back from everyone and heard a boy's laughter, felt the breeze flung outward by the torque of a whirling body.

Dazed, I stood and watched. All that summer, I felt different, but had no understanding. Everything outwardly, after all, seemed the same.

---

THE LADY OF FATIMA never strangled me: instead, she failed me.

Miss Gertrude Doyle ruled with a snarl and the threat of a leather strap.

One day, restless, I dipped my favourite pen in the small glass inkwell sitting in the right-hand corner of the desk. We were supposed to be reading; I dipped when I shouldn't have dipped. White-haired Miss Doyle tore across the room, grabbed my pen from my hand and threw it against the far wall.

"*You* LISTEN TO ME*!*" she said. "*READ!*"

My ears vibrated with her voice. Having become accustomed to Miss McLeod's hushed tones, I was in shock. Miss Doyle pointed to the corner of the room and sternly motioned me to pick up my pen. I did. The nib was bent, useless. This was my best nib. My eyes went back to the page we were reading, something about Dick and Jane. I tried not to cry, but a blur of colour floated from the book. The recess bell rang.

"Stay behind, Sonny," Miss Doyle said.

"Now you're going to get it," someone said, snickering, as the other kids pushed past my desk. I couldn't stop my lower lip from trembling.

Miss Doyle stepped out to escort the rest of the students into the hall, as she always did. Alone, I rubbed my eyes with my shirt sleeves. There was the teacher's leather weapon hanging next to the Neilson's Chocolates Map of the World. I knew I had to get ready to be strapped. Executed. Shot and decapitated. I hated school. I hated Miss Doyle. My ears roared with fear. I had never been strapped before.

Miss Doyle walked into the room and shut the door behind her. Best not to let the world hear my screams. She went towards the strap, and I shuddered. Miss Doyle turned to her desk and looked in a side drawer. She was probably going to put on her executioner's gloves, just like the ones the school inspector was said to wear when strapping delinquent boys. That was what one of the senior monitors told us boys in Grade Two. That's why all the boys and girls had to line up straight, not talk, and walk directly to our classes. However, girls were never strapped. They were just sent to the Nurse's Office. There was simply no justice.

I heard the big woman leave her desk and walk towards me. I didn't dare look up. She had a mean, red-cheeked face, eyes like bluish crystal that could bore through you. Her white hair told me she was the oldest woman I ever knew.

"Sonny," Miss Doyle said. Her voice was calm. "I'm sorry that I got so upset with you."

I lifted my head a little, just to peek at her. The voice remained calm.

"You know you should have been reading, don't you?"

"Yes, Miss Doyle," I said. I was holding the twisted nib and staring at it.

For a long moment, the big woman said nothing. Tears dropped into my lap. I hated feeling guilty.

"Here," she said, finally. "Wipe your nose."

I took the tissue and wiped my nose and dabbed my eyes.

"Go out and play, Sonny."

I stood up, barely glanced at Miss Doyle, and quickly walked out. In the school ground, I spent some minutes by myself, thinking and thinking, until some boys from my class noticed me under the stairwell.

"Did you get it?"

"Didn't hurt at all," I said.

Unfortunately, someone noticed the Kleenex in my hand; my cover was blown. One of the boys laughed.

When the bell rang, I waited for most of my classmates to go back into Miss Doyle's class first, thinking and praying that no one would notice me. When I sat down at my desk, my eyes widened with embarrassment: there was some more incriminating tissue on my desk. As I lifted my hand to sweep it off, Miss Doyle called for everyone's attention.

"I wanted you all to know," she began, "that I have pinned on the back display board the best writing for this month."

She marched to the back of the class.

Everybody turned their heads to follow Miss Doyle—everyone but me. I just pretended to turn my head slightly; my fingers crawled along the desk to snatch away the tissue. Miss Doyle always made a show of this event. Best Writing. Best Reader. Best Art. She unpinned the *Healthy Daily Foods* poster. Lined up behind the poster were four tidy pages of penmanship.

"Yes, you can now see who has done the very best work in this class."

Someone sitting near the back was told to read the name out. A barely heard girl's voice said, "It's Sonny Choy."

At the same time as I had been slowly dragging away the offending tissue with my baby finger, I heard my name being repeated. Everyone turned to look at me. *Caught.* To my horror, as every boy and girl stared at the cry-baby, the next nervous tug of my finger made the tissue on my desk open like a white flower. In its centre, gleaming like silver petals, were three brand new nibs. Corry and Sammy, both sitting across from me, saw the gleaming points. Corry smiled. I knew she liked me. Sammy looked envious. You could make arrows with extra nibs and fire them at tree trunks.

"Take out your writing books," Miss Doyle commanded. "*NOW!*"

All the boys and girls, even Sammy and me, quickly reached into our desks and picked up our penholders. I licked one of the new nibs, tasted the oil, and fitted it tightly into the slot. It felt good. Miss Doyle carefully demonstrated the new exercise we were to copy out, her large hand sweeping in chalky white curves between grey lines on the blackboard.

Ready to be broken in, my newly fitted nib flexed and creaked between the wide blue lines of my penmanship book. The curving, swinging arcs Miss Doyle drew were perfect exercises for training Grade Three writers.

"Be like birds swooping down," Miss Doyle said.

Everyone strained to think of flight, to be accurate, to be graceful. Miss Doyle warned Sammy and me to sit up straight—*or else.* I stiffened my back. The nib flew.

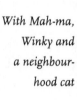

## Fifteen

*With Mah-ma,
Winky and
a neighbour-
hood cat*

T HE FIRST SATURDAY OF our Easter holidays, Mother promised me a nice surprise because, in spite of my complaints, I had survived Miss Doyle for so long and my report card
said: Good to Very Good. She said it was not chocolate bunnies—too much chocolate was bad for me—or hard-boiled
Easter eggs, which she thought was a waste of eggs. It was to be
a surprise.

That morning she left me alone to play in the backyard while
she was doing housework in the kitchen. She let me wear my

favourite short pants, torn ones made of a khaki twill that I could get as dirty as I felt like without being scolded. When I heard voices coming from the open window, I turned from my empire-building to look through the back kitchen window.

A tall man in a red plaid shirt and patched overalls was talking to Mother. It was Old Wong, a darkly tanned farmer who on some Saturday mornings drove his run-down Ford slowly along our street, the back and side of his fenced-in truckbed crowded with open crates of cabbages and bok choy, and baskets of snowpeas, tomatoes, cucumbers and lettuce. "*Fresh vegetables!*" he would shout. "*Morning fresh!*"

Mother called me in and pointed to the sink. She helped me hop up onto the broken-back kitchen chair and turned on the tap. With the tall farmer in our kitchen, I didn't want to make a fuss, like I was a baby.

"Use the soap," Mother said. "Did you say hello to Mr Wong?"

Her anxious smile told me right away something was going to happen. I quickly nodded my greeting to Old Wong, shook my wet hands the way Father taught me and quickly hopped off the chair.

"Dry yourself properly," Mother said, handing me a tea towel. She gently gripped me by the shoulders.

"Turn around," she said.

Old Wong reach down into a knee-high sturdy cardboard box and lifted out a paper bag filled with tins. With a rough, sunburnt hand, he quickly closed the flaps of the box. On its own, the flat side of the large carton facing me suddenly shifted, tilted.

"Look," I said, as if no one else had noticed.

The cardboard side began to bend, to push out by itself. The box yelped. There was a scrambling noise. Another yelp. I dropped the towel.

"What's that?" I asked.

"This is the food you'll need to buy," the tall man said. He was holding up some labelled cans. I didn't understand.

I thought at first the box contained one of those plump, red-feathered chickens to slaughter for Father's month-end home-coming. Third Uncle or Uncle Wally, or even Aunty Freda, would come over and do the job. I would stand there, squirming with bloodlust and breathless at the sudden *whack!* of the axe; I loved to hear myself squeal as the flapping headless creature staggered and heaved about our backyard, neck squirting.

But this was not the chicken man.

"Make sure," the man said, "you put out a bowl of water, too." He put the bag of tins down on the kitchen table.

"You haven't told him?" the man said.

Mother shook her head and wiped her hands on her feedsack apron; she gave me a push.

"Go and look inside the box."

I nervously walked over. The man flipped out one of the card-board flaps. The box shifted again.

"Go ahead," Mother said. "Take a look."

I peeked and caught my breath.

From inside the box, lit by a triangle of daylight, eyes as large as shiny brown marbles stared up at me. They blinked.

"A puppy," I whispered, as if no one else would have known.

Beneath a quivering black nose, a wet pink tongue slipped busily back and forth. I pushed aside the flaps of the box and the sunlight poured in. A chubby, thick-pawed, blond-headed mon-grel copped an attitude and looked up at me.

I said hello and then turned to Old Wong. "It looks shaky."

"He's a boy, like you. Take a closer look."

I knelt down beside the carton.

Standing on his squat hind legs, blinking furiously at the sun-light, the tubby, yapping creature hopped towards me, his front legs pumping frantically, as if he might fly. The triangular head dipped and shook, its roving, sandpaper tongue licking every-where—across his muzzle, across his oversized paws, across my reaching fingers. The beanbag torso slid, folded, skipped away, and careened back up, hopping, shaking its behind. Each time stubby paws bounced against the cardboard walls, the puppy fell backwards; the sides of the box bent, curved, buckled.

"Pick him up," Old Wong said.

Large brown eyes turned up to gaze at me; my own eyes widened. For the longest moment, the puppy and I faced each other. His warm, wheezing doggy breath matched my own breath-less disbelief. My heart pounded. I hadn't expected anything like this. *Was he my very own dog?*

With both hands, I reached right into the box and put my fingers around the pup's plush squirming midsection. His weight shifted like a small bag of rice. As I lifted him higher and higher, the twitching bundle stretched out his limbs.

"*Oh-kee-doke*," I said. Pudgy paws kicked in vain to balance itself.

"Don't drop him," Mother said.

At the sound of her voice, the puppy stopped moving. Blinking furiously at the bright sunlight, ears alert, tongue lolling, he looked about our kitchen. Lifting him higher, I could see the dog had a wee-wee. I rubbed my head and nose into its white belly and took a deep breath. Damp oily fur. Dog pee.

"Is he mine?" I asked.

"Hold him carefully," Mother said.

I panicked. What if Old Wong was only offering to sell him? What if Mother said no?

But Mother said, "Do you like him?"

I did not realize I had to like the puppy; I only knew I wanted him.

"You can keep him if you pass Grade Three," Mother said.

Miss Doyle's eyes flashed before me. Now I would have to really study, to practise my penmanship and my spelling and my arithmetic.

"What will you call him?" Old Wong asked. "Every boy gets to name his own dog."

As I held the wriggling, blinking beast, eyeball to eyeball, the name came to me at once.

"Winky," I said. "He's winking at me."

Winky yelped.

"He wants something," Old Wong said. He patted Winky's head with his farmer's hand. "He's talking to you, Sonny."

Winky's stubby paws frantically waved in the air; I held him tightly, turned him sideways. He was my very own.

"What d'you want?" I asked.

A stream of pee ran down my arms.

---

IF I HAD KNOWN Winky would turn into the kind of rugged and fiery dog he became, I think I might have named him Rover or Stampede. He had a rough-and-tumble spirit that little reflected the childish and puny name I gave him. He was a mixed Yellow Lab, the other parts of the mixture mostly unknown, a mongrel with short blond fur and a great appetite. Old Wong said he had been weaned and could eat anything we had.

"Here," he said, picking up a tin from the kitchen table. "Give him some dog food."

Mother opened up the can and banged half of its contents onto a plate. I put Winky's nose beside the grey chunks. In minutes, he gobbled up every bit of it and was pushing at the empty plate with his nose. Mother gave me a bowl to fill with water. I lay down on the linoleum floor and watched with growing pride as Winky slobbered up the whole bowl of water. Mother looked disconcerted, but I knew Winky wasn't going to be a prissy dog like the thin Whipper down the street. Before he left us, Old Wong looked pleased that Winky was hopping up on me and licking my face.

"The puppy will cry a bit tonight," he said to Mother, and left her staring after him. She must have had a few questions to ask, but Old Wong was in a hurry to sell the rest of his vegetables.

When Mother picked up the empty box, something pattered about.

"Leftover business," Mother said, mysteriously.

I looked inside. It was the rest of Winky's excitement—steaming fresh and rolling about like small chocolate eggs.

———

NEITHER MOTHER NOR I had any idea about how to raise a dog. Winky might have considered himself blessed, for he had fallen into a life of more freedom and less discipline than any spirited canine might dare to hope for.

It turned out he came from a litter belonging to one of Mother's mah-jong cohorts, a woman who thought I should have a companion. "Sonny's an only child," Mother was told. "He needs an only dog. Keep him company. Keep you both safe at night."

The whole of that day I fed Winky reddish-grey gobs of the leftover tinned dog food. My fingers smelled like salty baloney. He licked hungrily, growling with pleasure. I watched him slop his oversized head into the water bowl and laughed at his attempts to slurp and lick up the liquid. Mother let me take him out on our porch. The first week, every day I sat on our front steps and showed him off to every passer-by who happened to stop.

"I get to keep him," I told neighbours and strangers alike. "Because I'm going to pass Grade Three."

Winky licked my face.

---

THE NEIGHBOURHOOD children soon spread the word. Surrounded by the envious Lydia Chomyshak, who was already a teenage girl; Tommy Cheong; ooohing and aaahing Jen-Jen and Alvin Lee; and my next-door playmates, Phoebe, Henry and Fred John—that first week I held some power: I had the right to decide who could touch Winky, who might pick him up, and who could be my best friend for two minutes. Lydia Chomyshak, the oldest of us all, helped me to make up my mind.

"I'll do *one-potato*," she said.

Everyone lined up and held out their fists. Lydia launched in with *one-potato, two-potato, three-potato* . . . *FOUR!*, tapping each fist with her own. At *FOUR!* someone was eliminated. Finally, Fred John was the last one standing. Winky wriggled into his arms. Half of us sat down and formed a circle on the sidewalk and Fred let go of him. Winky bounced up and licked my face.

Already more than three handfuls big, Winky must have then been a few months old. He could stand up on his hind legs, busily bump his head against you, lick frantically and, if you molested him enough, even nip at your fingers. His handsome head, the thrust of his ears, the gleaming blond-whiteness of his coat and his quizzical round eyes made us all reach out to pet him.

"Is he a smart dog?" Henry asked.

"Sure he is," I said, and commanded, "Winky, *be smart!*"

Actually, I had no idea what would happen. But when I clapped my hands together, like a magician, Winky's tail shot up. Lydia snapped her fingers over his head. He bounced up on his hind legs like a circus dog. Phoebe and Henry applauded.

"Fall down," I commanded, slapping my hand on the sidewalk. Everybody else slapped their hands, too. Winky fell down and rolled about, trying to lick our fingers.

"He's *really* smart," Jen-Jen said.

I felt as if Winky and I were heroes.

———

THAT FIRST WEEK, Mother decided the puppy should stay in the kitchen, in a wooden crate she had set up beside the sink. As we walked away, and Mother switched off the kitchen light, Winky at once began to hop up and down, yelping and whining frantically. His half-barks pulled me back to him.

"I'm going to sleep beside the box," I announced. "He misses me."

"No," Mother said. "He probably misses his mummy. He has to learn to be by himself."

I refused to leave Winky. He was mine. I would gladly give up a comfortable bed. Besides, Mother had just mopped the kitchen floor, and I relished sliding my body along the cold, cracked linoleum, deeply breathing in the heady octane whiffs of Johnson's Floor Wax.

"I'm not leaving him."

At the sound of my protest, Winky's own yelps grew more hysterical. I ran back to the side of the box and knelt down, settling my hands around the warmth of my licking, pawing puppy. I mimicked Winky's whimpering. We were in this together.

Eventually, Mother gave in. Winky could stay with me until he was big enough to sleep by himself.

"He's going to guard the house when he grows up," Mother said. "He has to stay downstairs to do that."

Mother carried his box and I carried Winky up the stairs to my bedroom. She put a large towel in the box he came in, picked up Winky, and let him sniff about and push the towel into a heap. But after just a few minutes, he began yelping. He didn't quiet down unless I picked him up again and let him dig a space between the top of the bedsheets and my head.

"You'll smother each other," Mother said, taking him off the bed and putting him back into his box. She had heard that sleeping cats could suffocate babies. But I wasn't a baby. Winky wasn't a cat.

Finally, I shifted to the edge of the bed, looked down at him and dropped my left hand into the box. He licked my fingers, and curled up against the towel, head propped on the palm of my hand. We were both content.

"Good," Mother said. "See if you can sleep like that."

We did.

---

FOR THE FIRST FEW months, my puppy followed me everywhere. Unfortunately, Winky was fast becoming a nuisance.

Whenever the neighbourhood kids played Hide 'n' Seek, I was always caught. Winky followed me into the best hiding places, like the narrow space between the garbage bin and the back wall of the Good Shepherd Mission Church. He always barked whenever someone came close to our spot, so I was constantly "it." Later, playing tag, everyone was tripping over him as he hopped up against their legs to play his doggy version of the game. When some of us boys started to play King of the Hill and piled on top of each other, Winky bounded in and then got so excited that he peed on us. Finally, I had Mother keep Winky in the house unless I was doing nothing but sitting around.

"He's just being a good guard dog," Mother told me. "Winky's supposed to get excited if there's anything unusual happening."

One night, something unusual did happen.

Strange grunting noises from down the hallway had awakened Winky. He whimpered and hopped in his box, his legs now longer than his torso, and woke me up. I heard the noises, too, but had no recognition of where the grunts were coming from. Winky whined, then licked my wrist and nibbled my fingers until I had to get up.

Rubbing half-shut eyes with the back of my pyjama sleeves, I hopped off my bed and blithely sauntered to the side of my parents' double bed to complain that I couldn't sleep. That Winky was keeping me awake. Before I could say anything, I realized that something was happening: the mattress was squeaking, and Mother and Father were moving about on it. Neither one was aware of me standing there beside the bed.

The fog in my brain began to lift; I noticed that my parents were—quietly, gently–*wrestling*. Though unaware that parents might grapple in special ways, I was not at all surprised that they wrestled. At seven, wrestling with pals on the playground and with my cousin King in the parlour of Kam Yen Jan was a common form of play-fighting.

Whenever King and I were wrestling, tumbling off the sofas onto the dusty carpet, we hated to be interrupted before one of us had said, "Uncle!" Once King and I were trying to break a tie; the loser had to pedal the large tricycle that would speed down the long third-floor hallway of Kam Yen Jan. The winner got to ride on the back of the trike, yelling a cowboy "*Giddy-up!*" I was older and bigger than King, and usually won.

There were also those wrestling pictures in the sports pages that the older boys always looked at. The men who went to the Exhibition grounds at Hastings Park to take in wrestling matches came back and told us stories of the fights, how the good guys always won at the last minute, how the crowds always cheered.

That night, the few gentle movements that I witnessed between Father and Mother did not alarm me. Father arching his back and easing his head over Mother's shoulder, just seemed to be play-fighting, and he seemed to be winning the match.

"I can't sleep," I wailed.

Turning his head, Father looked annoyed at seeing me there. Mother peered over Father's bare shoulder, now unmoving, and pushed her chin up to see me.

"Go back to bed," she said. "You were dreaming."

The back of my fists scrubbed the sleep from my eyes. Father adjusted the bedding and pulled a blanket over himself. Mother sat up and held a sheet to her chin.

"Go back to your room," she said. "I'll get you some warm milk."

"Cocoa!" I said, and turned to stumble back. I loved my cocoa. With groggy head, I lay waiting in my bed. Father had looked upset, but that was understandable: Mother looked like she was about to say "Uncle!"

The next day in the kitchen, Mother reminded me how I had been sleepwalking.

"Do you remember anything?"

I caught Mother's eyes glinting at Father sitting beside me at the table. The corn flakes crunched between my teeth. I was not fooled: I knew I hadn't sleepwalked.

"Yes," I said. "You forgot to give me my cocoa before bedtime, so I couldn't sleep."

"No, I didn't forget," Mother said. "Here's proof." She held up my favourite Ovaltine cup. "You were very sleepy when you drank your cocoa."

She plunged the mug into soapy dishwater, swished it around, wiped it clean.

"Did I drink every drop?" I asked, marvelling that I could have forgotten.

"Every drop," Father said, beaming. "Winky had some, too." The taste of sweet cocoa skimmed over my tongue. The discussion ended. I hadn't thought to bring up anything else; my world was warm cocoa. Mother put a steaming full cup before me. I poured some cocoa into the saucer to cool. Beside my chair, hopping on his hind legs, Winky waited for his share.

———

BY THE END OF THAT summer, I was in grade four. The stern, humourless woman who taught us arithmetic was also my homeroom teacher. She controlled every detail of her classroom, every second of her students' breathing. Not only did she believe in the maxim that "silence is golden," she thought silence was eternal. Her rusty hair, classically knotted in a perfect bun, Miss Tight Lips peered over her firmly perched glasses, thin lips pressed shut, and dared any of her wards to fall out of line. Never mind out of their seats.

I couldn't help it.

As a consequence of Mother having used Sunlight bar soap to wash my underwear, an itching, burning rash had flared on my bottom. Since scratching was out of the question—we were never supposed to take our hands off our desks unless we were told to get our books out—my only relief was to push down with all my weight and slide back and forth on the hinged-back seat.

Back and forth my posterior glided, back and forth along the hardwood seat. Relief was palpable. Then the back-pocket button of my pants got caught between bum and board. Before I could stop myself, the pocket, threads and button tore away, assaulting the tomb-like silence with an Abbott and Costello's mummy's revenge: *rrrr-rippppp.*

Miss Tight Lips suddenly turned around; I froze. Her red eagle-eyes checked every boy and girl sitting in place, saw every hand folded in prayer. Miss Tight Lip's instincts were flawless. She took a deep breath and turned back to her row of chalked numbers. My face grew red. The itching now felt like a thousand biting ants.

I pushed my bottom harder against the plank seat. My cheeks wiggled with the rhythm, faster and faster, from left to right, right to left. The relief felt good—perhaps *too* good. I sighed—a little too loudly. Just as I lost control, scratching right to left, Miss Tight Lips turned around. I shot off the seat like a cartoon rabbit and crashed to the floor. The hinged seat flipped up with a bang.

A few giggles were quickled stifled by piercing, bloodshot grey eyes. Miss Tight Lips raised one eyebrow.

"*Sonnnny!* What do you think you're doing?"

There was no possible answer: the words for an itchy bum were not in my public vocabulary. When the bell rang, everyone left but me.

It was an unimaginable and wicked punishment, an unjust and foul penalty for something I could not control. I longed to be yelled at, or even—maybe—to be strapped. But the narrow woman in sensible shoes went to the tall cupboard at the back and took out her dreaded thick wad of three-by-five-inch cards. All the while, she shook her head with disappointment.

She took me by the ear and stood me beside her desk. *Three* randomly picked work cards slapped down on her desk. It was horrible: you got one card for talking in class; two for making unseemly noises, such as laughing or burping; and three for heinous crimes, such as falling off your seat. I looked at the long, long row of numbers on each work card.

"Add these up and check your answers carefully."

With Miss Tight Lips sitting beside me correcting papers, I forgot all about my itchy bum. Today, I have even forgotten her name. But I do remember every lyric of a big-band song that drove her crazy that year.

The senior Grade Eight class, rehearsing for their spring fashion show, played "Smoke Gets in Your Eyes"—the song selected for their catwalk—over and over and over again, every afternoon for two weeks. The school auditorium sat directly across the courtyard from our open second-storey windows. On the first day, it seemed to me those thin lips were silently mouthing the lyrics. By the end of an hour, her face was wrinkled with stress. Into the second hour, freckles stood out on her face like a rash.

By the second day, Miss Tight Lips shut all three windows. Still the stubborn tune came muffling through. By the third day, Miss Tight Lips shut her eyes and clenched her fists each time the opening bars were played. By Thursday, she began to put books along the crack of the window ledge. By Friday the books held down the blinds, and we sat in semi-darkness, still faintly serenaded from across the yard.

"Instead of doing arithmetic, we will all read aloud today," the stern voice announced from behind the dim desk in front of us.

And in the semi-darkness we tried to make out the words from our textbook. I don't remember why she never turned on the lights. She never did. Perhaps she felt the classroom was a kind of bomb shelter. And I don't even remember what we read, but in a chorus of every known accent, twenty-five or thirty voices read, each at its own bumbling, mumbling speed. We sounded like a Munchkin mob surrounding the Wicked Witch of the West.

"Keep reading, keep reading," the witch urged. "*Speak up!*"

Frazzled, jerking her head as if to shake off the music or to conduct our chaotic reading, Miss Tight Lips gripped the pages of her textbook and slowly, slowly, began to rip out one page after another—until, finally, the school bell rang.

———

AS THE WEEKS WENT by, mother grew frantic. Winky seemed incapable of being house-broken. All through the summer he had been playing outside with me, doing his business mostly in our backyard, in the alleyway, beneath local trees or in neighbours' yards, and on lamp-posts and corner hydrants.

But in September, when I was in school and Mother at work, that is, when no one was home, we tied Winky up to our old, empty garage. He waited for us to come home every day, barking and pushing his way through the broken garage door to greet us. Then, when he came into the house, he lifted his leg and peed against our kitchen wall. If Mother yelled at him, he darted away and found another wall. She asked our neighbours what to do. She asked her lady friends. One mah-jong lady said, rather too casually, "In China, dogs are for eating."

Her other friends told Mother to use old newspapers, spreading them out for Winky to sniff, for him to pee on, then slowly moving the newspapers outside.

"Don't waste your time, Choy Sim," another said to her. "Just roll up the newspaper and smack the dog on its behind. It works with children, too."

I suppose I didn't help. Some days I was too lazy to take my dog out for his walk. Gradually, he got the idea that the whole house was his toilet. Every time Winky did his business, I tried to hide the consequences. I moved chairs around, threw my trader comic books down to soak up the wetness, or delicately picked up the doggy goods with wads of newspapers; if I had to, I would bump into Mother's path if she came too close to the evidence. But, of course, time and my failing interest betrayed me. In a day or two, drifting odours would signal the location of Winky's last dumping target.

In spite of all the advice she got, Mother did not like to hit any living thing (except for her knuckling my head now and again), even if a boy or a dog might well deserve it. Instead, she compromised: Leong Sim told her to drag Winky to the scene of the crime and demonstrate her anger. At first, when Mother raised the rolled-up newspaper, I grabbed her wrist and, with my knee, pushed Winky away. She explained to me how she was just going to hit the soiled spot to scare him.

"You'll see," she said. "Winky will learn not to dirty the house."

"Teach him well," Father warned. He was tired of hearing about Winky's habits every third or fourth week when he came home. He was even more tired of smelling the consequences, which Mother tried to deodorize with a mixture of vinegar and soda, and splashes of Florida Water.

But every time Mother rolled up a newspaper to whack the latest soiled spot, shouting "*NO!*" to Winky, I held my palms tightly over my dog's ears. He would arch his back, his head struggling against my grip. When freed, he darted away, quickly turned, and growled at Mother and me as if we had gone temporarily mad.

That was when I discovered Winky was intelligent.

He accepted Mother's *NO!* and, being very smart, made sure he never, never, *never,* soiled the same spot twice.

"It's working," I said, pointing to another new spot Winky had just flooded. But Mother didn't see things my way.

Out of her limited understanding, her confused frustration, she took to tapping Winky on the nose with the rolled-up newspaper for doing what comes naturally. When I saw him pull back his head and snap at the offending paper cudgel, I pushed Winky away from her.

"Don't hit him," I said. "He just forgets. *DON'T!*"

Winky yapping, a newspaper club swinging wildly over his head, me shouting and pushing my way between them, Mother chased us both out the back door.

I complained to Father about all this when he was home one weekend, but he scolded me for having such a bad dog. I ran into my bedroom before a single tear could fall. Winky ran after me. We stayed huddled under my bed. As I whispered murderous plans to Winky, I heard Mother telling Father, "The two are *lat sing mah-lau!—unleashed monkeys!*"

"*A bang giu gau,*" Father said. "*A fool calling for a dog!*" Father meant that a dog or boy would always disobey Mother; she was too easy. They started to argue.

Minutes went by. No one bothered to come and get me or Winky, so I climbed up onto my bed with Winky and stayed there reading comics until, at last, Winky grew ravenous for his supper. We came downstairs and left the house through the front door, which I quietly closed, and then dashed along the side lane to the backyard. Winky barked, and I caught Mother looking at us from the kitchen window. We came in through the back door. Mother sighed, no doubt relieved to see that we had just both peed against the garage wall.

"Button up your fly," she said to me.

I could tell Mother thought Winky and I had both learned something.

I DID LEARN MORE about dogs at school. I always loved my comic books, even before I could read them. When I learned enough words, I read them every chance I could get, sneaking them under my shirt or sweater into Miss McArthur's Grade Four library period.

One fateful day, Miss McArthur reached behind a big geography book and firmly snatched away *Superman*.

"Read this," she commanded, as if she were quoting from Scripture, "What you read *matters*."

In place of *Superman*, a dark-blue book with a torn cover fell into my hands. The gruesome volume smelled of dust. I flipped through a few pages. It was discouraging, a dead weight of nothing but words. My eyes caught a few black-and-white illustrations. One pictured three large guard-dogs, each with eyes as big as saucers under the title "The Tinderbox." The wide-eyed mongrels provoked me to think of Winky. I grew curious. I didn't know dogs could figure in stories so prominently.

*A soldier came marching down the road: Left . . . right!*
*Left . . . right!*

I knew about soldiers. I struggled with some of the other words. I started to read.

The next story I read was about a Chinese emperor and his nightingale.

*. . . This story happened a very long, long time ago. And that is just the reason why you should hear it now, before it is forgotten. The Emperor of China's palace was the most beautiful one in the whole world . . .*

In those printed words, the Chinatown voices that told me stories of *long-ago* Ancient and Old China came echoing back to me. I read another story. And another. My eyes raced over new words that I had never seen before. I read a passage about a wicked witch who had "a lower lip that hung way below her chest"—I was elated: no one had to tell me what Andersen meant by "a disgusting sight."

If I stumbled on a word or a phrase, I saw Gung-Gung's finger on the page and heard his voice, "What do you *think* it means?"

The next day I asked smiling Miss McArthur for the same book and reread "The Tinderbox." I relished again the last sentence, how, "the three dogs sat at the table and made eyes at everyone." I looked up from the book and felt as if my brain had stumbled upon a secret, discovered a new world.

When I handed over the Andersen book to be checked out for three days, Miss McArthur said, "Here's another one," and waved a gold-printed title before my nose.

"*Grimm's Fairy Tales*," she said.

As I walked out the door with my two books, I paused to look at the librarian standing behind the counter, stamping each library card with military precision. I thought Miss McArthur could be a soldier, guarding with Andersen's saucer-eyed dogs great treasures beyond a boy's dreams. I thought of Winky and could hardly wait to get home to read him the story.

———

THEN, GROWING TALLER and stronger, forepaws and hind legs stretching out, his handsome snout lengthening, Winky's serious teething began.

When Father came home, sniffing the air to see what progress Mother and I were making with Winky, he discovered one of his favourite slippers in the corner of my bedroom. I had noticed the oddly shaped object, but never realized until I examined it up close that the floppy, split-apart thing had once been a felt-lined slipper. I thought it was junk, just one of the half-dozen toys I had surrendered to Winky's jaws.

After three months, collected in that corner of my closet where Winky carried his favourite chews were pieces of a rubber ball, an old cigar box (crunched for its pungent flavours), a gnawed limb of a rubber cowboy, some unidentifiable household item with wooden knobs, a torn shirt that Winky and I used for tug-of-war, a mess of hemp rope and, yes, Father's barely recognizable slipper.

"Clean this mess up," Father warned me, flopping his slipper at me and Winky. "Or that dog isn't staying."

I held on to Winky, who saw Father (because of Father's long absences) as a barely tolerated intruder. Later, I overheard Mother and Father have a serious discussion, and I was told the next morning that Winky was now big enough to be put into the basement at night.

At my own whining, Father hooked the security chain and left the basement door partially open. Soon after, though, to deaden the sound of his howling, Mother shut the basement door tight. Winky was firmly relegated to the basement, and I had to get used to that. My own howling over the matter would just get me a sharp rap on my head.

Eventually, Mother just had to say *Foon-lah, Sleep time,* and Winky would trot into the dark basement and I would shut the door behind him. Winky was down there faithfully guarding a tinderbox. Neither of us howled.

WHEN I THINK ABOUT Winky, I now realize how ordinary he was. He hardly did any tricks, except to lift his paw to be shaken, to sit when shouted at, to come when called. That was not because he lacked any intelligence. It was Mother and I who were lacking: we had no sense of what to do with a dog. Winky must have soon realized this and, after his first year of sharing our lives, concluded that he had to train us.

This insight must have first come to him when Mother sat down one day in tears over the latest mess on her parlour carpet. In those days, the parlour was kept as a special place, mostly untouched by human activity. It was the one room where you kept all the furniture draped in bedsheets, the lamps in their original cellophane, and lacy doilies to tell you where to place your hands, your head, or your teacups. We would never use the parlour unless we had company to impress. Otherwise, the glass-paned French doors were kept closed.

Winky somehow slipped into the parlour one day, finding one of the last places he hadn't yet soiled. A few days later, when I detected a familiar smell rising from behind the sofa, I used a comic book to push some of Winky's oblong "leftover business" out of reach. How was I to know that Mrs Jung was coming to our house for tea that afternoon?

I was called into the parlour. Mother broke into tears.

"You can't let your dog do this," Mrs Jung said to me calmly. "See how it's breaking your poor Mother's patience."

Just as I nodded, Winky blundered by me and started pawing at the front door.

"Does he do that often?" Mrs Jung asked.

"Now and then," I said, thankful for the distraction from my weeping mother. Winky kept scratching at the door.

"He's trying to tell you something. Pay attention, Sonny. You be responsible. Make him do his business outside."

I was, most of the time.

Mrs Jung rolled up a newspaper and followed us out. Winky looked at her, saw the roll of newsprint, darted away and barked angrily.

"Sonny, you be the Number One Boss," she said. "Call him."

Winky came, after my fifth commanding call, his head down, eyes wary. Mrs Jung gently tapped the edge of our front yard, calling his name in a friendly, authoritative way. Winky went up to her and, where she tapped the newspaper, he lifted one leg and did his business.

"You see, Sonny," Mrs Jung said. "He just wants to be told where, that's all."

She left Winky and me outside. I could hear her talking to Mother, calming her down. When Mrs Jung stepped out, Mother was less upset.

"You can keep him," Mrs Jung said, "if you make sure he goes outside. I'll talk to your father, Sonny."

Winky stood by and barked at Mrs Jung as she left.

"Good watchdog," she said.

"Good dog," I said. "No one's going to take you away."

Winky barked, licked my face, dashed over to the side of the front yard and lifted his leg.

---

WHENEVER ADVICE CAME about handling Winky, I was always mindful of what Third Uncle had taught me.

"In Old China, animals were rarely pets," he had informed me, disapproving of my having Winky. "Creatures," as he called all animals, "are fed precious grains only if they do muscle work, like oxen."

"What about chickens?" I asked.

"They're fed scraps from the field, some of the good grain; the pigs are fed leftovers, if there are any."

I wasn't satisfied. "What about dogs in China?"

"Chickens and pigs were fed," Third Uncle went on, "because they're food for people."

"What about dogs?"

"They're fed, too." Third Uncle looked over my shoulder at Mother, who was making signs at him. "As long as they're not pets. Very rare to see dogs as pets in China."

"Very rare to see any dog at all," Father said. "The war in China, the famine and droughts..."

When advice about handling Winky came from any of our family or Mother's mah-jong ladies, I refused to cooperate. I knew what Third Uncle meant. Why he thought my having Winky was spoiling me. But this was Canada, where dogs were not parts of recipes. I was told again and again: dogs were better fed in Gold Mountain than people were in China.

# Sixteen

*A reluctant
scholar*

ONE SATURDAY AFTERNOON, Mother met me at the corner
of Princess and Keefer. We stopped at Leong Sim's for
a snack.

"Look at your *dai goh*," she told her youngest son. "Look at your
*big brother*."

Garson, who had just started Grade One at Strathcona, liked
my new black leather school bag that I had slung over my shoulder. I felt proud to tell him how, from now on, every day after
English school, I would rush directly away for a couple of hours

of Chinese school. We wouldn't be able to play together like we used to. I was grown up.

All respectable Chinatown families felt obliged, even coerced, to send their sons and daughters to one of the half-dozen private Chinatown schools. A Chinese boy or a Chinese girl must be taught Chinese, in the formal Mandarin or Cantonese dialects. Village dialects like Toisanese were not taught at all.

Being in "Grade Three or Four English" meant you were old enough to walk by yourself to any of the Chinatown schools; you were mature enough to be responsible for crossing streets and still young enough to avoid serious trouble with the gangs of senior boys. If you had older siblings, you might even start Chinese school at age seven. As for me, I started at eight and, when I turned ten, was a Chinese-school drop-out.

"After today," Leong Sim said, "you make sure you remember the way."

Going to Chinese school meant a new adventure, and Mother was advised to take me through a kind of pre-school rehearsal.

It was easy. Mother and I walked past the familiar Keefer route, headed towards Kam Yen Jan, but at Gore we turned north. The school was in the big brick building with the high balcony at Gore and East Pender. American Cleaners was on the ground floor, and at the corner of the structure huddled Sun Lee Tobacco, where Father had bought me the supplies. Part of the same building held the Jong Wah Company, where Grandfather used to get his Chinese patented medicines.

"*Hai-lah*," Mother said in Toisanese. "*Look up.* Your classroom will be up on that top floor. Aren't you lucky?"

High above my head, alongside a Union Jack, a Chinese Nationalist flag flapped in the wind. I could see two rows of blind-drawn windows like monster eyes bordering the scalloped mouths of open balconies. Stepping inside the enclosed Gore

Street entrance, we walked up and up and up echoing marble stairs, my new briefcase slapping against my thigh.

The place smelled of soot and dried papers. Shut doors greeted us on every floor. We stood at the top of the building, opened some double doors and peered inside a large auditorium. Two old men were painting signs in Chinese. Mother quietly shut the doors and we turned to walk down again.

"When you come by yourself," Mother said, holding my hand tightly, "be careful on these steps."

I wanted to skip and jump, hear my shoes slam onto each stone-hard step, but Mother would not let go of my hand. The rehearsal was over.

Later that afternoon, Shirley Lee came for a visit.

"You have to be well behaved in Chinese school," she warned me. "Naughty boys are hit with stiff bamboo rods and yard-sticks."

I had tough Miss Doyle at Strathcona, so I knew I could handle tough teachers. Besides, there were other enticements that seemed more positive. Checking a list written in Chinese, Father bought me new pencils and two pointy-tipped brushes, a sealed bottle of soot-black Chinese ink and an ink stone, three thin writing books with pages stitched back to accommodate a master sheet from which to trace Chinese characters with pencil and brush. All of these I placed inside my brand new briefcase.

"Looking like a real student," Father said to me one day.

"Tell Father you'll study hard," Mother said.

"I'll study hard," I promised, "just like Gung-Gung did."

"Yes, *dai gai tong-yung!*" Father said, smiling. "*We all be Chinese.*"

BY THE TIME MOTHER could take me to my first official day—her overtime work at the factory had been demanding and I wouldn't let Third Uncle take me—the second week of the Chinese-school term had already started. We were fifteen minutes late. Mother rushed me double-quick up the cold, grey-veined steps. We could hear children's voices already settling down. When we reached the main assembly hall on the top floor, the frowning headmaster directed Mother to the area walled-off on the north side: the Kwomintang Chinese School Junior Class.

As Mother stood humbly beside my teacher's desk, I handed over an envelope of money. The slim, narrow-eyed lady told me to sit in one of the three remaining front seats. The dark-haired Chinese lady spoke politely with Mother and asked if I had brought my reader and copy-book. Mother smiled shyly. Her son had everything he needed.

I clutched my satchel. Looking at the ink bottle and reader on the teacher's desk, I could hardly wait to unseal my own bottle. My fingers ached to grasp my new pointy brush, to send it swirling in patterns, like I did with the nib in Miss Doyle's class. I was *Best Writing*. Mother waved goodbye and scurried off to the factory.

Boys and girls sat patiently at long wooden tables with tops that lifted up to store bags and hats. Coats were to be hung in the entrance hallway. The teacher told us to stand up. We stood. The class moved out into the main assembly room, outside our walled-off area. We sat in rows on chairs at the front of the room. Older children marched in from the other floors below and, pushing past the double doors, began to fill up the rows and rows of benches and fold-up seats that were behind us.

In minutes, the hall filled up. Two of the men teachers sat on carved chairs on a small platform, with the headmaster between them. When they stood up, everyone in the hall rose as one. Catching on, I quickly jumped up. The three men on the platform solemnly turned to face the Republic of China flag and a picture of Sun Yat-sen, the founder of the Republic of China. My lady teacher, seated at a piano, struck a note, and the half-dozen teachers on the floor and all the older students began singing an anthem. I didn't know the Chinese words but very softly mumbled the only anthem I knew: "God save our gracious King, long live..."

After the singing, the headmaster, a retired military officer from China, recited the principles of the Republic of China. His clipped, formal Cantonese sounded authoritative, imposing. I couldn't make out a single word. Finally, everyone sat down. Chairs and benches and student voices rumbled together. The teachers on the floor began patrolling the classes, rushing up and down the middle and two outside aisles, demanding immediate silence.

I kept turning my head, half-sitting in my corner seat along the inside-wall aisle, impatient to see everything. If I stretched my jack-in-the-box neck I could see outside the scalloped balcony and glimpse the hilly rows of houses and the distant tops of trees along East Pender Street. Looking over to the back corner of the hall, I could see, between the rows and rows of student faces, the long bench desks that belonged to another class to be taught later in the main room. I bobbed and twisted and stretched to see if I could find any familiar faces, and then, halfway out of my seat— without warning, a powerful hand gripped the back of my neck and held me prisoner. I was too stunned to cry out.

A youthful male teacher glared into my surprised face. His oily hair was slicked back; his sickening cologne burned my nose. As his grip tightened on my neck, his other hand slid purposefully along my thigh, then pinched me so hard I yelped. His hostile eyes said, *Sit still*, but his odd curving mouth said something I could not read. When he dropped me back into my seat, I was gasping. Quietly, the young teacher went up and down the aisles, looking for other miscreants to choke or pinch or both. I later learned that Mr Cologne taught the third senior grade.

One of the other lady teachers was a stocky, white-haired woman who taught the next level. The students whispered her hair had turned white overnight when the Japanese took Canton. Hidden in the ceiling, she had looked down and witnessed bayonets kill her family. Everyone liked her because she never raised her voice, smiled warmly, and was patient with even the slowest students.

As luck would have it, the narrow-eyed teacher standing before my desk turned out to be the other lady, the one everyone did not like as much. She had tightly curled hair, and a lean, hungry face framed by large glasses; she stood tall and slim as a willow trunk. She wore a red sweater over her plain *cheong-sam*, her bony arms protruding like sticks. The older students gave us an English pun on her Chinese name. Behind her back, she came to be called Miss Tree Trunk. She taught strictly according to the old way; her thin lips rarely smiled.

We read Chinese characters with her, repeating Miss Tree Trunk's words as she pointed out each line on the blackboard. Then she told us to open our readers. There, the same words were printed in a row. We placed our fingers over each word on the page and repeated aloud, ten times, each sing-song line.

The first term went easily enough. If I didn't quite recognize the Chinese ideograms, I needed only to hear one or two rhyming sounds, and I could "read" the rest. For the elementary grade, every text was a simple nursery rhyme:

*Siu, siu mew.*
*Tew, tew, tew!*

*Little, little cat.*
*Jump, jump, jump!*

Miss Tree Trunk taught us how to hold a brush properly, how to dip into the squat bottle and load the point with ink; how to "touch-press" a downward or upward stroke; and how to quickly lift the brush before the thin rice-paper blotted badly. I loved sniffing the ink; it smelled of coal pitch and soot, just like an old garage. However, trying to make the stroke-and-dash markings wore out my patience. It took pages and pages of repeating one downward stroke, two dashes and a third cross stroke before some of us caught on. I was one of the slower ones. I craved quick results, the kind I could get in Miss Doyle's Speedball Penmanship class.

Instead, I got black blotches everywhere.

How could pointy brushes and smelly ink compete with efficient, no-nonsense steel nibs? How could ten thousand complicated ideograms compete with the clarity of twenty-six letters of the alphabet? How could a language divided by so many confusing dialects and tonal accents compete with the lyrics of "Cruising Down the River"? Or be belted out with such force as the Andrews Sisters' rendition of "Don't Fence Me In"?

I was doomed.

---

ONE SATURDAY AFTERNOON, after my morning Chinese classes and a long lunch at the B.C. Royal Café, Uncle Dai Kew took me to the Orpheum on Granville Street to see *Snow White and the Seven Dwarfs*. My big ears had overheard his telling Mother one evening that, if I saw the Seven Dwarfs working so hard in the diamond mines, I might pick up the idea of working hard, too.

When he thought I wasn't looking, Uncle pointed at my school bag on the floor and winked at Mother. After the movie, we went home and had tea with Mother. Uncle asked me if there was anything I noticed about the Seven Dwarfs.

"They were funny," I said. "I like them."

"Yes, yes, Sonny," Uncle Dai Kew said and glanced at Mother. "Didn't you see how hard they worked?"

"Yes," I said, "because they don't go to Chinese school."

Mother frowned. Uncle asked for another cup of tea.

---

TWO WEEKS LATER, for my birthday, and because I had asked for it, Uncle Dai Kew bought me a Walt Disney hand-puppet. He was reluctant to buy it for me, but I wanted the toy the very first time I saw it in the store window. When I unwrapped the present, there, in a gift box from Woodward's, was my new toy, my favourite of the Seven Dwarfs dressed in a blue flannel nightgown, with a smile and a bald head topped by a floppy nightcap.

"What is the name of this one?" Mother asked. The kitchen blind was down; Mother strained to see the cherubic blue eyes.

"Dopey," I said.

Mother frowned. Uncle Dai Kew raised the kitchen blind to brighten up the situation.

But I was happy. I treasured Dopey as much as I treasured my Chinese opera puppets. I adorned the Disney creation with a Chinese warrior's gilded cape by safety-pinning one of Mother's embroidered handkerchiefs around his thick neck. In his right cloth palm, I taped a thin bamboo skewer Mother had used for cooking, and tied a miniature hand-made pennant to it. Though his eyes remained sky-blue, Dopey was now as Chinese as I wanted.

AFTER THE FIRST FOUR-MONTH Chinese-school term, as I continued to struggle to control brush and ink, and paper, Mother despaired. She herself had never been to school. Father was never home. I had no older brothers or sisters to help me. Mother took me to Leong Sim's house, and sisters Lil and Shirley helped me when they could, but I preferred playing marbles with Garson or racing down the street, playing Kick the Can.

As for reading the Chinese ideograms, I was very efficient. I hardly looked at the junior reader after I had glimpsed the picture on the page. Instead, I counted on my memory of every rhyme to do the work, just as I did when I first began to read English words. I was proud of myself. I could "read" every page by glancing at the simple drawings and parroting a rhyme.

Tree Trunk soon observed I could not identify most of the ideograms. One day she wrote a many-stroked word on the blackboard and asked me to name it. I said *cat*. The word was *jump*. Then she asked Penny sitting next to me to write on the blackboard the two simplest words in the whole Chinese language: *yung* and *dai*—*man* and *big*—each formed by a couple of simple strokes. Easy.

Miss Tree Trunk's chalk scraped down some extra strokes and made the word *forest*.

A blind person could figure out those words, but Tree Trunk decided to give me the toughest one to write—*"I"*, a killer ideogram, drawn with seven breathtaking strokes. One *upward-dash*; two long, opposite-facing *curves-with-hooks*; and three *criss-crosses*—or was that two *dashes* and three *criss-crosses*?

I could never comprehend the exact number or the exact order for putting them down. It was humiliating.

Then there was "Homework Inspection."

Tree Trunk took her ink-soaked brush and marked up my writing. Her red-inked brush slashed pinkish circles around my incorrect copying. However, I knew there was a row of near-perfect writing on the next page.

"Who did this for you?"

"I did," I said, proudly, remembering how one of the Lee sisters tightly held my hand as I gripped my brush, how she guided me down the page. The next two lines—completed entirely by myself—were not as good, but I was catching on. It was the best that I had ever done. I felt pleased the teacher noticed and waited for her compliment. Instead, she angrily slashed a line of red ink down each of the rows.

"You're cheating," the voice said. *Slash. Slash.*

Everyone laughed, except me.

———

SOMEHOW, I WAS passed into the next level, but I did not get the kind lady with the white hair. Everyone said she had retired. The new teacher was a man, not an unkind person, but all his patience didn't help me. Unable to sit still, to pay attention, to do my homework properly, I sank like a stone. Before three weeks had gone by, after being punished on both hands with a bamboo rod, I, finally, one afternoon decided to skip Chinese school.

Strathcona was holding a White Elephant Sale that afternoon, a fundraiser for the library. I paid my two cents to get in. Adults paid ten cents. Eyes alert, I quickly looked everywhere, but there were no elephants to be seen, not even a plain grey one.

There were, however, tables of wonderful used books to pick out, countless used toys and knitted goods to buy, and lots of food. Bags of buttered popcorn and baskets of B.C. apples scented the air. A pot of boiling water held dancing hot dogs beside open jars of mustard and relish. Bottles of pop stood in ice cabinets. From the side door, adults and students carried in hot steaming trays of exotic Italian and Ukrainian food and familiar Chinese chow mein. My stomach growled.

There were dart games, yoyo and bouncing bolo-ball contests, a circus of activities. There was a noisy, non-stop mungo-sungo competition the Hall Prefects had organized. With the sides of their feet, boys and girls were batting into the air ringed and knotted paper shreds. The mungo-sungos bounced off their heels to rhythmic counting: *ah-five, ah-six, ah-seven* . . . The highest count won. I had stumbled onto a secret world. Jealousy and envy gripped my heart: everything happened when I was locked away in Chinese school.

Red and blue balloons jostled everywhere. A ping-pong table was being set up. Mr Barclay, as tall and lanky as Ichabod Crane, played a few notes on the piano. A violinist began tuning up in front of Mr Patterson and Mr Glass. At the TELL YOUR FORTUNE table, one of the lady teachers presided, dressed as a gypsy. I thought it was Miss Farrington, but I wasn't sure. On one big table alone, Miss Schooley and Miss Eastman arranged trays and trays of dessert cakes, sugary doughnuts, chocolate squares and butter cookies. Fresh steaming apple pies wafted by me. And everywhere, stacked on tables and chairs, and in piles on the floor, second-hand goods waited to be sold.

I reached into my guilt-heavy briefcase, tore open the monthly tuition money that Mother had given me to take to the Kwomintang School, and looked around me. I heard my stomach growl . . . felt the crisp dollar bills between my aching fingers. There were books by the dozen, toys I wanted, but how would I sneak them home?

My larcenous instincts were keen: I would play the games— maybe even have my fortune told—but I would not buy a single thing that I could not swallow. I marched up to a tray of butter cookies and pointed to three of them. They crunched between my teeth. Delicious. I pointed to the two largest Rice Krispies squares and asked for a bottle of cream soda. I made my way to the steaming trays of spaghetti and chow mein and sausages.

No one would ever know.

---

"THE HEADMASTER CALLED me at Kam Yen Jan," Mother said. "You weren't at school?"

"I was so," I said, trying to make my way to my bedroom. It was true. I had been at ... a school.

"What were you doing?"

"Helping the library."

"Kwomintang doesn't have a library."

"Helping the Strathcona library."

Mother rolled her eyes. This was the third time she had been informed by phone about me and it was only the fourth or fifth week of school. The first had to do with my missing homework. The second had to do with a fight I got into and lost. I was always losing fights. Mother shut her eyes for a moment, then she marched me upstairs. I wanted to shut the door to my bedroom, but she held it open. Her eyes fixed on the mysterious carton around the corner at the foot of my bed.

"What's that?" She walked in and looked down. "What's all this stuff?"

I was caught.

Mother pointed to a stockpile of newspapers I had gathered and crumpled up into careful balls and stuffed into the large carton.

"Just newspapers."

She poked into the box. The papers made protesting noises. "Why are they all crumpled up like this?"

"Not telling," I said.

Mother knuckled me hard. The top of my head stung like blazes. She hunched her shoulders up; she was getting ready to strike again. I had to tell her. If I told her, then she would really kill me. Chop me to death. My head began to spin; nausea crept over me. The walls of the room seemed to shift. My eyes blurred. An awful taste seeped into my mouth.

*Yes,* I thought, *Mother would murder me in cold blood. Everything would be over. Even Chinese school.*

My stomach ached with all the food I had eaten; every breath I took began to torture me. I gulped for air. Acid seared the back of my mouth. No escape. I would confess and then willingly die. One immense intake of breath, a half-gulp, I felt my cheeks puff out. Suddenly, in a rush of breath beyond my control, my voice erupted,

"I'M GOING TO BURN DOWN THE SCHOOL!"

At the very moment of confession, I doubled up, bent my head over the carton of crumpled newspapers, grabbed the rail of my bed—and a day's worth of half-digested cookies, popcorn, cream soda, spaghetti, garlic sausage, tomato sauce, apple pie and chow mein splattered out of my mouth.

That same night, from my bedroom, I could hear Mother and Father discussing my case. I heard my name over and over again, and the words "thief" . . . "dangerous" . . . "liar." Finally, Father came up to tell me I was not to think I was getting away with anything.

"How did you think you were going to burn down the school?"

"With matches and newspapers," I said, weakly. My stomach was still sore. That was how one of the bad cowboys burned down a barn. You threw in papers, you threw in some matches.

"What," Father said, slowly, "is the Kwomintang building made of?"

I thought of the solid marble stairs, the solid red bricks, the solid plate-glass windows. Father made his point. Nothing would burn. Defeat was written everywhere on my face. I had had weeks of delicious dreams, of flames consuming the building, of hated teachers screaming for rescue, their hair on fire. My dreams had come to nothing. I closed my eyes.

"You will finish this term," Father said. His stern voice pierced my heart. "You Chinese."

———

I DID FINISH THAT term. I failed everything. Father went to the school and spoke to Lai Lock Hin, the headmaster. They both agreed that I had to repeat the grade.

———

ONE DAY, AWAKE before Mother was—she had been at Betty Lee's mah-jong party till dawn—I tried my hand at making the morning porridge. I had seen how Mother boiled water, poured in the dried cereal, shook in some salt, and waited until it was ready. I switched on the gas jet, listened and watched it pop into a blue ring, and waited for the almost full pot of water to boil. I nearly forgot the salt and shook some in. Shook again, in case.

I poured out the Quaker Oats and waited. The cereal swirled about the surface of the water, than gradually sank; but everything looked too much like a cloudy liquid rather than steaming, bubbly porridge. Perhaps it needed another dash of salt. Nothing much seemed to happen. I picked up the cereal box, tilted it, and kept pouring until the thick, gruel-like substance bubbled at the

surface. Steam began rising from the pot. The porridge thickened, looked almost right, but suddenly began to clump together.
Smoke rose in puffs that broke through the bubbles of porridge.
The gluey stuff expanded, then as quickly contracted, like a living organism. Now the smoke smelled of burnt enamel. A hot,
foggy mess began to cloud my vision. The pot made hissing
noises and bounced and churned by itself. I had to rub my eyes.
Everything was going wrong. The pot was attacking me.

I screamed.

Jumping away from the smoggy heat of the stove, I shouted for
Mother. I hated to use my baby voice, but I had no choice.

Mother came rushing down, struggling with her bathrobe. At a
single glance, she surmised what damage I had done. She turned
off the gas jets and, with a dish towel around the pot handle, she
pulled the smoking pot off the stove. Her bathrobe flapping
open, Mother scrambled to the sink, turned on the tap, and set
down the heated pot, which snapped and crackled in the swirl of
splashing water. I didn't even get a chance to explain anything.

After my punishment—two hard knocks on the head with her
knuckles—Mother examined the bottom of the pot. It was sal-
vageable. I was sniffing with the pain caused by her knuckles; she
didn't pay me any attention. When everything cooled down,
including her temper, Mother scooped out with a wooden spoon
oozing clumps of solid porridge and gave them to Winky to eat.
He sniffed at the food, lifted his tail, looked up for an incredulous
moment at Mother, then me, and turned away, tail hanging down.

"He'll eat it," Mother said, "when he gets good and hungry."

But Winky didn't. Hours later, when Mother tapped at the large
bowl of clumps, Winky repeated his sniffing and walked away. He
went to his water dish and lapped furiously.

"He's eating his water up," I said. "Winky's starving to death."

Mother wasn't sympathetic at all.

That night at supper Mother made a beef stew with extra gravy. When we ate our share, and everything had cooled down, with Winky, famished, jumping on her to get at the stew, Mother tilted the pot and poured the meaty-brown gravy over the porridge clumps. She let the rich broth soak into the oatmeal.

"You'll like that, Winky," I said. I put his bowl down on to the floor beside the sawdust box.

Winky gobbled everything up. Then I filled up his water dish, as I always did. He lapped at it greedily, paused, and then went back to gobbling up the clumps of beef-cereal. He ate everything up, pushing his long tongue in his bowl until he knocked it against the sawdust box. Then he noisily slurped up more water.

"Did you put salt in the cereal?" Mother asked me.

I did. Lots of it. Forgetting she had calmed down, Mother knuckled me.

---

THE NEXT MORNING, when we opened the basement door to let Winky out, we heard a whimpering down at the bottom of the steps. Turning on the light, Mother could see Winky lying stretched out, in agony, his stomach grotesquely distended. At the sight of my dog in anguish, I ran down the steps. Winky struggled to get up, raising and dropping his head. Every move my dog made caused him to shake and whine with pain. I burst into tears.

The porridge in his tummy had swollen to at least ten times its volume. There was a knock on the door. Salvation. Upstairs, Mother talked urgently with the vegetable man. I heard Mother say, "Yes, yes, the same dog."

Old Wong came down the basement steps. He patted my head, then knelt beside me and gently pushed on Winky's belly.

"Have you anything like a rubber hot-water bottle?" he asked Mother in Toisanese.

We had. The old man went to his truck and came back with a pile of newspapers and some rubber tubing. He helped Mother spread the papers around Winky's business end. I held Winky's head in my lap, stroked his jowls, stilling my boy's panic at his moaning. Mother gave the water bottle to Old Wong. He compared the rubber tubing to the bottle opening; he looked satisfied.

"Don't worry, Sonny," he said. "Happens to horses and cows, too. Winky needs an enema."

He explained to Mother what needed to be done, how she was to fill the water bottle with cooking oil. As much in shock as in disbelief, Mother knotted her kimono belt three times, listening with widening eyes to Old Wong's careful instructions. After some hesitation, Mother reluctantly took the water bottle upstairs.

The farmer pressed gently on Winky's distended tummy. Winky groaned. Mother came back and handed Old Wong the bulging container. He pushed one end of the thick rubber tubing into Grandfather's bottle, twisting and jamming it in tightly. He then held the whole contraption above Winky.

I watched the cooking oil gradually ooze out of the open end. When Old Wong was satisfied that a steady stream was flowing, he pinched the tube and slowly, steadily, pushed a long section of it into Winky's bum. Unable to move, Winky moaned. Mother grimaced.

"That's it," Old Wong said and matter-of-factly handed the rubber bottle to Mother. The old man had a no-nonsense attitude.

"Compress it gently," he instructed Mother. "*Like this.*"

As I held Winky down, Mother slowly squeezed the rubber bottle with all her might, then let go.

"That's it," Old Wong said, laughing. "Keep up the rhythm!"

He patted me on the shoulder as he stepped over Winky and climbed up the stairs. We could hear the front door close. Suddenly, some farting noises came from Winky's back end.

"It's working," Mother said, keeping up the rhythm. "I can feel the cooking oil leaving the bottle."

With the liquid seeping into his overstuffed bowels, Winky's underbelly began to push out even more; his paws shook uncomfortably.

Mother hated every moment of this, but whenever I thought she was slowing down, giving up, I cried out, "More, Mommy!" Winky's breathing became harsh; I could feel his heartbeat racing against my arm.

Finally, Mother said, "No more oil!"

The water bottle was as flat as a pancake. But I remembered Old Wong's instructions.

"Now rub, Mommy, *rub the belly!*"

Mother put down the water bottle; she tugged at the rubber tubing until the one end popped out. She leaned over, brushed back her hair and slid both hands along Winky's downy white distended tummy, gently pushing, stroking, pushing. . . .

Winky made endless spurting and greater and louder farting noises, and then, just as it seemed that Mother wanted to give up, the dam burst: S*luusssshhhh.*

"*Yipppeee!*" I laughed and hugged Winky's lolling head and stroked his suddenly sinking tummy. Old Wong said if everything came out, Winky would recover. Mother shut her eyes, as if she were afraid to look.

"He's OK," I said. "Winky's going to be OK."

Mother sank to her knees, her eyes still shut. Winky raised his head and began licking her hand. Much to my surprise, Mother kept her eyes closed.

WHEN EVERYTHING WAS done, the basement mopped and cleaned of the soaked newspapers, Winky washed and towelled, bright-eyed head lolling on my lap, Mother sat on the steps and wiped her brow, looking like the rescue had almost killed *her*.

We put Winky on a blanket, and Mother struggled to carry him up the basement steps to the kitchen, where the fresh air would revive all of us. I stretched out on the ice-cool linoleum floor beside Winky. He huddled against me.

Still dressed in her morning kimono, slumped on the kitchen chair, Mother stared blankly at the empty Quaker Oats box protruding from our garbage pail. She pushed a curl of hair off her forehead. I knew what she was thinking.

To show my remorse for having wasted all that cereal, to discourage her from possibly reporting me to Father, I knew I had to say something. Winky growled softly. I rubbed his nose.

"Doesn't matter, Mother," I said, not even looking up at her. "I hate porridge."

Mother raised her head slowly. Seeing that she still looked discouraged, I added, "And I'll work hard at Chinese school."

# Seventeen

*Chinese
school*

Mother tried everything to help me succeed at Chinese school. She had an older girl, Jen-Jen's cousin, come some evenings to help me with my homework. Even Chulip Sim's son, Norman Wong, from Ming Wo's hardware store, stayed in our house to finish his last year at high school, studying every night—an example to me. I hardly saw Norman, except to catch him sitting at his bedroom desk, poring over his books under a gooseneck lamp. He graduated at the top of his class, but I was unimpressed. That was *English* school.

Jen-Jen's cousin had little interest in my success. When Mother was out playing mah-jong, her boyfriend drove over in his second-hand Dodge, with a half-carton of hand-scooped ice cream from Benny's. They sat and held hands in our parlour and made sighing sounds, while I sat in the kitchen, the Italian ice cream melting in my mouth. Besides, when the two yearned to be alone, I could easily convince both of them I was too sick to read and go upstairs to bed, close the door and read my English books. Other evenings, sitting at the dining-room table, I didn't mind the writing and tracing, but Jen-Jen's cousin wanted me to be finicky about every stroke so that she would have something worthwhile to show Mother. Finally, at her boyfriend's urging, the cousin gave up on me.

Mother tried threats, rewards, even shame, but nothing worked. She and Father had loud arguments downstairs when I was in bed. I could hear their voices even when my door was closed. I never knew what the shouting was about, only that Father disappeared for longer and longer periods of time. At last, Mother let me be. She went to work, and came home exhausted. Told me to do my homework and otherwise ignored me. I was free.

Some evenings, getting home later from school than I should have, I would push my key into the door and discover Mother was still working at Kam Yen Jan. The huge underground cook-and-dehydrate rooms that slowly readied the sausages for final wrapping and shipping determined Mother's work schedules. If hungry, I would eat whatever Mother left me in the icebox. I could always empty a box of Ritz crackers, slather them with thick gobs of butter, and drink three glasses of milk. Then I would burp contentedly and read my English library books or go over my pile of trader comics, always shoving aside my book bag of Chinese-school homework to make more room on the kitchen table.

At Kwomintang Chinese School, not one of the China-born

teachers understood that kids like me were simply different. Many of our Chinatown parents came from the poorest districts of Old China, from farming villages, but the teachers themselves, many of them refugees from the Sino-Japanese War, came from the modern cities of Canton and Hong Kong. They were barely able to tolerate our Sze Yup dialects. They saw our peasant Chinese faces, but not our in-between souls. Rather, many of them felt the in-between, local-born children were *mo-no juk sum—brainless bamboo stumps*—truly spoiled and utterly stupid. From their feelings of superiority at being traditional and Chinese, many of them saw us as beyond redemption, deliberately disrespectful, and needing more beatings than lessons.

Beatings, in fact, *were* lessons.

One Saturday morning, an older, in-between boy refused to take his public punishment—a ritual the militaristic head of the school insisted upon. During the weekdays, the names of delinquent boys (it was only boys) were collected for this ceremony. At Saturday assembly, each such boy carried a bamboo rod and presented it to the participating teachers, mostly male. Each teacher whacked the offending boy on the palm. It set an example for all badly behaved children. One day the ceremony fell apart. After the first stinging smack on his palm, one boy suddenly snatched back the bamboo rod and threw it hard across the room. The weapon hit the far wall and clattered to the floor. His face red with rage, the boy tore down the aisle and slammed open the double doors, so forcefully that they jammed. In the shocked silence, we heard his footfalls slapping down the marble steps. No one said a thing. We could hear each other breathing. Finally, the headmaster gave instructions to the boy's teacher to phone his parents, to tell them of the boy's expulsion.

Never did I have the nerve to do anything like that. But the second time I was publicly punished, as the bamboo rod fell the echo of those heroic footfalls sustained my courage. No doubt, as I was a smaller and younger boy, the teachers did not hit me too hard. One of them even nodded his head and let me walk past him.

Instead of feeling grateful, something tightened and seethed inside of me: I wished desperately to snatch the rod out of his weak hands and toss it, and him, over the balcony.

———

BY THE SECOND TERM of Level Two, I had started skipping class again. One day, while I was playing hooky around the Carnegie Library building at Main and Hastings, I wandered in with a group of children and discovered the City Museum. It was wonderful. Before my eyes, thousands and thousands of things that I had read about were displayed, like toys in Woodward's windows. I could press my nose against glass cases full of strange insects, peer into dim displays of ancient weapons. There, one fateful day, I ran into a Chinese boy with a crew-cut and thick glasses. I remembered him from my kindergarten class. We met on the third floor when I interrupted his intense study of the scale model of the Canadian Pacific liner the *Empress of Asia*.

"Want to see something better?" I swung my book bag off my shoulder. Marbles rattled against the ink bottle. "Follow me."

We skipped past some displays and stopped at a small painted coffin. It sat beneath a cat sculpture, between statues with vacant eyes.

"Look," I commanded. I let my briefcase fall to the floor.

Larry Wong looked. He was not overly impressed.

"It's a wrapped-up dead person," I said. "*Dead*."

"So? Want to see something even better?"

"Show me," I challenged.

Larry quickly turned, and we both ran down the curving flight of stairs. We ended up at the back of the Modern Silk Shirt shop, half a block from the Carnegie. This was Larry's home, fitted into the crowded back quarter of a tiny store, where he and his father lived. His mother had died when he was a baby, and his older sister and two older brothers were now working and living on their own.

In the front were the store's long glass counters, with stacks and stacks of boxes of shirt samples, piled high. Larry's father, Wong Quon Hau, made and sold expertly hand-tailored shirts. He had a crew-cut like Larry and wore a plain Chinese-style shirt. His customers liked the idea that he was a tailor of the old school, perhaps too humble to wear his own first-class work.

Mr Wong, *Wong Bak*, worked in one crowded corner. As long as we didn't bother him, as long as we didn't make too much noise, we could sit on a dark sofa beside an oilcloth-covered table and play. Across from the table stood a sink, with exposed pipes, and a hot-water tank, and, beside it, a small kitchen burner that served as the stove. The small, dark bathroom was next to the door to the alleyway. Mr Wong slept in a three-foot-high loft built above his working area. Bolts of fine cloth, smelling slightly of camphor, jutted everywhere from shelves above our heads. A naked bulb hung over Wong Bak's work area. Shaded lamps lit up other areas when he needed the light for fine work. Half-finished shirts, backs and sleeves, flopped over ironing boards and hung on a tailor's dummy. Wong Bak looked up and studied my school bag for a moment. I held my breath; he said nothing. The sewing machine whirled away.

Looking around, I was not too impressed. It was a store like all the Chinatown stores, where people lived in crowded conditions in the back, or upstairs, or huddled in the damp basement. I was expecting to see something better.

I kicked my briefcase aside and flopped down on the sofa. Mingling with the dust were the pleasant smells of silk and cooking oil. The sofa springs squeaked.

"Careful," Larry said. "That's my bed."

From somewhere under the right angle of his father's L-shaped sewing table, Larry pulled out a Bell and Howell projector. My eyes widened. Using three clothespins, he hung up a white sheet. It hung perfectly flat just above the table. With agile fingers, he threaded a strip of film from one reel to another. He calmly plugged in the cord and smiled at me. The machine hummed, then the reels began to turn. White light flashed, and the numbers 5, 4, 3, 2 . . . *Castle Films Presents* . . . appeared on the cloth screen. In seconds, Charlie Chaplin was steadying his feet on the sloping deck of a large ship.

My mouth fell open. This was better than anything I imagined a boy could ever own. When the ten-minute silent reel finished, I grew suspicious.

"Don't you go to Chinese school?" I asked.

"I don't have to," Larry said, picking up another reel. "I have some kind of TB and the doctor says I have to rest."

"Don't you go to school at all?"

"Sure," he said. "Strathcona. I see you around sometimes."

Tom Mix flashed on the screen. Larry and I became fast friends. For my truant afternoons, by some miracle, I had found a perfect sidekick.

The Modern Silk Shirt shop on Main Street became the place I visited during my impulsive absences from the Kwomintang school. I discovered Larry liked books, too. We went to the Carnegie together, roamed the side streets so that no one could discover me, the shady refugee from Chinese school.

Skipping my Saturday classes worked out perfectly. Once, however, on my way to meet up with my sidekick, I had to dodge

Leong Sim and her friends coming out of American Cleaners. I ran into the butcher shop, then darted into the poultry warehouse and pretended to take an interest in the squawking, doomed chickens.

Larry and I went to the movies, using coins shaken out of my piggy bank. Leaving my school bag at Larry's, we snuck our way down Hastings to the Lux or Rex, dodging any Chinese person who looked even faintly familiar.

There were Saturdays that started off with good intentions. I'd even head for those hated marble steps leading up to my hated stuffy Chinese classroom. Other days, however, with the sun bright and the North Shore wind cool on my back, it took too much of a boy's energy to fight temptation.

---

THE TEACHER AT Chinese school eventually grew tired of being mean to me. His furrowed brow and dutiful anger obviously had no effect, so he focused instead on his other students, using me as his bad example. Many of the others worked studiously, had real tutors at home, older family members to encourage their progress; in short, I felt sorry for all of them. When I told one girl how much fun I had at the museum or at the library, or at Larry's house, she looked at me curiously.

"Don't you want to be Chinese?"

I knew what she meant. If I could not read or write the language, if I could not learn to speak the Sam Yup Cantonese dialect that was being taught, how could I ever be Chinese? I thought right away of giving up on being Chinese.

"I'm Canadian," I said.

Her braids wagged behind her as she laughed pityingly.

Larry never laughed at me. I never laughed at him. We ran

reels and reels of movies backwards and laughed at Laurel and Hardy jumping out of the water back onto diving boards; at cowboys leaping up from the dusty ground, bum first, limbs flying, back onto their saddles.

At Kwomintang Chinese School, when all the students bent their heads in unison, brushes dashing perfectly stroked Chinese characters, I barely felt that I was losing out. When the teacher phrased the monosyllabic tones to be repeated, I repeated them with an easy heart. I no longer felt I was a failure, because I was no longer going to be Chinese. I was going to be Buster Keaton or a Keystone Kop... my head buzzed happily with new scenarios for movies that Larry and I would star in.

The Cisco Kid, Hopalong Cassidy and Roy Rogers galloped their horses across the prairie desert of my desk. In my radio ears, Jack Benny whispered funny things, and Fibber McGee and Molly's closet stuff came crashing down; the Lone Ranger galloped off with Tonto, and The Shadow knew everything. The Happy Gang sang songs, and I hummed "The Teddy Bears' Picnic."

I spent hours practising squawking voices inside my puppet theatre in the upstairs back room, and my older cousin Donald came over one day and helped me attach a light bulb to the top of the box. Aunty Freda stitched some curtains together and showed me how to work them. My extra Chinese brush was dipped in opaque watercolours to paint scenery. After I got home, my Chinese-school bag stayed shut, but life held unlimited possibilities.

Finally, out of the blue, at the beginning of November—it was a Saturday morning—Mother said I did not have to go to Chinese school any more. My spoon crashed-landed into the cereal bowl, splattering milk and Shot-from-Guns Puffed Oats. Mother went on, her voice strained.

"Why throw money away?"

I didn't know how to tell Mother not a penny had been wasted. Besides, I could see she wanted the last word.

"You've been seen everywhere. The school just gave up calling me."

I bowed my head, tried to look sorry, bit my bottom lip. It didn't stop Mother. Months of silent, intense frustration propelled her forward; she wiped tears from her eyes. She had been playing mah-jong at the back of Betsy Lee's grocery store on Hastings Street. Playing mah-jong and spying on me.

"Every week, Wong Bak told me everything."

Mother's voice cracked; her heart broke. She had been doing her best, she sobbed, and all of Chinatown had been laughing at her. There were concerns expressed at the mah-jong tables.

"Watch out," the ladies warned her. "Way Sun's not going to be Chinese any more."

The butcher laughed and asked Mother how her young scholar was doing at the Rex Theatre. The vegetable man wondered aloud from the back of his truck if they were teaching Chinese at the Carnegie building. Mother wrung her hands, twisted her apron. She had failed; her only son had failed. Hearing all this, Aunty Freda shook her head: What would Father think?

Against the sound of Mother's rattling, tearful voice, my head conjured up a black and white image—Mother and I slipping wildly on a banana peel—feet flying, limbs akimbo, tumbling down marble steps. I knew better than to smile: I held intact my serious, downcast face.

"Why waste more good money?" Mother repeated.

Right there my head began to buzz. I knew what I would need to do with my free time. Earn money. I would start my own puppet show, using my Dopey and Cantonese Opera hand-puppets, and using the humped-nose one I made at school in Miss McGlashan's papier mâché class. I would ask Aunty Freda to make curtains for a puppet theatre, copying the one I saw at the White Elephant Sale. It was just two orange crates with curtains and a light bulb on top, with the whole contraption sitting on two spread-apart chairs. I would invite Phoebe and Henry and Freddy from next door to come and watch. I would make tickets that Garson could sell to all the kids on Saturdays and Sundays. I could even show silent movies with Larry's projector. I could make lemonade and sell stuff to eat, too.

Mother suddenly caught my eyes. She had my full attention. She stopped talking, swallowed back her tears and took a deep breath; she waited—her hands smoothing out her apron—to hear my words of apology and regret.

"Ah-Mah," I began, thinking carefully, the crackling sounds of my enterprise already in my head. "Can you make popcorn?"

———

IT TOOK FATHER AT least three visits home to get over my dropping out of Chinese school. He yelled at Mother, and then at me; then, after talking to Third Uncle and Aunty Freda, he spluttered and then began to calm down.

"Send him back to China," Third Uncle said," if you want Way Sun to learn properly."

"Everyone talks English here," Aunty Freda told him. "What do you expect? Sonny lives in Canada, not just Chinatown."

And I knew Father could never send me back to China, even if he wanted to. After all, we were neither a wealthy merchant family nor the well-off who hired teachers from China to tutor their children. There was just enough money between his and Mother's salaries to have me farmed out to sitters and to keep his family living in a house. Mother just wanted some rest from the problems of my bad behaviour and told Father so.

"You stay with Sonny," she said. "I'll go to work on the ships!"

That, too, was impossible. By Father's third visit home, there was barely any mention of Chinese school. My report cards from Strathcona began to improve; Father could at least take some comfort in my reading English books, and, as I never played hooky from English school, I seemed to be staying out of trouble.

Mother soon discovered that the sons of her friends were also having difficulties with Chinese school. In frustration with one of the disparaging teachers, Mrs Wing's son flung an ink bottle and cracked one of the school's windows; the famished Yee boy, Jack—fearful that he would be caught—tossed over the open balcony a take-out box of vinegar-stinking fish and chips, and the ketchup-smeared mess fell three storeys before slopping onto the head and shoulders of one of the patrolling staff below. And rumours went from one household to the next about the young teacher recently hired from Hong Kong who was fired for pinching the girls.

Less and less was said about taking Chinese lessons. There were other ways to be Chinese.

# Eighteen

*Father at work*

Wᴴᴇɴ ɪ ᴡᴀs ᴏʟᴅ ᴇɴᴏᴜɢʜ to listen at last to Father's stories about his labours on the CPR ships, I came to understand better his bouts of drinking and his roving eye.

The combination of twelve- to fourteen-hour shifts, cramped working conditions and the superior attitudes of his white supervisors created in him a bursting rage that he had to struggle hard to contain. There were a dozen daily humiliations that he had no chance to dispute. Chinese crew must leave last, always stand aside for others, take the worst bunks and sleeping cabins, and never be taught any other duties beyond those fit for no-class, half-salaried labourers. Every day, Father had to swallow his bitter frustrations. He came home with a hair-trigger temper.

Father was not entirely helpless. His pride often saw him through unjust situations and won him some respect. One of his favourite stories, typical of his instinct to fight back, he repeated over and over.

"Captain complain every morning his breakfast cold!" Father shook his head with renewed anger every time he began this story. "Captain just come two weeks to ship. New captain. Don't know I best chef!"

Father was a perfect chef, the kind who challenged everyone else to keep up to his standards. He took immense pleasure in his skills as a chef; he enjoyed the spontaneous compliments of the crew, who fed off his table, and remembered every guest who'd sent a note to thank him for his attention to their orders. Each day, when the last round of cooking was done, Father and his assistants left the galley spotless. The bottoms of hanging pots and pans shone like mirrors. Before the former captain had left the ship, he had shaken Father's hand and told him, "I wish I could take you with me, Toy."

Father was proud to be recognized by his first name.

But the new captain was displeased.

Blunt typewritten notes arrived every day by two p.m., just before Father's two-hour break; day after day, the notes came, written for a simpleton to comprehend.

"Porridge cold!!!" read one note, the three exclamation marks, like daggers, underscoring the captain's displeasure. "Coffee—ice!!!"

Father recounted the paper litany of complaints that the captain sent for his attention. "Eggs and bacon cold. Toast cold. Coffee like goddamn ice!"

By the second week, the complaints turned into reprimands too insulting for Father to bear. Father began to read them aloud to the crew. A war had been declared between Captain and Chef. "What the hell's going on in that galley?" one note read.

There was, of course, a reason for the chilly breakfast trays that eventually made their way to the captain's private cabin. As the new executive officer, the captain had changed the way things worked. He didn't want Father's lowly assistant, a shuffling galley Chinese, to be seen anywhere near the officers' quarters. Father's helper was now commanded to deliver the breakfast tray to the captain's chief officer or, if he was not available, to find his assistant, one deck below. In turn, and in full uniform, the assistant officer would ascend to the captain's cabin, knock on the door, wait five seconds, enter, and leave behind the full tray.

Father was furious. But his galley status did not allow him an opportunity to respond, and it was no use waiting for the captain to drop in for any explanation. Except for his first visit to announce who he was, it was clear from his pompous, nose-above-the-smells attitude that the new captain would not be caught dead among the lowest-paid crew, the Chinamen.

"I fix Captain," Father told his crew. "I fix him good."

Father spent an evening heating up a series of dinner plates and coffee cups in the oven. When he had figured out how long a plate and cup would hold heat without glowing or cracking, he gave the mate specific instructions about delivering the captain's breakfast. Father knew the captain always went for a morning walk on deck before he returned—promptly at 7:15 a.m.—to his waiting breakfast.

One morning, on Father's strict instructions, the mate bypassed the First Officer and his assistant, slipped into the captain's quarters and laid out the full breakfast tray. The mate told Father he had, with oven mitts, carefully put the main dishes on the woven table mat, and everything looked fine. Father went on with the business of the galley, cooking, and ordering others to follow his schedule of breakfasts for the crew and guests. In the midst of a humming galley, everyone was astonished to see the new captain blundering through the swinging double doors, bellowing for Father.

"Where the hell is Choy!"

Father stepped up, wiped his hands on his long apron, tilted back his chef's headgear, and looked the red-cheeked captain in the eye. The man's eyes blazed back at him.

"The plate singed my fingers!" he yelled. "I almost scalded my tongue with the goddamn coffee!"

"You want hot!" Father said. "I give you hot!"

"Damn it, Choy—" the captain started, but Father took over, his fists hitting the stainless-steel surface of the galley counter.

"Every morning—*bang!*—breakfast leave my stove hot!" Father pointed to the eggs sizzling in the pan. "You breakfast leave my stove hot, yes? Egg from stove hot, yes?—*bang!*—Toast hot, coffee hot—*bang, bang!*—Leave hot." Father paused, rested his fists on the counter, then quietly finished: ". . . and you get cold." Father looked at his crew, then back at the broad face before him. "*Who you blame?*"

Whenever he recalled the look on the captain's face, Father roared with laughter.

"After that," Father repeatedly told me, "no more shit-you noise from captain."

———

WHEN FATHER CAME home, he seemed more a visitor to me than a parent. There would always be *sui-yah, late supper*, with my favourite chicken chow mein and sweet-and-sour spare ribs.

"Mother says you've been a good boy," he would invariably say, giving me the first dish of food. Then, afterwards, I would receive gifts of Rogers' Chocolates or a toy someone on the ship had helped him pick out for me. If he came home during the afternoon, we would go out for dinner that night with Aunty Freda and Uncle Wally, or with some of my Chinatown uncles and relatives. After I turned eight, we no longer hugged when we met, and we never kissed.

When I turned ten, I still did not know Father well, except to observe that he and Mother, when I compared them with other mothers and fathers, seemed more coolly apart than together, and that Father was seldom at home. Many Chinatown fathers were away for long periods, earning money in lumbering and fishing camps, so I didn't feel too deprived. My world seemed complete with Mother by me, with my visiting aunties and the uncles who took me out, and with Winky.

———

I REALIZED FATHER'S concerns about my missing Chinese school were completely gone the day he brought me wind chimes from Chinatown.

The chimes made a nice sound when the knotted tassles were gently moved, but Mother could not stand the rattling whenever a strong breeze sent its glass pieces crashing together. I had Father hang it on the back porch, but, during windy nights, its discordant music disturbed even the patient old lady next door. Mrs Joe sent her foster daughter, Phoebe, to ask Mother, politely, if she would mind removing it. Mother liked Phoebe, who wore pigtails and was always studying her Chinese, always polite. Mother was only too happy to tell Phoebe to tell Mrs Joe that the wind chimes were as good as gone. She promised me a Li'l

Abner wind-up toy, with Mama Yokum playing a tinny piano. Later that day, I found the remains of the wind chimes in the trash bin and salvaged one of the tassels.

The red tassel was tied like the rest, but this one had a beautiful knotted design in the middle of it. I was puzzled by the intricate way its diamond-shaped strands wove in and out, seemingly without a beginning or an end. I wanted to learn how the knot was done. I showed it to Fifth Aunty and she told me it was too hard to do. You needed a special pin board, then you had to weave the strands together so tightly that only an expert would see where you began and ended. Then you would end up like those women in China who went blind embroidering stitches so fine that soon they no longer needed their eyes to continue their work; their fingers could trace how each stitch would *feel*. I thought of Mother's cronies playing mah-jong, how many of them never had to look at the tile they had picked up. They only needed to run the pad of a finger across its surface to know at once whether they would discard the piece.

"This is the endless knot," Fifth Aunty told me. "Very common in China."

"Why no end?"

"Oh, stupid boy." Fifth Aunty laughed. "Life like that! Love like that! Everything like that!"

"Is it lucky?"

"Always lucky," Fifth Aunty said. "You keep it safe."

Father said nothing about the missing wind chimes when he came home. But two days later, when he left for his work on the boats, Father noticed the woven endless knot tied to one of my warrior opera puppets. He held the toy in his hand for a moment.

"Did you do this?"

I said I did, thinking he was going to be upset. Instead, Father looked pleased.

WINKY ACHIEVED A handsome height, his back reaching my hips. As far as Mother was concerned, if a stranger approached our house and climbed up our front steps, and Winky barked and bared his teeth, he was earning his keep. Mother began to notice how much I loved reading my comic books in bed with Winky by my side, just before bedtime. One night, in her new flowered dress, Mother said to me, "Would you like some more comic books to read tonight?"

I nodded enthusiastically. Even Winky barked happily. This could stretch out our time together, before he would be sent down to the basement.

"I'll give you some money," Mother said. "You go to the corner store, buy three comics and tonight . . ." Mother paused. I could sense from her manner, she wasn't sure about *tonight*.

"Three comics and tonight *what?*" I said.

Mother took a deep breath. "Tonight you stay home with Winky by yourself."

I looked puzzled.

"Winky can stay upstairs with you."

"Where're you going?"

"I'm"—Mother took another deep breath—"I'm going just down the street to Mrs Lee's—Betty Lee's."

I was getting to the age when I was too big and rambunctious to be dragged along to Mother's thrice-weekly mah-jong parties. She had been saying all week what a big boy I was, now that I was nine years old. Almost ten.

Mother reasoned that at my age I didn't need any babysitter, certainly not some young girl who might gossip about her late-night mah-jong habits to the wrong Chinatown ears; besides, she told Leong Sim, "Sonny has Winky."

Mother looked uneasy.

"I want five," I said. "Five comics and an ice-cream cone for me, and one ice-cream cone for Winky."

Mother said I could have the ice cream, and share the cone with Winky. That was it.

"Don't tell your father," Mother said. "He'll say I'm spoiling you too much."

That was the first of many nights Winky and I curled up among a growing pile of comics, sleepy heads resting together on my island bed; together, we guarded our house from thieves, intruders and other lawbreakers.

Winky stirred awake and growled at the slightest noise in our backyard, which my bedroom window faced, and if he woke me up, I would holler, "Get 'em, Winky!"

We created a chorus of barking and shouting. With my added imitations of a howling, mad dog, any prowler would think twice before stepping into our backyard.

Mother didn't need to come back into the house to peek into my bedroom now and then, but she did anyway. Her hasty inspections only caused Winky to lift his head, shift his furry weight and crush the neatly piled comics on my bed. (If a cover got folded or crushed, the comic became a trader. My favourites, such as Classic Comics, I kept in my closet on a shelf. They were sometimes worth three traders.) To make things more irritating to me, if Mother lingered in my bedroom doorway Winky would sit up, and growl long and loud enough to wake me up from my deepest sleep. He never barked at her. He was just annoyed. So was I. The comics, neatly piled beside me, would spill across the bed like a multi-crayoned quilt.

Mother used to tell Leong Sim and Mrs Jung about the time I woke and sat up when Mother was checking on me, and how I spoke very clearly before I plopped back into a deep sleep. Mother told the two women that I said, "*TEN comics!*"

———

SEEING THAT I WAS perfectly safe with Winky at my side, Mother went out at least three times a week, sending someone like Fifth Aunty back to the house to check on me.

But when Father's schedule at the CPR became more complex, Mother was less able to predict when he would come home. Whenever he discovered Mother absent from the house, Father, with too much drink in him, would initiate a round of shouting as soon as her key clicked into the front-door lock.

Awakened, I used to go and sit at the top of the stairs, with Winky by my side, listening to the rising, angry tones coming from the kitchen. After five minutes, the hollering would tumble into the dining room, until the front door slammed with such force the whole house shook. At last, wearied and perhaps guilt-ridden, Mother would call out to Winky and he would trot down the stairs and into the basement. Then I'd run back into my room and duck under the covers.

———

FOR ALL THE YEARS I lived at home, I never saw my parents spontaneously hug or kiss each other; few Chinatown children ever did. The community considered such affectionate displays vulgar, more appropriate to certain tea houses or for those no-mannered barbarians, those Caucasian outsiders. Until I was nine, I never even thought sex had anything to do with my parents' lives, or for that matter with me.

One Saturday afternoon, playing marbles at Strathcona, four of us younger boys were interrupted in our game by Tommy Soon and a white boy, Alfie. They were kicking dirt at each other and came crashing through our game of Hit the Steely. As they kicked at each other, laughing their heads off, our marbles went scattering out from the centre of the circle we had drawn. The game wasn't over until the steely itself was knocked outside the circumference, but anything else you could aim for and knock out was yours. If you knocked out the steely, all the other players "paid up" whatever was agreed upon—usually, three marbles—and you got to keep whatever else was still inside the circle. I was winning, too, having pocketed five marbles that I had managed to hit out of the circle. Then Tommy and Alfie broke our game up. We started to complain, even though we knew it was hopeless to do anything about it. They were much taller than any of us, and everyone knew that Alfie was training to be a boxer.

"C'mon," I said, "leave us alone!"

Alfie gave me a slap to the head.

"Wanna fight?" He put up his fists like Joe Louis and started punching at me. Tommy Soon started punching my other friends. We tried dodging them, because it was useless to do anything else. Then Alfie stopped, laughed even harder, and said, "Hey, Tommy, look over there!"

He had been distracted by two dogs sniffing each other. By design or by chance, the larger black dog began mounting the smaller whisky-coloured one. I had caught Winky trying this with one of our neighbour's dogs, but always managed to pull him away. Whenever Winky tried to mount her leg, Mother kept him in the house, locked in the basement.

"No fighting!" Mother scolded.

Tommy Soon had another word for it.

"Holy Moley!" he said. "Look at 'em *fucking!*"

Blackie and Whisky were raising dust. I had often noticed dogs wrestling this way, the dog on top desperately trying to pin down the dog below. Mother always pulled me away from such sights, warning me the animals were crazed and dangerous; if you came too close, they might bury their long fangs into your flesh, spittle flying, ready to tear you apart. Now Alfie said, matter-of-factly, "That's how people fuck, too."

Four uncomprehending boyish faces stared back at him. My mouth dropped open.

"You know where babies come from, don't you, Sonny?"

Babies came when you were grown up and got married. You went to the hospital, Mother told me, and got one. But something in the air warned me to keep quiet. Everyone else was quiet, too, except for Tommy, who giggled. Alfie rolled up his sleeves, picked up a stick and started to draw some pictures in the playground dirt. The bent stick cut deep, clear lines. There was the man, he said—and paused to think what he would say next—with a *peepee*. The picture took only seconds to scratch out. There was the woman. She had a *peehole*.

Alfie took obvious pride guiding four drooling brats past the throes of innocence. The *f*-word sprang rapidly from his lips as if it were the most legitimate verbal currency, a coin to be freely spent on a good cause. He continued with his explicit illustrations, quickly erasing and animating the exaggerated male part, till the man's *peepee* poked into the woman's *peehole*. The rapid-fire playground show-and-tell took less than three minutes. Our guardian instructor threw away his stick and stood back.

"Show how," Alfie commanded Tommy.

Four boys watched Tommy Soon form a circle with the thumb and middle finger of one hand and poke the forefinger of his other hand in and out, in and out.

"That's what those dogs are doing," Alfie said, pointing out the two panting mongrels, still too engaged to pay attention to the human voyeurs. We stepped over to take a closer look. A yelp startled me. Alfie had roughly pulled the top dog away and lifted him into the air. Frustrated, the panting dog bent its head down; its long-nosed tongue tried dementedly to lick the length of anatomy stretched beneath its underbelly.

As Blackie promptly climbed back on, Alfie explained the procedure in more technical terms—how the *pee-nis* went into the *regina*. For years, I wondered about the geography of Saskatchewan.

Eventually, the dogs separated, huffed and barked and hopped about. Whisky bared her fangs to warn us off. Except for Blackie cheerfully licking himself, the show was over.

———

THE IMAGES OF Tommy Soon's moving forefinger and the rutting dogs suddenly made perfect sense. But what made perfect sense also made me feel perfectly queasy. Alfie laughed to see some of the startled looks of recognition on our childlish faces; my stricken face sent Tommy into convulsions. They seemed mysteriously to have enjoyed the show; I, for one, was nauseated.

At the dinner table that evening, I secretly stared first at Mother, then at Father: my stomach churned with disgust. Their homey parental faces—so smoothly swallowing honeyed pork from their chopsticks, so soundlessly sipping broth from porcelain spoons— betrayed nothing of the nocturnal doggy activities Alfie insisted all parents enjoyed while their children were fast asleep.

My thoughts wandered back to those yelping, panting mongrels in the playground, the vivid drawings scratched into the dirt. A piece of pork caught in my throat; I could barely chew. My turned-down lips scorned the very thought. *How could they?*

Mother put down her spoon and touched my forehead with the back of her hand to test for fever. My eyes shut against their will; blood rushed to my cheeks. I dropped my chopsticks, pushed my chair out, said I wasn't feeling well and wanted to lie down. As I darted upstairs, I heard Mother saying to Father, "It's all those plums and Bing cherries he ate this afternoon."

Of course, those half-dozen tiny plums, the half-pound of cherries had nothing to do with things; it was the apple dropping from the Tree of Knowledge.

For many nights thereafter, I lay in bed listening for any sounds like those I remembered from when I was seven; but I never again heard such sounds from my parents' bedroom.

# Nineteen

*Lil, Garson and*
*Shirley Lee*

WHENEVER GARSON AND I played together as boyhood friends, even the most callous adults would be distracted by his bright-eyed charm. His genuinely shy smile would melt grown-up hearts. Though undersized, even for an eight-year-old, Garson mirrored his older brothers' tough-guy stance that made young women swoon. Men, like friendly giants, bent down to lift him up, up... *up*... tossing him giggling onto their shoulders. While he flinched, doting women knelt down to pinch his cheeks. Everyone wanted to hug or pick up Garson. Dawdling beside him, I was the ugly duckling waiting to be noticed.

I wanted to crush him.

Almost two years older than Garson, I was half-a-head taller, his unofficial big brother, and I hungered for the physical affection showered so lavishly on my smaller pal. Being a Chinatown son, I was expected to have outgrown my need for physical affection, and any feeble attempts on my part to get the same kind of attention that Garson abundantly attracted—like stupidly raising both my arms in expectation of being lifted up—were met with disdain. I was absurdly too tall for picking up, too bony for hugging. I had just turned ten and hated to look like a stranded fool, so I soon quit trying. My arms stayed stiffly by my side. Jealousy clung to me like cobwebs.

Besides, whenever we were compared as boys, Garson always won out. He was smarter, slim like his sisters, athletic like his older brothers Gar and Spike. He had bright intelligent eyes and a vocabulary equal to mine.

Grown-ups said to me, if they noticed me at all, "Sonny, you watch out for Garson. You take care of your little brother."

If they really knew Garson, the agile one, the smarter one, as Mother had pointed out a few times to Father, people would be saying instead, "Garson, you take care of Sonny."

Mother never said she would have actually preferred Garson for her own son, but I could guess what she sometimes thought.

Even my mother betrayed me.

Garson, decent even then, never really took advantage of his drawing powers; he himself hardly noticed them. He said to me, "You are my best buddy." I agreed. Whenever someone picked on him, I stood up for him. Once I tried to defend both of us from Stan Yee and his two older brothers. The three boys shoved and punched me, and, laughing, tossed me into the bushes for my puny efforts at self-defence. Garson ran away.

"You should be as smart," Mother said, removing my torn shirt and ignoring my tears.

After that episode, we smaller kids kept watch on each other, screaming "*Run! Run!*" if we spotted any one of "them." I would bang on our front door; Mother would quickly let me in; and Winky would dart out, race down the steps, barking wildly, and chase them away.

In the hierarchy of children, we picked-on kids did our share of picking on others. There was an older boy—he looked to be twelve or thirteen—who sometimes wandered down our street. He softly sang to himself and spoke in a funny-sounding, snorting way. One of his suspenders always slipped off his shoulder, and the other was safety-pinned to his shirt. If one of us pulled at the tail of his shirt, he spun about, dancing like a clown St Vitus, his legs wobbly, his arms waving. We were drawn to him, as we were drawn to the sideshow tents at the Pacific National Exhibition.

Giggling with our collective power, we threw sticks and kicked dirt at this gentle, dream-like figure who visited our street, but who never understood how ordinary boys thought. We distorted our faces to mock his own, and he always smiled, gap-toothed, to think we were his playmates. At first, I ran away from the sight of him. Then I stood to watch him go by. Most times, we would merely mimic his motions and let him go on his way. Sometimes Mr Kelly or Mrs Mah would yell at us to leave him alone.

One day, one of the older boys threw a rock at him, missed, and pushed him down onto the cobbled road. Something like bloodlust infected the pack of older boys that surrounded the fallen outlander.

"C'mon and have some fun," one of the older boys shouted at us kids standing on the sidewalk, watching. First one, then, two, then all five of us darted into the road. In the screaming mêlée, most of my childish kicks missed their mark; arms flailing, my blows fell upon the backs of other boys. We didn't stop until a honking car horn warned us away. Everybody scattered, shrieking like hyenas.

When I got home later that afternoon, Mother was on the telephone in our hallway.

"He's just walked in," she said in Toisanese to whoever was on the phone. She held the receiver away from herself and began to look me over.

"Did you do anything bad today, Sonny?"

"No," I said. I hadn't stolen anything or broken any windows. Winky jumped up and down on me, licking my face.

Mother continued to look me over carefully.

"That skinny white boy that's funny-looking," she said. "The *sung-khin* boy—you know the one I mean?"

I nodded my head, expecting to be knuckled on my head for taking part in beating him up.

"Don't touch him again," Mother said, her voice trembling. "Don't go near him. You don't want to be crazy, too, do you?"

"No," I said, and walked away.

The poor boy never showed up on our street again, nor did he show up anywhere else. The neighbours told Mother his family had him put away in a place with tall cement walls and a locked iron gate, far from boys like me.

In dreams he came back to visit me. Against his jerky, gentle ways, his questioning face, I have never had an answer.

HOWEVER BADLY AND shamelessly I joined in attacking that boy, my secret ambition was to be a brave protector of the weak. I wanted to be a protector, a hero, but I wasn't even a contender.

My arms and legs were never coordinated for sports or fighting. "But you have a tiger's heart," Fifth Auntie said. "You grow up to be a tiger."

On the other hand, I was not beyond using Garson, commanding him to go, hands out, to ask for a third or fourth round of cookies or candy. Nor was I beyond bullying him to play games strictly as I commanded, under my own ever-changing rules. "*This* time," I told him during a game of kickball, "you have to score three times in a row to win." If I were to protect him, he had to see life my way. The point was, we almost always had the most fun together: we were best friends. His mother, Leong Sim, always called me Garson's big brother, his *dai goh*.

I would normally have rushed into the Lees' home and grabbed Garson; then we would have dashed out into the front parlour to get away from our mothers. But that morning, before we left for the Lees', Mother had warned me not to go near Garson, not to bother him. "Stay by me," she sternly warned, as she threaded my arms through my spring jacket.

"Why?"

Mother's face darkened. "Garson's been hurt." The way she half-whispered, a runaway truck might have hit Garson. "Look at me," Mother said. She took me by my shoulders and held my chin. "Last night, someone tried to kill Garson." My eyes widened. *How?* Mother put her hands gently around my throat. "Like this."

The way Mother said "Like this," her voice catching at her throat, her hands brushing across the nape of my neck, thrilled me. Charlie Chan movies had given me my first impression of murder victims who were strangled; they all looked close-eyed, smooth-skinned, especially the women, their hair dishevelled, necks extended, mere unblemished sleepers.

As we walked the block and a half west on Keefer to the Lees', I gripped Mother's hand.

"Remember to stay by me," Mother said. "There's no playing today."

I resented the fact that Garson was once again getting the attention I craved, but looking at Mother suddenly wiping tears from her eyes—"*Aiiyaaah*, it could have been you, Sonny!"—my jealousy was quickly overwhelmed by a sense of dread.

Leong Sim sat down with us at the dining-room table. My best friend sat across from us. His older sisters and brothers were putting on their coats and jackets and getting ready to leave the house. Mr Lee had already left for his office at the Chinese sausage factory.

When Mother took stock of the small huddled figure, her mouth half-opened in shock. I had kept my head bent down, afraid to look. Finally, I stole a quick glance, and shuddered.

Garson's eight-year-old head looked as if someone had smashed a baseball bat across its lower half. Dark bruises, like ink stains, splattered upwards from his throat to his cheeks; the pupils of his eyes, congested with blood, jutted out like fish eyes, jellied with shock.

Staring at Garson, I gradually absorbed what had happened to him.

"Say hello," Mother said to me.

I said nothing.

Garson sat staring blankly back at me. His slight body unconsciously shifted whenever someone moved abruptly, mistrusting even Spike, who brushed too closely by him.

"You'll be okay," Spike said, patting his brother's head. "Tonight,

I'll bring you back a winning pari-mutuel ticket." The two oldest boys were off to the races at Hastings Park.

Last night, they had taken Tiny, a large mixed German shepherd, and roamed the neighbourhood for two hours, looking for the tall, pale, thin-faced man in a dirty brown suit who had assaulted my friend.

Garson and I sat staring at each other.

Leong Sim and Mother spoke above our heads in hushed tones. I got off my chair and stood beside Mother to stare at Garson as if he were one of those Catholic-church gargoyles Uncle Kan had pointedly warned me about. "This is the demon place," he used to say, "where they eat bread and say it's human flesh."

Looking at Garson, I felt at first fear mingled with helplessness. I had not been there when a demon attacked my little brother, mutating his face into a gargoyle stare. I had not taken care of him the way I was expected to as his *dai goh*.

I felt discomfited, confused. Thinking of myself, I confronted the impact of someone's murderous hands tightening around my own throat, squeezing. No one was blaming me; no one said the incident was my fault. Nevertheless, I heard comments and took them to heart. Garson's mother was distraught, tumbling over the details of a mother's worst nightmare. And then, my name came up.

"If only Sonny had been there," Leong Sim said, shaking her fist, her Toisanese words suffused with anger. "That monster wouldn't have dared pick on *two* boys. Garson wouldn't have suffered this." Leong Sim cleared her throat. "One of them would have gotten away."

Mother nodded. "One of the boys would have gone for help."

I pushed closer to Mother, looking across the table at Garson. *I was not there.* Leong Sim, her voice edgy, took long pauses to look at her youngest child, as if to will away the disfiguring welts and bruises on his face and neck. Mother put her arm about me. Tugged me closer.

The abuse of children happened a lot in Old Chinatown. But it wasn't always abuse in today's terms. Physical discipline—employing leather straps, belts, bamboo rods, the back of the hand—was the Old China way, something Vancouver's ghetto children took for granted. Our Strathcona schoolteachers, for example, swung leather straps across our hands; our Chinese schoolteachers wielded bamboo rods that vibrated on our palms; and our parents thought nothing of giving us the full back of their hand across our head, sending us sailing. The few bruises we boys showed off in the playground, whether we were Chinese or Irish or Italian, were like merit badges. But it was a fine line. If you had too many bruises—*two* blackened eyes or an arm seared by a hot iron—you hid from others. After all, there would be vicious gossip, people insisting your parents were shameless drunks or, worse, that they were crazy.

---

THE POLICE WERE CALLED that night Garson was attacked. Two uniformed officers separated Garson from his family, and drove him around in the patrol car, so he could show them where the incident had taken place.

At first the cops didn't believe Garson. There was no doubt that somebody had beaten him up, but maybe they thought he had been battered at home.

Evenually, though, the two officers found the groceries scattered near the alley entrance, where Garson said he was attacked. Now, looking more closely at Garson, the bruises and welts darkening in pools on his face, his eyes bulging, the police had no doubts that someone had tried to strangle him. One of them, out of habit, took out his notebook.

"What'd he look like?"

With shaking voice, Garson described the man who had attacked him. The two policemen looked at their watches, sighed. They didn't take notes. There was no suspect. Other than a frightened boy's words, there was no evidence.

———

SOMETIME LATER THE family physician, elderly Dr MacMillan, pulled back Garson's shirt collar and inspected the boy's neck. He noted the swelling and bruises that marked Garson's pale throat; he recorded the boy's still-racing pulse and shook his head.

"Your son will be fine in a week or two," Dr MacMillan told David Lee, Garson's father.

Every grown-up said Garson would soon forget this terrible experience; everything would be safe, would be the same again. Familiar. At least—and wasn't it the way fate worked?—Garson would now be a more cautious and wiser boy.

"Sonny should learn from this, too," Leong Sim said.

Until I caught my name, I had not been paying much attention. I was busy trying to make sense of what had happened. Boys could die, I knew, but not boys like me, like Garson. We had been raised to respect those who would guarantee our safety. And yet one night, in an alley, a boy like me almost died.

That afternoon at home I shouted at Mother, "How come Leong Sim and you and everybody always tell us to listen to grown-ups?"

"But a *white demon* attacked him," Mother said, "a *bak kwei* in the guise of a grown man."

And I remembered: *there are demons everywhere.*

GARSON HADN'T WANTED to go out the night he was attacked, but his two sisters had begged him to. Shirley and Lil needed walnuts to complete a cake recipe, and the pantry was running low on flour and baking powder.

"Go to the Georgia Street store," Shirley had urged her little brother. "It sells the right kind of walnuts."

Garson had hesitated, but Lil said, "You can buy yourself a candy bar and a big bottle of pop."

"Hurry before it gets dark." Shirley slipped two dollars into her brother's hand.

That fading August evening when Garson walked out of the Georgia Street corner store, a lanky, brown-suited man emerged from the shadows of MacLean Park. Garson instinctively turned away, holding his bag of groceries in one hand and a bottle of Kist Orange in the other.

Walking rapidly north on Jackson, the eight-year-old heard footsteps rushing up behind him. At the corner of Jackson and Keefer, the boy was ready to turn left, homeward, when, all at once, a shadow rushed by and a fedora-hidden face, gulping the air, stood in front of him.

The face smiled in the falling dark and flashed an envelope in the air. It had stamps and writing.

"Hey, kid, where's the mailbox around here?"

Garson pointed towards Hastings Street. The man pleaded for the boy to show him where exactly, as he was new to Vancouver. The man walked a few feet ahead of Garson, watched to see that the boy also crossed Keefer, watched until they were both standing at the Jackson alleyway entrance between Keefer and Pender. The stranger quickly turned and headed into the alley, stopping at a backstairs landing.

It was just light enough for Garson to see the fawning stranger standing there beside the waist-high landing, twenty feet away, to see him crook his finger, urging him to follow. Clutching his groceries, hynoptised by the beckoning finger, Garson nervously, reluctantly, obeyed.

The gaunt giant lifted Garson up and plunked the boy on the landing, finally pulling himself along by the railing. A strangely cheerful voice broke the momentum.

"*Hel-looo*, boy."

A moonlit face smiled confidently down at Garson.

"You're a pretty little boy."

The man's tawdry brown jacket reeked.

"You'll help me," the deep voice said, quickly putting away the envelope. "You'll be a nice little boy."

Petrified, Garson's fingers tightened around the Kist bottle.

"I just need to know, boy, where there's a mailbox."

"D-down the street, sir. . . . H-Hastings . . ."

A sudden powerful grip yanked the boy against thin, curling lips; the breath was foul. Garson lifted the club-shaped Kist bottle and began flailing. Undeterred, the man grabbed the boy's neck and began squeezing. The pop bottle went bouncing off the landing.

As Garson was blacking out, a car noisily drove up the Dunlevy end of the laneway. Its approaching headlights shone down towards Jackson. Startled, the strangler fled.

Garson stumbled into the glare of lights.

———

*If it were me*, I thought, *what would I have done?*

*Nothing.* At least, that was the consensus.

I remembered someone saying to Father a few days after the

news had gone around Chinatown about the attack, "Well, lucky that man didn't grab Sonny."

I listened carefully.

"Yes, yes, Sonny would have been dead for sure," Father agreed. "Not as tough as Garson."

I remember the resentment that caught me when I heard my father's words. *Not as tough as Garson.* I remember, at that exact moment, wishing my father dead.

His big brother, and I was not there. I would never know what I would have done.

# Twenty

*With Larry at the
train station*

ONE DAY MOTHER WAS ON the telephone, talking very clearly. She always spoke more quickly and more loudly when Father called long-distance from Seattle or Alaska. Long-distance calls, like telegrams, were serious business.

Father had not been home for months. He had taken his holiday to travel to the East with wealthy friends such as Gordon Lim. He and his friends—some of my uncles, too—were looking for opportunities. Everyone was sick of working for the CPR. Aunty

Freda told me that Father had taken Third Uncle's advice to save his marriage and go East.

"Where will you be without a wife and son?" he told Father. "Find a business where you can both work together and be a family."

That was what the long-distance call was about.

"We're going to leave Vancouver," Mother said, hanging up the wall phone. Her voice was steady again. "How would you like to ride a train all the way to Ontario?"

It sounded exciting. I always looked at the trains running parallel to Main Street when we walked down that way towards the Georgia Bridge, where Fifth Aunty lived. I put my sacks of trader comic books down.

"When?"

"Very soon," she said. "We're going to a town in Ontario, a place called Belleville, to help Father run a restaurant."

I thought of the restaurants in Chinatown, the ones like the Blue Eagle or the B.C. Royal Café, the ones with soda fountains and ice-cream freezers. Winky was jumping on me. I pushed him down.

"I want to go," I said.

Three months after that phone call, Mother put the house up for sale. It sold in one week to the Wong family. Mother quit her job at Kam Yen Jan and spent two weeks packing everything.

Winky spent most of the days tied outside beside the garage and was finally put into the basement to keep him out of the way. He growled ferociously when he heard voices coming from the yard or he barked loudly when someone walked into the house.

Mother had a second-hand sale and give-away day when her mah-jong cronies went through our house, buying our furniture or taking away what wouldn't sell. No one wanted our round

solid-oak table—everyone had been throwing theirs out and buying the new plastic-surfaced tables—so we left it and a few pieces
of bedroom furniture behind. When Winky was finally let out of
the basement at the end of each night, he ran frantically around
the empty rooms.

Some of the mah-jong ladies went through the stored bundles
of paper, reading the Chinese and English words and telling
Mother which documents were important to keep. The rest of the
papers and the last of Grandfather's books were piled along our
hallway or tossed into a box.

I remember Mother finally emptying Grandfather's two remaining trunks and packing the bound books into cardboard and
crated cartons for the garbage pick-up. Uncle Wally had taken away
those few volumes he thought were interesting, such as the geography books. Two large half-filled boxes of loose papers waited on
our back porch. Mother thought these fragments might blow away,
or the rain might soak them and leave a mess before pick-up day.
No one else was coming that evening. Winky sat by the back fence,
guarding Mother and me. Though he had no way of knowing that
it would be one of the last times, he whined and moped and
refused to leave my side.

"We'll burn these," Mother said. "Don't play with Winky."

Before I tore any papers apart, I quickly examined everything.
Mother let me save the postage stamps from China letters. We
worked swiftly.

Unstitched bound books were pulled apart. Three-folded
official documents, some embossed with government stickers,
others with red seals over Chinese writing, Mother instructed me
to rip into three pieces. There were shoeboxes of bills and bank-
book receipts with excise stamps, string-tied packages of airmail
letters, unidentifiable photos, greeting cards and business cards—

all were crumpled and pitched into the oil drum that sat at the back of our laneway on Keefer Street.

Last to go in were Grandfather's notebooks and diaries. The countless minutes, hours and years Grandfather had spent writing down his thoughts into these string-bound and stapled pages meant nothing to an eleven-year-old boy who was eager to see the fire lit. They meant nothing to Mother, who could read neither English nor Chinese.

Mother tossed in the flaring match.

The fire started slowly, built up gradually, and finally began to roar. Winky and I stepped back from the heat. After ten minutes, Mother dumped another load into the gaping, rusty mouth.

The sudden warmth radiating from the steel drum forced even Mother to step back. The licking, crackling flames aroused the dormant arsonist in me. I hurled two more crumpled handfuls in. All at once, a burst of acrid-tasting, greyish-blue smoke coiled skyward. A ballet of ash-grey tails sparked and floated above us. Winky jumped up to snatch at large pieces that came scudding down. Finally he settled on the warm grass, exhausted. The night was quiet, except for the steady crackling.

Mother stared at the fire. I thought she would be happy to see everything disappear in smoke and flames. Instead, with her mouth half-opened, she looked as if she were deep in thought.

Spinning higher and higher, the tendrils of curling paper-ash quickly blackened and dissolved into the early-evening air. Mother and I looked at the darkening sky. I strained to see the vanishing drifts of smoke.

"Straws in the wind," Mother said, sadly.

THE NEXT DAY, I made Mother carefully pack away Lady of Fatima and my puppets, but I had to surrender my boxy theatre with the curtains that Aunty Freda had made for me. I untied the silk tassel with the endless knot from the head of my warrior puppet and, along with my other favourite things, put it in a cigar box. She let me take twenty of my favourite comics, plus some books, such as *Beautiful Joe* and the picture book of the mountains; the rest I gave to my friends. Mother promised me I could buy new books and comics when we were in Belleville.

———

FINALLY, THE MORNING came when the taxi arrived to take us to the train station. I was so excited I had hardly slept the night before. I told Winky all week how he had to be a good, good dog since new people were going to take care of him from now on. The Wongs had promised to keep Winky as their own watchdog. Winky whined at all the noise when the last piece of furniture started to leave our house, but Mother let me feed him a whole one-pound package of wieners and he was soon happily distracted by his treat. I was so excited and so busy thinking about the long train ride ahead that I hardly noticed when Mother asked me to say goodbye to Winky, and shut the basement door one last time.

Just as we walked out the front door, Third Uncle was rushing up the steps to help with our three pieces of luggage. He was dressed in his best suit. Mother handed Third Uncle the house key to give to the Wongs. The new owners were arriving later that afternoon. Rushing down the steps, then getting into the taxi, I could hear Winky's frantic barking.

———

TOM'S TAXI TOOK THE three of us straight to Kam Yen Jan. I sat restlessly in the backseat. I was told to help Third Uncle guard the luggage.

"We have five minutes here," he shouted to Mother. "We're late."

Mother's fellow workers waved goodbye to her as she left the front office. She said goodbye to Leong Sim on the office phone because she couldn't make it. The cab turned north on Main and drove us past Star Rooms, Atlantic Junk, past the Beach Avenue Shipyards, the Ivanhoe Hotel, and towards Terminal Avenue, before it stopped in front of the Canadian National Railway station.

The train station was huge. I had only seen it walking along Main Street, from across its expansive lawn, and never taken any of the criss-crossed paths that led up to the station. I looked up at the huge pillars supporting the sloping roof. When I looked down again, Aunty Freda, with her three daughters, and Larry Wong, emerged from the crowded end of the building and were waving to me. Larry had skipped school to come and say goodbye.

My friend handed me a present. It was a 1950 souvenir picture book of British Columbia. Slipped between its covers, there was a lucky packet of money for me to spend. I opened it right away and looked. Ten dollars.

"Write me," Larry said. "My address is inside the book."

There was a train whistle, and a track number was announced over the loudspeakers. Mother pulled me away. Aunty Freda and the girls waved goodbye.

"*Fah-dee lah, fah-dee lah!*" Third Uncle shouted. "*Hurry, hurry!*"

Third Uncle found our car and climbed on the train, and then he helped Mother up. The porter took our luggage from the redcap.

I looked down the long tracks. The engine was far away in the distance, but I could see the trail of steam rushing out from its side. I waved to Larry, clutching the book, then turned quickly away and climbed onboard.

In the railway car, Third Uncle was giving instructions to the porter about the luggage. The porter's face lit up when he showed him his two-dollar tip. I glanced into our sleeping compartment while Third Uncle helped Mother settle in. Then Third Uncle tapped me on the shoulder. "You take care of your mother now," he told me, and was gone.

The door to our compartment was open and Mother was sitting down now. She looked tired and shut her eyes. Out on the platform, Aunty Freda, her three girls, Larry and Third Uncle were looking at me, all of them waving, all of them moving away from me as the train thumped, threw me back, then slowly began to gather speed. Beneath my feet, I could feel the hard, vibrating wheels beginning to *click, click, click.*

The car's vibrations pressed my body hard against the window wall of the car. A thrill went through me. I was leaving Old Chinatown, catching glimpses of familiar buildings as the train went speeding by. Though I didn't know it then, we would be gone for six years: I was leaving a world that would never be the same again.

# Part Three

## Twenty-One

*Toy and Lilly
Choy with
Baby Way Sun*

I TOOK A DEEP BREATH AND looked out the hotel window at the familiar Vancouver vista, at the grey sea and snow-topped mountains. My conversation with Hazel haunted me; later that same October afternoon, she and I exchanged addresses and promised to stay in touch.

"See you in the spring," she said. "Write me."

The idea that someone I had never met, a mere phantom voice on the phone, had just told me my mother was alive, my *real* mother, sent my mind whirling. As far as I was concerned,

Mother had died in 1977—eighteen years ago. I resisted jumping to any conclusions.

Besides, I was getting ready to leave Vancouver and return to my home and my teaching career back in Toronto. I thought it best to let sleeping dogs lie, at least for now. And if, indeed, I was adopted, how would that alter the life I had shared with Mother and Father? Nothing would change, I assured myself.

"Signs," the elders used to tell me, "pay attention to them!"

How could I have written a novel about the secrets of Chinatown, and, if Hazel were right, failed to notice my own Chinatown secret? I was fifty-six years old, caught unawares, dumbfounded.

---

THE FOLLOWING SPRING, at the Vancouver airport to catch my flight back to Toronto after a reading engagement, my Vancouver relatives had a luncheon for me. Hazel could not make our appointment. I cornered my two aunts, Freda and Mary, to whom I had dedicated *The Jade Peony*. Was I adopted, I wanted to know, as this mysterious Hazel had told me? My two aunts looked sheepishly at each other. Surely Aunty Freda and Aunty Mary knew the truth.

Eyes full of loving concern, they turned to look at me. I said nothing. At last, Freda confessed, "Yes, yes, you are adopted." Mary quickly added, "So what? To me, you're just as much a part of our family."

"You're even better than that!" Freda laughed. "You were chosen! We just got born into the damn family."

I didn't laugh. Hearing them confirm Hazel's claim made me pause: all those years that I had taken "home" and "family" for granted.... A long-drawn-out sigh escaped from me. I had become a kind of orphan three weeks before my fifty-seventh birthday.

"Maybe Hazel will tell you more when you meet with her," Freda said. "I was just a kid myself in Victoria when you came into your parents' lives."

I glanced at the date registered on my watch.

"Tomorrow is April Fool's Day," I finally said, voice maudlin. Then, barely able to contain ourselves, we all three burst out laughing.

———

AS ARRANGED, LATER that summer, in Vancouver, Hazel and I sat down together for tea, some dumplings and bowls of *jook*. Hazel Young proved to be a friendly, talkative woman in her late sixties, wisps of grey hair floating about her. I asked her what made her phone the radio station to tell me about seeing my real mother.

"Oh, I was just leaving the house, putting on my coat, and was going to turn off the radio. Then I heard your name mentioned, started listening to you talk about the old days, Chinatown days." She looked thoughtfully at me. "You know, Way Sun is unusual name."

In 1939, when Hazel herself was in her teens, she had taken care of a baby named Way Sun. Her family home had been a kind of short-term foster home for in-transit Chinatown children. It was 1939, the year of the Royal Visit, and Hazel's own mother had desperately wanted to see the King and Queen parade down Hastings and Granville streets.

"That's why I remember your name," Hazel said. "Unusual name, Way Sun. My aunt Helena recalled how your new mother worried that you wouldn't have a birth certificate."

"But I have one," I insisted.

"That was because *my* mother was a midwife," Hazel said. "My

mother probably told the government clerk you born at home."
She sipped from her tea cup and laughed. "What do they know?
What do they care?" Her eyes sparkled with memory. "Those old
days! Here was a China baby, just a few weeks old. They maybe
think things done differently in Chinatown. Anyway, my aunt
Helena says that nobody care about one more China baby. Everybody worry about the war."

"Can I talk to your aunt Helena?"

"No," came the blunt answer. "I already asked. Aunt Helena
says we should let old days rest."

One single phone call had shifted all the pieces; I felt trapped
between fact and fiction. This real-life drama beginning to
unfold, this eerie echo of the life of one of my fictional characters,
struck me as the ultimate irony. Suddenly, nothing of my family,
of home, seemed solid and specific. Nothing in my past seemed
to be what it had always been.

———

I DID NOTHING AT first. After all, whoever my actual parents
might have been, I understood perfectly well that Toy and Lilly
Choy had been my *real* parents, for all my life. But, of course, I
had a few questions.

"Is my mother still alive?"

"I made a mistake," Hazel told me, sipping her tea. She
brushed back a strand of grey hair. "That wasn't your mother I
saw on the bus."

I gasped, but Hazel blithely ignored me.

"Aunt Helena says your mother died many years ago. That lady
was someone else's mother."

"And my natural father?"

"I tell you what I know." She took a deep breath. "He was a member of the Cantonese Opera company."

The news caused my mouth to drop. For three summers before Hazel's phone call and before our meeting on Salsbury Drive, I had been researching the Chinatown theatre companies, obsessively collecting details at city and museum archives and interviewing the old-timers. Hazel rested her fingers on the rim of her teacup and stared out the window to give me time to think.

I thought of the photograph of the chubby baby on Lilly Choy's lap, of proud Toy Choy, the father, standing behind his wife and son. I thought of those first seven years of my childhood when Mother routinely took me to the Sing Kew Theatre. Half a century later, like shards of glass in a kaleidoscope, old patterns of memory shifted, bringing strange shapes and shadows into view.

"My father," I said, my eyes as wide as a startled child, "was in the opera?"

"Yes, your real father," Hazel said. "A member of the opera company."

I swallowed, took a deep breath. There were signs. I had studied dozens of theatre photographs from old Chinatown collections and from the archives at the Museum of Anthropology. Among those stage pictures, in sepia tones, I must have caught a glimpse of my biological father.

"He was one of the actors," Hazel continued.

Cymbals and drums invaded my inner ear: I suddenly imagined my biological father sing-shouting, moving like a mythic warrior, his eyes outlined in thick black, his face painted in slashes of blood red and ghost white. As a child, when I played with the opera dolls backstage, a tall man came by to show me how the puppets could be made to move, how the warrior doll could be made to tilt its jewelled head or wave a tiny sword. What haunts me and remains with me still is that man's lingering patience, his kind eyes. Some women were there, too. My actual mother may have smiled at me, may have touched my cheek.

"Can you tell me more?"

"No names," Hazel said. "Those times were so different from now. That's all Aunt Helena will tell me—no names."

The way Hazel responded, I felt as if I had no right to press for more. Already, she seemed to suggest, Aunt Helena had told her too much, more than she had intended. Elderly Aunt Helena, I somehow understood, had secrets and promises to keep, covenants made in 1939, when I was finally sold, and waited, in transit, in her niece's home.

I thought of those pre-1945 days—a period I had researched when writing my novel—when Chinatown children were often bought and sold. Fifth Aunty told me boys cost up to ten times more than girls. Girls were bought cheaply, given false papers, and were often trained as housemaids to serve the rich merchant families. And boys were bought by childless couples to continue the family name. That was my adoptive parents' case: Toy and Lilly Choy wanted a son. And with a British Columbia "Registration of Birth" document—verified on May 16 by a midwife and using their *gai-gee* names, Yip Doy Choy and Nellie Hop Wah—a three-week-old baby boy became, officially, their son.

"You don't need to know any more," Hazel said. "Those days long gone."

The couple I had called Mother and Father died believing their son would never find out that he had been adopted. I didn't spend much time wondering why they decided not to let me know, nor did I wonder too long why, in a family of eight surviving blood-relatives, not one of my five stepuncles and four stepaunts ever told me anything about my adoption. As for all the other Chinatown aunties and uncles who took care of me, who knew the truth and kept their silence—*Well*, I thought, *that was the way things were.* The past was another country, where they did things differently.

There was nothing more to know.

———

TWO YEARS AFTER MY meeting with Hazel, as I sat with Aunty Freda, I thought back sixteen years, to the afternoon the old man I knew as my father began to slip away. I had spent two years looking back at my Chinatown childhood for this memoir, and was sharing the results of my research.

Mother had died five years before Father died, and Father's last words, I explained to Aunty Freda, were to call out to my mother, invoking the endearing term he used whenever the two of them had shared a tender moment: "Mah-ma... Mah-ma..."

Aunty Freda looked surprised. As she quietly sipped her tea, she gave me a thoughtful look, as if she were making up her mind whether to tell me something. I had seen that look before, two years ago, in Hazel's momentary hesitations.

At that time, Hazel and I had repeated all the clichés to each other: *The past's the past . . . Leave well-enough alone . . . No use evoking long-gone ghosts . . . Why bother the dead?* But when Hazel removed her navy cardigan, I noticed that she was wearing, with much dignity, a *Phantom of the Opera* T-shirt. A sign.

It was now two years later, and Aunty Freda stirred uncomfortably in her chair. All at once she asked me, "How much do you know of our family history?"

# Twenty-Two

*Great-Great-
Grandfather,
merchant*

*Great-Grandfather,
scholar*

I SHOWED AUNTY FREDA THE two photographs left by Father
to me of scroll portraits handpainted in the middle 1800s, one
of Great-Great-Grandfather and the other of Great-Grandfather.

A successful businessman, Great-Great-Grandfather sits confidently dressed in a brocade jacket and merchant's beads. His
son the scholar, my great-grandfather, wears a long white silk
robe, holds a book, and sports long nails on his elegant fingers.

"Your great-grandfather never laboured," Father used to tell
me. "Look at his rich man's hands."

By the time Grandfather was born in 1877, fortunes in Old China had been altered by the Bible-inspired Boxer Rebellion of 1845–1864, during which some twenty million Chinese lost their lives. After the fall of the Imperial Qing Dynasty in 1911 and the rise of the Republic of China in 1912, countless middle-class families in Grandfather's home province of Kwangtung were devastated by civil chaos and government corruption.

My family's downfall was due in large part to the fact that my great-grandfather, more scholar than businessman, had invested heavily in currency, a slippery, unpredictable business during those revolutionary times. During the ten years between 1880 and 1890, the copper cash that was the common Chinese currency had been drastically devalued; a silver *tael* that once was valued at 2,000 copper cash now cost 8,000. By the 1900s, the strings of copper were worth more made into toy souvenir swords for overseas markets. Such a coin sword, two feet long, used to hang on my wall in my bedroom.

Middle-class fortunes were also depleted, if not wholly destroyed, by the cycles of drought and by the relentless famines that stalked Southern China around the turn of the century.

"Terrible times," Aunty Freda agreed with me. "Some people ate their own dead children. The old men in Fan Tan Alley used to tell me those stories."

Grandfather Choy's full name was Tuey Duk-Lin, the family name, Tuey, came first—a name transliterated to "Choy" on his B.C. documents—and his birth name, Duk-Lin, a Confucian phrase meaning "refined virtue," was meant to guide him in his life. But virtue alone could not feed his family. So, like countless men of his educated standing, by the time he was in his twenties, Grandfather set sail to Gold Mountain, probably around 1903.

With some financial and clan backing, the details of which are lost now, Grandfather Choy made the month-long journey to the other side of the world to rally overseas support for the growing Reform China Movement and, equally important, to discover what opportunities might be available overseas for a man like himself. Left behind to wait for him in Old China were his First Wife, and a five-year-old son, my father.

Like his own father, Grandfather Choy had been educated as a scholar, but he would work for most of his life as a labourer.

"No more rich man's fingernails," Father used to tell me, laughing. "Everyone in Sunwui work in those days. Even me. Go to school sometime, work on a farm or in town, just work, any work."

Then, when my father was almost nine years old, and my grandfather had been away for almost four years, First Wife, my father's mother, disappeared. Those were difficult years, and I assumed she died of some terrible illness, probably related to malnutrition. Grandfather soon returned to take care of Father and, in the next ten years, re-established the family funds, probably through exploiting the contacts he had made in Gold Mountain. Through his business deals and his schoolteaching, he saved enough money to think of starting another family. When my father was eighteen, seeing how hopeless China was politically and financially, Grandfather married his Second Wife and prepared to return to Gold Mountain.

My father would have been twenty years old in 1918 when he joined Grandfather and his Second Wife, along with Second Wife's nephew, my uncle Harry Young, on the deck of the *Empress of Russia*. Along with their three metal steamer trunks and five leather suitcases, Second Wife packed extra pairs of shoes to be shipped to Victoria. They were tiny shoes, no longer than four or five inches, made to fit her bound feet.

Finally, with trunks and baggage in a safe harbour, the four of them settled in the port city of Victoria. Grandfather and Second

Wife began their Gold Mountain family of ten children, my father's stepsiblings, nine of whom would survive their childhood.

"That's what I know," I told Aunty Freda.

"Where did you get all that money detail?" she asked.

"Father told me some of it when I was growing up," I said. "And I did lots of research."

Aunty Freda uttered a long sigh, the kind her stepbrother and her sister-in-law, my father and mother, used to give me when it was clear I knew everything and nothing at the same time. A China-town sigh, given to *mo-no*'s like me.

"Well," she said at last, "tell me more."

# Twenty-Three

*Yune-Shee*

Disembarking from the *Empress of Russia*, the four were probably placed in the "pig pen" stockade for Chinese immigrants. After waiting for their papers to be cleared, they eventually settled near Victoria's pioneer Chinatown community, in crowded rooms along Pembroke, four blocks from Fan-Tan Alley.

In the B.C. Archives, the listing of arrivals for 1918 did not include the "travelling names" of Grandfather, Tuey Duk-Lin, or of Second Wife, *née* Young Yune-Shee. Nor could I find any reference to "Choy King" and "Toy King," the names officially recorded on their death certificates in 1945 and 1968. There wasn't any listing for "Yip Doy Choy," the name my father signed on my birth certificate. All four, including Uncle Harry Young, undoubtedly came to Gold Mountain with "bought names" on false papers, *gai gee* documents, now lost or burned.

There is no record of their paying the Chinese Head Tax originally imposed in 1886—a surcharge that rose from ten dollars to five hundred dollars by the time my family arrived. Of course, they might have paid the tax under names now lost to our family memory, or have been exempt from paying because Grandfather was a scholar: Ottawa made an exception of those who were "merchants, their wives, and children, wives and children of clergymen, tourists, men of science and students."

Whether peasant, merchant or scholar, the secrets of Old Chinatown families are buried among these hundreds of assumed names that were left behind to be hidden or forgotten, in shame or humiliation.

I never questioned Father's long absences from us. That was the way things were. Nor did I ever question why he never left us for good, or if he ever wanted to. Until fifteen years after his death, I never knew my father had kept from me his desolate and grief-ridden secret.

And I never would have known, except that something in me does not like the dark. Something pushes towards the light.

———

I NEVER CAME TO know Grandfather, except as my docile companion—after his strokes—when I was finishing kindergarten. Yet I know now that the old man had dreams and talents; his life was passionate and difficult, with one fault line that came to undermine my own father's acceptance of the past. One tragic event came between Grandfather and my father, one event that burdened Father so much it divided him from everyone he loved. And he kept it to himself until his death.

Shortly after settling in Victoria with Second Wife and my father (Uncle Harry took a room by himself), Grandfather earned a local reputation for his political ideas about reforming China. He soon became known as the community calligrapher, someone consulted on his knowledge of the classics, a political reformer willing to debate Chinese philosophy and politics.

Meanwhile, he shrewdly adopted the Anglo-sounding name "Peter King" to win his first job interview, and in the years that followed learned enough English words and *chop-chop* kitchen skills that the CPR shipping lines looked to him for recommendations when they were hiring other Chinatown men. "King," not "Tuey" or "Choy," became the family name for his Victoria household.

"In those days, using 'King' meant fewer problems," Uncle Len told me. "Lots of English people didn't want to sell property to anyone Jewish, Irish or Oriental. With a Caucasian agent as a go-between, the seller wouldn't know Peter King or Len King was oriental."

My father, for his own reasons, stayed with the name listed on my birth certificate, Yip Doy Choy, though he was known by family and Chinese friends by his birth name—pronounced "Tuey Choy"—later to be transliterated on official documents as "Toy Choy."

At age twenty, Father began working in wealthy private homes as a houseboy, and soon picked up enough English to work as a bellboy at the James Bay Hotel and, later, at the Empress Hotel. Five years later, he worked alongside Grandfather and Third Uncle on the CPR ships to Alaska, apprenticing his way until he himself became Chief Cook.

Grandfather's dream of a Gold Mountain family would come true, but bitter resentments were already beginning to seethe between my father and Second Wife.

---

YUNE-SHEE WAS THIRTEEN years younger than Grandfather Choy King's thirty-nine years when he started to look for a wife to take to Gold Mountain. She had been introduced to Grandfather by a village matchmaker who knew her family.

Even at their first meeting, Grandfather told my mother, and she later told me, the petite candidate from the Young clan was not too shy to stare directly at him; village gossips suggested the small woman had a spirit and temper to match Grandfather's, which, in fact, should have warned him. Two sparks could only mean fire. However, the community accepted that Choy King was a widower who needed a new companion, and approved the match.

The new wife, to be chosen from Grandfather's village of Sun-wui, would have to be older and experienced enough to make a life in Gold Mountain, and young enough to bear him children. The petite Yune-Shee had been given a middle-class lady's education, so it seemed appropriate to match her with a well-off suitor. I imagine those clear eyes, unyielding before his reckoning glances, made him aware that she was not weak. After all, she had known suffering.

When she was three, the Young family took steps to assure that Yune-Shee would find a suitable husband. They began wrapping her feet with strips of binding-cloth while her young bones were still malleable. The binding distorted her toe bones, slowly breaking them, wrenching them under the foot in a second-by-second, slow-motion crush; the progressively tighter and tighter binding then gradually, painfully, pushed her arches upward, creating two humps.

Every evening, in spite of the helpless child's agonized screams, the bloodied bandages were replaced; and after a burning salve was applied, a new roll was first knotted around the child's ankle, then stretched across the foot to the toes, and tautly back, again and again. The bones cracked. The hired servants trained in such duties were relentless.

"Do you want a rich husband?" the *amahs* used to taunt their young charges, and pull even harder.

Through such pain, a girl-child like Yune-Shee began to understand her place in Old China. Her own mother's incapacitated hobbling now revealed to the daughter how she, too, would come to depend upon husband and sons and, with good fortune, command countless servants. When such a daughter grew up, she would pray to give birth to sons and frown at, if not curse, the birth of daughters, those useless "small joys."

By the time she was twelve or thirteen, the process was complete: each foot, from bent-back toes to adult heel, should measure no more than the ideal three inches in length. These "delicate golden lilies" were signs of class that gave a woman an erotic grace, made her seem more voluptuous and vulnerable. In the same way that stiletto-heeled shoes emphasized the buttocks of Western women, bound feet created a sashaying hobble that sexualized a young Chinese girl.

In her girlhood, Yune-Shee wore finely embroidered silk gowns and long brocade jackets; hand-shaped starched shoes covered her tiny feet. Yune-Shee was given a lady's education and commanded her own household servants. When times were good, she oversaw the cooking and the festival servings of dim-sum dainties and sweetmeats. Later, when famine and drought raged across the land, the family fortune and her good life would change forever.

Yune-Shee's encumbered feet must have appealed to Grandfather's own sensibility and his own sense of rank. As his wife, she would not leave the house and work, not like a *kay-toi neui*, those indentured Gold Mountain women who laboured in North American laundries and restaurants, and often "served" in strangers' beds as well; she represented another class of immigrant Chinese women, whose duty would be to raise a family.

Most girls were married by the time they reached sixteen. Yune-Shee was twenty-six, and set in her ways, when she married Grandfather. They hardly knew each other.

"Your grandfather and grandmother were already fighting with each other on the ship over," Uncle Harry Young told me. "Crazy! Choy King couldn't stand the fact his new wife knew so little about philosophy or politics! What did he expect?"

But Yune-Shee had her expectations, too.

Of those years living with his own father and stepmother, Father remembered trying to keep to himself. From the beginning, he did not like his new stepmother's attitude towards him. She barked out orders as if he were her servant. "Next time, buy fresher vegetables!"

"I just turned twenty-one," Father explained to me. "Two days after we landed in Victoria, I went to work in a restaurant kitchen. I come home late, I come home early, I get yelled at. '*Get me my walking-stick!*'"

During that first year among the port-city Chinese women, Yune-Shee's exquisite embroidery work, her dim-sum cookery and her razor-edged temper were equally famous.

Perhaps my father, who inherited Grandfather's quick temper, snapped at her once too often.

"If these are not fresh enough," he used to shout back, "grow your own vegetables!"

He knew that would outrage her, a woman who once had servants to work in the family plot. Against his retorts, she slammed doors and cursed him.

As for Yune-Shee, she must have been desperately homesick, feeling herself abandoned in a strange country without knowing a word of English. Her ornate silk robes and China-style leggings were of little use in a country where clothes were deliberately plain and utilitarian. The leather shoes made especially for her feet did not cushion her steps as well as the padded cloth ones, embroidered, shaped and starched by an artisan hand. Even the wedding bed was empty of splendour and, as often, empty of her mate. Choy King worked longer and longer shifts on the CPR, leaving both her and my father, on shifts himself, to sulk about the house.

Within the first two years of their arrival, Yune-Shee gave birth to her First Son, my uncle George. Having saved some money, and with the addition of Father's own growing earnings, Grandfather Choy King rented a larger place, at 644 Cormorant Street. The four of them moved into the two-storey structure. Soon after, Yune-Shee King's face grew pale, then flushed. She was expecting her second child.

Grandfather's dream of a Gold Mountain family would come true, but bitter resentments were already seething between my father and Second Wife. As the months passed, she became even more demanding, as her feet ached with the added weight of the child she was carrying.

"Toy! Tell the herbalist I want some salve for my feet!"

By day, Father, a proud man, catered as a houseboy to household mistresses and as a bellboy to the whims of hotel guests; by night, he did as much as he could to take care of the house, and cook and clean, while tiny Yune-Shee complained of aches and pains, and demanded this ointment be mixed in honey, or that dried herb be boiled for tea.

By 1921, the second child had arrived, a girl, Aunty Freda; within a year, a third child, Uncle Len, was born. Three children in four years. Where were the servants to help her raise them? Where was the time to work her embroidery? Away from the luxuries she had taken for granted in China, and having, too, to manage her life among strangers and barbarians, Yune-Shee began to detest her fate.

Perhaps Grandfather had not told her the entire truth about life in Canada. In the crowded rooms of their first place together on Pembroke Street, Choy King might have expected Second Wife Yune-Shee to adapt as he had done, both thrown into the new world to survive or perish. By the time they had moved to the Cormorant Street house, everyone in Victoria's Chinatown knew of their conflicts and of her disappointments.

Victoria tenement homes could be stifling in the summer heat, and draughty and damp with evening fog. Yune-Shee complained she was dizzy every day. Her stomach lurched. The women of Chinatown listened, nodded their heads with great sympathy. But none of them could do much for her.

"This place my death!" she yelled at Grandfather and her stepson, and they yelled back at her. The children grew up hearing these adult voices wielded against each other and railing against fate.

Perhaps Yune-Shee had not listened to Grandfather when the truth was told, or had failed to pay attention to the cautionary words of those who returned to Sunwui, penniless, broken in spirit and body.

"Go rich, stay rich," they used to say. "Go poor, stay poor."

Gold Mountain dreams were built upon the success of the very few, and upon the plentiful sweat of China-born families like hers. There was some craziness in almost every ghetto family in those days, a tension exacerbated by the racism that forced a whole community to live among their own kind. Choy King, Yune-Shee King and my father could not run away from one another's dreams and hopes. They lived in the in-between world of those first immigrants who, unable to compromise or fully comprehend their circumstances, were doomed to *yum foo-chai, drink bitter tea.* Waving her sandalwood fan and complaining to anyone who would listen, Yune-Shee came to focus her frustration on my father.

"Make me some pig-feet ginger soup," she demanded. She turned pale. Suddenly, her stomach heaved. "No, no—get me to the sink!"

Father half-lifted her to the porcelain basin and watched her empty her stomach. Yune-Shee was pregnant again.

---

EVEN THOUGH HE WAS twenty when he arrived in Canada, Father was bound by tradition to live with his father and stepmother until he himself married. Besides, knowing so little English, he could not survive without Grandfather's labour contacts.

More important, there was his loyalty to his own father; there were ancestral laws about filial obedience, Confucian edicts so ingrained in him that he could not simply break them. He turned his salary over to Grandfather, and endured, mostly in silence, his stepmother's complaints.

The second Gold Mountain child, Aunty Freda, was born with allergies. Her skin broke into burning rashes.

"Get me someone to help me!" Yune-Shee demanded of Grandfather and my father.

It was a reasonable request. Grandfather had already been asking around for such help in *Hahm-sui-fauh, Salt-Water City*.

Arriving on the overnight ferry from *Hahm-sui-fauh*, a slim woman in her early twenties soon came to stay with them. Speaking Toisan, a related Sze Yup dialect, she settled in a small room of her own.

"Just big enough for a bed and table," I remember her telling me.

The slim, pretty woman at once took to Freda and helped to comfort the crying child. That woman, embracing Freda as her own, was to become my mother.

---

MOTHER HAD COME TO Gold Mountain around 1922 as a "paper bride." She used the birth document of a married woman born in Canada. This woman had died on a visit to China, but her death was never officially noted. Such deaths were rarely reported, as the papers of Gold Mountain residents were invaluable "passports" to be bought or resold. Her birth certificate and travel papers gave Mother the chance to assume the dead woman's name and to book a "return passage" to Canada.

My mother's *maaih-ji mengh*, her *bought-paper name*, appears on my birth certificate as "Nellie Hop Wah," whose birthplace is "New Westminister, B.C." Her family name, according to this paper, was "Wah."

In fact, Mother was born in Toisan, a village south of Sunwui, in the Sze Yup district. Her family managed to arrange her passage to Gold Mountain. She promised to send remittances back to China to help her elder brother. He had just married, and a child was on the way.

In those days, families in China sometimes "sold" their daughters to Gold Mountain settlers, to overseas jobbers brokering cheap labour or to well-off merchants seeking a family house-servant, a mistress or a concubine. These women were called *kay-toi neui,* "*stand-at-table*" *girls,* serving girls or—for immigration purposes—"waitresses."

It seemed a Mr Hop Wah, Mother's "paper husband," had sub-sequently died, leaving her "a widow." Whether or not she had ever been a companion of any sort to Mr Wah, no one has told me. When exactly Hop Wah died, before or after Mother's arrival, remains a mystery. However paper-phoney her widowhood may have been, the Chinatown community expected Mother to behave in a suitably mournful manner; otherwise, the immigra-tion officials might get nosy. Many of the elders cautioned that the real Nellie Hop Wah might come back to haunt Mother.

When Mother came to stay with the Kings, Father at once fell in love with her. They had seen each other before among mutual friends in Vancouver; he began his courtship when Mother came to Victoria, and became a part of Father's family. Grandfather seemed to have approved of the situation, but Yune-Shee protested. Mother, this common *kay-toi neui,* was beneath her class.

Living with the Kings, Mother helped to take care of the first four children born to Grandfather and Second Wife. There was no other work available for someone who spoke no English; she bore Yune-Shee's commands by holding her breath and keeping busy. She bathed the children, washed the diapers, paid special attention to Freda. Mother was permitted some evenings off, spending many of those evenings waiting on tables at a local late-night tea house.

On his days off, when both had evenings free, Father took my mother out to see Victoria's beautiful gardens. That cost nothing. He was careful to take her only to places where the Chinese were tolerated. Otherwise, they would be made to feel unwelcome, or bluntly told to leave. Many stores and cafés would ignore or sneer at Chinese customers, taking their money as if the coins and dollars were filthy. Eventually, Father discovered a dockside hotel with a long bar, a band, and a small open floor for shuffling about after 10 p.m.; the place tolerated anyone who would pay for exorbitant, watered-down drinks.

"Dancing and drinking were not done in those days," Father told me. "Respectable Chinatown marriages were always arranged. Your mother and I were fond of each other. People talked. Stepmother talked. We danced."

## Twenty-Four

*The handsome
couple*

MY PARENTS' MID-1920S wedding photo depicts, in sepia tones, a young man with a broad forehead, his elegant features defined by high cheekbones. And my mother, with her shapely eyes and soft mouth, her slender waist, is as beautiful as Father is handsome. Anyone could see why Toy and Lilly Choy were together.

"It was time to be married and time to move out of that house," Mother told me. "Your father and I had saved some money, and we wanted to start our own family, our own home."

My parents moved out of the Cormorant Street house into a set of rooms above a tea house, located near the corner of Fisgard and Government. They worked at the tea house, selling dim sum and Chinese pastries, which Mother had learned to make herself during the years she spent with Yune-Shee. Father now worked regular shifts with the CPR, and by 1932 he was promoted to Chief Cook, to work in the galleys of the ships that ran the overnight triangle route: Seattle, Vancouver, Victoria. On his days off, he worked with Mother in the restaurant. They also took turns helping with Grandfather's growing family. By 1933, Yune-Shee had given birth to six boys, one of whom died as a baby, and four girls.

"We work five times as hard as anyone else did," Father told me. "No choice. Work harder or someone else take your job." Father would clench his fist at the memory, his voice choking. "*Five times as hard!*"

Second Wife's hard-eyed resentment of my father's modest success was raising tensions in the family. Yune-Shee was a powerful, domineering woman, with a will to match, and whenever she felt her own first son's status threatened, she and Grandfather would openly clash. Perhaps Second Wife feared the rigid Chinese tradition that would have my own father, as First Son, inherit everything, leaving herself, her own First Born, indeed all her children, destitute.

"George will not do common work," she declared in defence of Uncle George's seeming inability to hold a job. She made her First Born, in his teenage years, the head of her household and kept him by her side to police the activity of his siblings. But nothing could make up for the fact that Uncle George hadn't been educated in China. Born in Victoria, Uncle George was a *mo-no* because he didn't have an Old China education. When Grandfather wanted to discuss China and Chinatown politics or articles in the Chinese newspapers, he talked to Father instead.

There must have been good years between Grandfather and Second Wife. But by the time I was born, in 1939, all of Victoria knew only of the couple's shouting matches and Yune-Shee King's demands for perfection in embroidery and baking. These were neurotic fixations, weapons of perfection she wielded against her own daughters.

"Oh, none of the girls could do anything right," Aunty Mary recalled. "She screamed at her four daughters, shaking her fist, '*In China, I would sell you girls cheap! Sell you today!*'"

By 1936, the Princess Line ships changed their main crews in Vancouver instead of Victoria; Father and Mother packed their bags, moved out of the rooms above the tea house and left behind the Victoria family. At last, they would have their own life in Vancouver.

After twelve years of marriage, in 1939, the son they had wished for arrived. Not surprisingly, only Uncle Harry and Grandfather came over from Victoria to celebrate the event. No words of good wishes came from Yune-Shee.

# Twenty-Five

*Toy Choy's first Gold Mountain portrait*

FATHER SUFFERED A stomach complaint in January 1980, which he at first considered to be indigestion, a minor nuisance. He ignored it. By the summer, his Chinatown herbalist had suggested that he see his Western doctor. I got the bad news in Toronto.

"*Jeul say-la!*" he told me on the phone from Vancouver. "*Die soon!*"

He went on and on in Chinese. The cramping in his stomach, he said at last, was cancer. I struggled with my Toisanese to interrupt, to tell him not to worry, everything would be fine.

"*Mmh ho kong kom-toh!*" the voice on the line shouted back. "*Don't talk so much!*" His Toisanese clipped away at me. "*Eighty-two—die soon.*"

I flew out that summer. Father's emergency operation proved successful.

After the operation, I made arrangements for Father to come and live with me and my extended family in Toronto. The nearly two years he spent with me, arriving under my care when I turned forty-two—the same age he was when I first settled into his life—was a difficult and sometimes joyful time.

I could not do everything for him, certainly not the way Mother had when she was alive, or the way Aunty Mary had in Vancouver: meals were not on time or to his liking, conversations were sometimes abrupt or cut off, and the room he had at the back of our house was too tiny, too unaccommodating. The new three-piece bathroom—my home partners Karl and Marie Schweishelm had built it for him—was the only room he liked. The walls were painted a fiery dragon red, a ghost-fighting colour.

"He's old, Sonny," Aunty Mary told me during a long-distance call. "In Vancouver, he complained the house was too big. What do you expect from an old man?"

The joyful times were enough, however, to keep me reasonably composed. Karl and Marie came to love him, to appreciate him for his wit and dignity. They helped care for him, in ways that made us family. Marie thought it was nothing to help cut Father's toenails and to cook many of his meals, and Karl took it for granted that he would fix up the old Saulter Street house and drive us around in his Ford pick-up. With his pension cheque, Father sometimes splurged on a restaurant dinner for all of us; he loved the hearty Roast Beef Tuesdays at the St Lawrence Market. When Marie announced she was pregnant, Father insisted on a celebration meal. The four of us headed for the Market diner, crammed inside the truck cabin like a sitcom hillbilly family. All we lacked was an old rocker tied to the roof.

Once, after I had heard one too many of Father's complaints about my inefficiencies and was feeling as if I wanted to push my poor father down the stairs, Karl turned on me.

"When you're eighty, Wayson, *believe me*, you're going to be *worse*."

That did not exactly humble me, but it shut me up.

Marie gave birth during my father's stay with us. The next evening, Father heard nine-pound Kathryn Elizabeth Schweishelm wailing through the thick glass at St Michael's Hospital and told me, her godfather, "She smart baby. Tiger spirit."

At the end of that second year in Toronto, and five months after Kate's birth in November, Father decided to return to Vancouver. The long, treacherous Ontario winters, the icy streets and roads, had kept him caged in our Saulter Street house for months, and, frankly, the father–son proximity was getting to both of us.

I had tried my best to care for him; my house-partners Karl and Marie—truly more my family—had grown very fond of Father and gave their best to care for him, too. The last months with us, slumped in a plush armchair, he cradled newborn Kate in his arms, nodding off with her.

But Father was too independent to be taken care of by anyone. Besides, he now felt fully recovered; he longed for his regular jaunts down to Vancouver's Chinatown social clubs. Snow and ice covered Toronto streets, but flowers were blooming in B.C. He felt fine and had me pack his bags.

Father flew back to his two-bedroom home on 62nd Avenue, the house he had shared with Mother. Again, Aunty Mary and Uncle Toy faithfully watched over him.

"I die in Vancouver," he had told Marie, hugging her goodbye.

I FLEW OUT TO Vancouver to be with him for a week. Back in his own familiar living room, the picture windows reflecting back the shrubbery and sloping lawn, our relationship was on comfortable ground again. Although he was still shaky until he steadied himself on his cane, Father's cheeks glowed, his voice was strong and his eyes alert. Every evening, as a concession to my fretting, when I came in to say goodnight, he let me tuck his blanket under his chin. Though a housekeeper came by twice a week and relatives visited, Father was left mainly on his own. We had been apart for three months, and it was comforting to see him doing well. I felt less guilty.

His regained independence had renewed his spirits, but it was clear from the way he leaned upon the back of the kitchen chair to go from table to sink, the way he stepped unsteadily with his cane, he was not doing as well physically as he let on.

I had come with a purpose. I felt the need to learn more of our family history before it was too late, before his memory or his eighty-five-year-old body, or both, would completely fail him. I had been too busy denying his mortality. It seemed I had never been ready to listen to him before, never been as interested in his past as when he seemed now to be leaving me. He had grown frail, smelled of dust and dying, and, at last, I thought we were going to talk.

For most of my life, neither Father nor Mother was willing to talk about important matters. We lacked the language and seemed to lack the will. The truth was, we were reluctant to give too much of ourselves away.

When it came my turn in my teenage years to be tight-lipped with them, to ignore their prying questions, I had by then learned from Father how to convey the same silence, how to look as grim and as secretive. How to behave so they would mind their own business. Every family, I believe, has their way of conveying "M.Y.O.B." to other family members. Whenever Mother asked me questions that I refused to answer with any specific details, like what part-time salary I was pulling in or who I was dating (so she could tell her mah-jong associates), she would say in her village dialect, after noting my stiffening silence, "You can stop looking like your father."

As I grew up, our family of three learned well enough not to probe each other too deeply. We became mutually secretive. We became beloved strangers. In my thirties, I noticed that we could go on for months, if not years, without speaking of anything personally meaningful, the natural condition (I now understand) of most families. But I had not counted on the will of ghosts; I had not realized that there were ghosts who do not always care for silence, who will not stay unremembered. With our shared Chinatown background, Father or I should have seen the signs that ghosts were drawing near. But I noted only the obvious: the old man was dying. It was time to ask about the past.

When he was in Toronto reminiscing with me, Father didn't mind too much my periodic note-taking, but had objected to my using a tape recorder.

"Too much trouble," he said, waving his hand over the small machine. The Sony unnerved him, hindered his free-wheeling talk. I put it away and, eventually, my notebook, too. Father grew flustered when he couldn't answer certain questions, such as: "What year did that take place?" "When did you work on the Princess ships?"

His face darkened.

"Just listen," he scolded.

Still, I was nagged by the need to record at least some of his talk.

That last spring break with Father, I didn't ask, but set up the Sony recorder on the kitchen table while he watched without protest.

We had been sitting kitty-corner. The cassette recorder hummed between us. Ever since the Sony had double-bounced off the airport floor, it had given me some trouble, but the thing seemed to be working again.

I wanted to ask Father about his boyhood in China. He didn't seem troubled by the idea that one day, my dream, everything would go into a book. Then again, neither of us guessed that some dark force would come between Father and me.

---

THREE WEEKS BEFORE I arrived that last summer, there was bad news. Father had been told that his stomach cancer of two years ago had returned. His medications now needed to be constantly monitored, adjusted. The day after I arrived, we went together to the clinic at St Paul's. The young specialist looked sombre when he turned from the vague shadows on the x-ray.

"Mr Choy," he said, tapping his stethoscope, "we could still try another operation."

"No," Father said. "No more." Then he smiled. "Thank you."

Father turned to me and interrupted whatever else the doctor wanted to say, "*Mo sau sut.*" Without my translating a single word, the doctor bowed his head. He understood: *no more cutting.*

We rode silently home on the bus together. I had never remembered the North Shore mountains so clearly, nor seen such a blue and cloudless sky. As the bus stopped at Granville, people jumped on with shopping bags, as if the world would never end.

In the living room, I took Father's coat. He put down his cane, settled on the sofa and turned on the record player to hear the last act of his favourite opera. The needle rose and fell. Through clashing cymbals, through the rising falsetto voice of the desperate heroine, came the thundering drumbeat prologue announcing the arrival of the hero. Father shut his eyes.

Sitting in the kitchen, nursing a drink, I closed my eyes. I was five years old and back in the Sing Kew. The yellow curtains shimmered. Mother's voice whispered in my ear.

———

UNLESS FATHER HIMSELF volunteered to tell me an anecdote that brought on laughter about "the good old days," days that were in fact rarely good, I knew enough not to ask too much. I had been wondering why I never really got to know all of his five stepbrothers and four stepsisters; why nobody except Aunty Freda and Aunty Mary visited us when I was a boy.

"The others listened to Yune-Shee," Father said, shaking his head at the memory of the tiny woman who so maliciously divided the family. "Tough lady."

He told me how the rancour that had existed between Grandfather and Second Wife had grown more vicious in the years after he and Mother were married. She resented my mother, favoured Uncle George and fought with Grandfather. The hostility between Yune-Shee and Choy King eventually divided the family, and she bought her own house with the salaries from her grown children. That was why, when I was in kindergarten, Grandfather came to live with us in Vancouver.

Yune-Shee told each of the King children, "If you visit your father in Vancouver, *I throw you out!*"

I remembered meeting Uncle Len and his wife, Daisy, at Grandfather's funeral. My aunts and uncles were forbidden to attend, but a few came over for his burial anyway. Yune-Shee stayed in Victoria, keeping the youngest ones with her.

I never quite understood the deep animosity between Grandfather and Second Wife, but it divided my Father and Mother from the Victoria Kings, and kept the three of us from ever becoming a family with them. Except, that is, for the oldest and youngest sisters, Aunty Freda and Aunty Mary, who, defying their mother, visited us quite often.

"Yes, they always spoiled you." Father laughed. "*Ho sum, ho sum! Good hearts, good hearts!*" His Toisanese flowed with grateful memories. "They were both very fond of me, of your mother, of you. Besides, Freda was independent enough to think for herself. She wasn't afraid to stand up to her mother or to George. And Mary's heart was too good to leave her stepbrother's family out in the cold."

"Did Grandmother kick them out?"

"Yes." Father sighed. "Freda left first, then Mary come to live in Vancouver. We make up our own family."

Father's openness about the problems between Second Wife and Grandfather led me to ask him about his own mother. It struck me as odd that he had said so little about her, even though he told me about other details of his village childhood. Whenever he felt disinclined to answer any of my questions, or could not, or if he felt discomforted by what he remembered, he would brush back the wisps of white hair above his ears and shake his head.

"I don't remember that," he'd say. "Too, too long ago."

I knew enough not to press him.

Father's reluctance was so dignified, his look so tellingly solemn, that he convinced me how impossible and meddling I was being, and how disrepectful.

"No good to know everything," he would say in English, then meditatively repeat in Chinese to himself another four-character epigram, reaffirming his judgement, his voice rising with finality, "*Dou se loh haaih.*" I pictured his meaning in my mind: *A basket of crabs let loose.* It always shut me up.

When I was ten, I once asked Uncle Wally to translate one of my father's cryptic sayings.

"*Gai sihk fong gwong chung.*"

"Your father just quoted an old saying," he said, and translated: "'*A chicken has eaten a firefly.*'"

"Meaning?"

"The firefly glows inside the chicken, not outside." Uncle Wally laughed. "Someone knows something not known to others."

"I don't get it," I said.

"Your old man's usual meaning, Sonny: *mind your own business.*"

In spite of the years of silence, I wanted to learn about that phantom woman, the mother he lost while still a boy in China. I assumed she was left behind because she had died in the famine, and that Father didn't talk about her because the loss was so painful.

"Where was your own mother?" I meant to ask, in my awkward and barely remembered child's Toisanese: What kind of a person was she? Why don't you ever mention her?

"Number One wife," he said, as if it should have been obvious who she was. "The one back in China."

He had deliberately misunderstood my question.

———

THE SONY HUMMED when I plugged the cord in. Father sat comfortably bent over in his favourite kitchen chair. A square of sunlight from the window behind me reflected off the dark Arborite table. The kettle on the stove gave its last burbling whistle. I poured the toast-coloured tea, and breathed in the sweet, flowery scent. Father's hands circled the steaming cup; the sudden heat made him smile. Settled, we were ready to talk. For the first time, he seemed comfortable letting me tape his words.

Father was amused by his own stories; his eyes flashed with remembered mischief. He once climbed the tall, thick-branched tree in the middle of the school courtyard and his old teacher, looking up into the sun, could not make him out. Father sat most of the afternoon and watched the distant fields of farmers moving behind their oxen.

"Did you skip school often?" I asked.

"Oh, no." He frowned. "I didn't mind school at all. I just wanted some time to myself."

Refreshed by the tea, Father thought we might go on talking "just a few minutes."

I pressed the *record* button.

I hadn't been thinking of much more to ask about his school days, but it came to me that he might now like to tell me something about his mother in China.

"Bah-ba, tell me about her," I said, softly, in Chinese. "Tell me how you remember your mother in China."

Father started to say something, as if he would, as usual, casually or curtly, dismiss me. But instead, his lips tightened. Seconds ticked by. Perhaps his throat was still dry. Clenching his fists, his eyes widened. For a moment, I panicked—*a stroke?* All at once, I had the oddest sense that *someone—something*—was standing before him. The sensation made me feel queasy. To see what Father was staring at, I turned my head.

There must have come to him without any warning—as can happen to anyone at any time—so exact a remembrance that *something* took hold of him. His lips were trembling; his pupils focused on nothing but air.

Yet, *something—someone*—had stood before us.

Father physically shrank away. Huddled in his chair, his hand reached out to grip the edge of the table, as a little boy might hang on for safety.

"I—I can't," he said, his face collapsing, choking back tears.

I quickly turned off the Sony.

For a few minutes, we sat at the table, saying nothing. I had not expected anything like this. The silence felt suddenly uncomfortable, unforgivable. What had I been thinking? The need to discover more, to know more, suddenly left me.

After a few minutes, when he had recovered from my intrusive question, Father reached for his cane, stood up and shakily walked out of the kitchen.

Disturbed by what I had unknowingly provoked, I shut my eyes and pressed the *rewind* button.

# Twenty-Six

*Father with
Aunty Mary (left)
and Aunty Freda*

"Y OU KNOW, THE SPRING before Father died," I began, "he broke down and cried when I asked him about his mother. Then he wouldn't say why. Do you know anything?"

Freda sighed: old news, old ghosts. I persisted.

"It's a shameful story," she said, sadly. "The family lost face. At least your father thought so."

"Shameful?" The word skipped over my head, as if I hadn't heard correctly. "I don't understand, Freda. He would just say that his mother left him, that she died in China; isn't that true?"

"Yes..." Freda hesitated, her own seventy-seven years reaching back into the past. She finally said, "She had to leave your father. No choice."

Thinking for a moment, Freda frowned.

"No, after what she did, there was no choice. It happened during that first time my dad—your Grandfather Choy—first came to San Francisco in 1902. Or was it 1903? I can't remember exactly when. It was the time he travelled from California by coastal ship all the way up the West Coast to Vancouver and Victoria..."

That was the time Choy King first sailed to Gold Mountain to seek opportunities, and left behind his First Wife and First Son in the family compound in Sunwui.

"I think your father told me he was five or six years old at the time."

As First Wife and First Son, the two were to wait patiently for Grandfather Choy's return from his trip. To stabilize his rapidly depleting inheritance, Grandfather decided to try for new work in California. Grandfather heard there were not only gold mines, but golden opportunities in *Gim San*, in *Gold Mountain*. Making his contacts, pursuing job opportunities, earning his way in all kinds of work in mills and on ships, he stayed away from China for more than three years. Remittances were sent home to support the family. When he came back to China, interrupting his sojourn, Father was almost nine years old.

"Something happened." Freda's youthful face wrinkled with concern. "He had to come home."

I could see Freda struggling to tell me, as if she were betraying a confidence, finding the words.

"The more I think about it," she said, "the more I get angry about the way... your father's mother—" She shook her head.

"Why did she leave? Why did Grandfather go back to China?" I searched for dramatic straws. Nothing came up. "Why did she leave her son?"

"The mother was found out," Freda said, finally. "Your grandfather was away for three years, and she got herself pregnant. She was having an affair."

I was dumbfounded.

"She was pregnant?"

"Yes, that's why she had to leave."

In Old China, adultery was the worst betrayal any woman could commit against her husband. A wife was expected to remain faithful; if attacked, she was expected to defend her virtue with her life. And if she could not fend off her attacker, however it happened, she was to do the honourable thing afterwards: as proof of her loyalty to the family, she was to kill herself.

But for any woman willingly to have sex with another man, to betray her own husband, her own son, a First Son, that was beyond shame, beyond dishonour.

Freda was not at all happy to have told me all this.

"You know what they used to do with adulterous women?" Freda shook her head in disbelief. "Around your grandfather's time, they used to tie the woman up to a post in the village square. With knives and cleavers, official executioners carved her up into pieces. My mother told me that. Nose first, just like that, then the ears. The fingers. The breast. The whole body. Piece by piece. In those old days, they thought a woman who betrayed her husband cursed the whole village."

In a sense, that was true. If the stay-at-home women, married or single, failed to set examples of virtue and patience, their betrayed husbands and sons in North America would have no reason to send money back home. Villages depended upon these overseas remittances: Gold Mountain money bought seeds for crops, fed families, funded wells and villas and schools.

As for the "agony of a thousand cuts," more civilized laws were passed by the Senate of the Republic of China in 1912 as part of President Sun Yat-sen's attempts to modernize the country. No one during First Wife's time, neither man nor woman, would have been executed in this horrifying manner. But every man and woman would have remembered the punishment.

"What happened to First Wife?"

Freda answered, matter-of-factly: "The villagers threatened to stone her. They wanted to kill her. One night, she just disappeared. Ran away to another village."

Her boy, my father, was left in the care of family members. He was old enough to realize the shame his mother had brought upon the family. But worse, probably, was the knowledge that his mother had deserted him. The betrayal shattered Father, ripped away his carefree boyhood. Shortly after that, he left school, unable to take the taunts of the other children or to focus on his studies. Silence about those years grew around him like a thick shell, its walls locking away his anguish.

"Did Dad tell you some of this?"

"Your father never told me any of this. My mother told me, and your mother later confirmed it. Can't blame your father. He was only a boy, only nine years old. The only person he ever talked to about this was your mother. Before your mother died, we got to talking about the old days and she told me what he said, that his mother broke his heart." I started to ask another question, but Freda anticipated me.

"He never did know what became of her," she said.

My storyteller's mind whirled with the melodrama. My father's history had somehow been passed on to me, father to son, however long and circuitous the journey. Why should this story finally fall into my heart and brain? Ghosts are to be wrestled with, if not subdued.

I knew that whatever the injury, the burning wounds seared into my father by his mother's leaving him, this private sense of loss had made him into the man who was to love and care for me: he never, *never* deserted me.

The sin of his mother, if it had indeed been a sin, was never visited upon me.

Yet I was convinced that his mother had not entirely left him. Father had not expected her to return. She had shamed and betrayed him, her only son. He had not wished to see her again. But though he did not ask for her, seven decades after his mother mysteriously disappeared, I believe she came back to him, a penitent ghost. I thought back to our last interview together in that house in Vancouver.

———

AFTER THAT LAST INTERVIEW with my father, when he broke into tears and left me in the kitchen, I recall pressing the *rewind* button. The machine resisted. I pressed again. It clicked and churned, rewinding at last. When the tape was completely rewound, I pressed *play*.

*Testing, one . . . two . . . three . . . Bah-ba, tell me about . . . oh, no, I didn't mind school at all . . .*

For a few more minutes, I listened to our two voices laughing about his school days; then, without warning, the tape spewed out static. All the rest was static.

At the end of my subsequent visit that August, as I was carrying out my suitcases to my cousin's car to fly back to Toronto,

Father asked me about the tape we had made. I told him the machine had not been working.

"Just crazy noises," I told him. "Just static."

"We'll talk again," he said and leaned his feather-light frame against his cane to embrace me.

"I die in Vancouver," he declared. "No more worry."

———

IN THE SECOND WEEK of September, 1983, I was summoned to St Paul's Hospital. My father, now skeletal with disease, had had enough of living. Ravaged by multiple cancers, barely conscious, he began to ease away from me.

Bending over to kiss his forehead goodnight, I accepted at last that he would soon be gone. My father's last attempt at speaking gurgled from his throat. With every attempt to speak, his Adam's apple rose and fell. A wetness came to his frosted, unseeing eyes, and when I pulled myself up to listen, with his last energy he lifted his head.

I heard him say "*Mah-ma . . . Mah-ma . . .*" then watched him fall back down, eyes closed.

For the last time, I tucked his blanket under his chin.

Five years ago, at Mother's funeral, he had reached into the open coffin to embrace her. "*Mah-ma,*" he had said, kissing her. Some of us had watched, astonished and discomfited. When she was alive, when they fell into a rare contentment with each other, he would brush her hair with his hand and say, "*Mah-ma,* you look lovely."

In St Paul's, as Father called out his last words and fell back into semi-conciousness, I was at peace to think that he had called out his final endearment to my mother, his companion of forty-five years. When I think back to this moment, I remember thanking him, and Mother, for my life.

The next morning, at 8 a.m., I was awakened by a phone call from the family doctor.

Father had just died.

Now, sixteen years after my father's death, as I consider everything Aunty Freda has told me about his history, I think of my father's dying words differently. As I kissed him goodnight and he tried to raise his head, I believe that Father saw not one woman, not just my mother, who never deserted him, but... *two*.

After all, did he not say "*Mah-ma . . . Mah-ma . . .*"?

Could there never be forgiveness?

# Part Four

# Epilogue

*A last Chinatown
portrait*

THERE WERE TIMES IN my twenties when, out of curiosity, I questioned my parents about my birth.

"We waited a long time for you," Father always said to me. "*Mah-ma* and I were so happy! We had a big dinner. Birthday presents! Lucky jewellery! Grandfather officially named you. Everything!"

Mother, blushing, told me they had tried to have children for ten years, but nothing happened until I was born. Mother would point to my baby picture again, shaking her head.

"*Gum dai! So big!*" she would say, eyes rolling. "Weighed eight or nine pounds!"

"Why didn't you have more?" I always asked.

"You were enough." Mother would laugh and Father would nod in agreement.

Another time, my university friend Dennis Yandle was attempting to do my astrology chart. Knowing the exact time of my birth would be crucial.

"Mother, you have to remember the time," I said. "After all, it was a big event for you and Father."

Father shrugged. He was always bad with dates and times. Mother thought for a long moment.

"Oh, *neigh-ka* birth," Mother finally said, looking helpless because she knew so little English and had to fall back into Chinese. She thought a moment. "*Leung-dim jung* . . . yes . . ." She looked away, then held up two fingers. ". . . yes . . . two a.m."

"That means you're on the cusp," Dennis said. "You're transitional, Sonny, between Aries and Taurus."

"He lucky?" Father asked.

"Oh, very, very lucky to be on the cusp," Dennis answered. "The best of two worlds." He drew some lines on my planetary chart. "Mars rising, too. Sonny won't starve."

Mother smiled. Her son would always have enough to eat. Putting down his *Chinese Times*, Father looked pleased, too. Dennis stayed for supper.

———

MY PARENTS' TRICKS were common enough. Countless adopting parents of their generation must have behaved with equal poise.

But what amazes me is that the truth of my adoption was in fact known by so many relatives and friends, yet no one broke the news to me. Not once. One of my oldest friends, Larry Wong, *fifty years after the fact* laughingly told me that, when I was playing hooky from Chinese school and first went to see those silent films in their store on Main, his father knew at once who I was. Larry's parents, while his mother was alive, had been part of the opera community.

"That boy's adopted," Larry's father told him, as I left the shop that first time.

But Larry never thought to ask who my real parents were; he only understood, without his father saying any more, he was not to tell me.

For fifty-six years I had no idea that I was not my parents' biological child. I lived all my life with Toy and Lilly Choy, never doubting that I was their flesh and blood.

At the thought that the very beginning of my own life might be harbouring a secret, I felt abashed, a little giddy. I had dared to live as if I were safe from surprise. Whether or not Hazel's news was true, my gut told me: something had happened. I had written a book exploring the secrets of Chinatown; why wouldn't the gods of Chinatown strike back? I saw myself skidding on life's banana peel, heels in flight.

I had heard a hundred times, "Signs are everywhere!" All I had to do was to open my eyes and see what was there. More to the point, why was I so surprised?

---

"THIS IS FROM Sam-Gung for you," Mother said to me as she put in my hand a small package, a sheet of brittle paper, envelope-folded in the old style that Chinatown jewellers used to wrap up gemstones.

"Sam-Gung left it for you the last time he visited Vancouver."

I had not seen *Sam-Gung, Third Uncle,* for almost fifteen years. The last time I met him he was with his younger wife, a small woman with perfect teeth who smiled shyly and covered her mouth when she laughed. We hardly spoke. I was in my twenties, and the old man and I had very little in common except for our memories of my Chinatown boyhood. At the sight of my jeans, their knees torn, and plain T-shirt, he didn't make any comments.

Dressed in his best suit, shoes immaculately polished, Third Uncle proudly showed me pictures of his grown-up Hong Kong family standing in front of their walk-up apartment. He had moved back to Hong Kong in 1969, just as he had always wanted, and his lifetime pass with the CPR allowed him this chance to return to B.C. for a visit. I was happy for Third Uncle, but I never quite got over the fights Mother and I had over the prickly Irish tweed she insisted I wear before I could go out with him.

I was a little sad to miss his last visit with the family.

"Third Uncle said goodbye to all of us," Mother went on. "He left this for you."

The brittle mulberry paper opened crisply. Out fell an oval, ring-sized piece of rare Burmese jade. It was apple green and semi-translucent. A milky cloud sat at its centre. Back when I was eight or nine, Third Uncle showed off his jade pieces in our kitchen on Keefer Street. He asked me to look them over. A half-dozen green and white jade stones glowed in the afternoon light. I instinctively reached out for one of them, perhaps this one, and held it to the light. Then they were put away and nothing more was said.

But as precious as this gift is to me, more valuable is the time he spent with me when I was a boy and he was being himself, a stick-in-the-mud, stubborn and annoying. And most valuable of all are the unseen gifts that have stayed with me all my life.

Third Uncle firmly believed that the world was inhabited by unseen presences. Many of Chinatown's citizens believed in ghosts. They spoke discreetly around non-believers, of course, pretending the wind was only the wind, the shadow only a shadow, however it moved. But among themselves, the Old China citizens talked quite naturally about the ghost-inhabited universe. They often heard the moaning spirits of departed men and women drifting in rooming-house hallways and glimpsed them lingering beside dank portals.

Third Uncle took me on his walks and sometimes he did volunteer work for the Benevolent Association. Probably before I entered kindergarten—that is, before I started becoming a know-it-all and seeing the world as a more sensible place—I was a natural part of the elders' world. The fact that Third Uncle would periodically shout questions to someone unseen never troubled me. In fact, it made me more alert.

"Is that you, Wah Bak?" Third Uncle said during one of our visits to the recently widowed Mrs Wah in her Jackson Street walk-up. Third Uncle was carrying a shopping bag of groceries donated by the Tong Association. We stopped at the landing before a long dim hallway. Uncle held my hand tightly and again addressed the warm, still air.

"Wah Bak, is that you?"

From the empty hallway, a voice, like wind, came back to us. Uncle seemed to understand and said, "We bring food."

Nothing stirred. No one seemed to be in the hallway, though Third Uncle stared ahead as if he could see something.

"Whenever you around a *ho kwei*—a *good ghost*—" Fifth Aunty had instructed me, "make a wish."

Third Uncle's gaze was steady, fearless and matter-of-fact. Wah Bak's ghost must be friendly.

I closed my eyes. I had just been given a large piggy bank for my birthday. I liked the way dropped coins *clink*ed in its hollow belly. "Money," I whispered, crossing my fingers behind my back, just as I was taught to do when I made a wish over my birthday cake.

Later, after thanking us for our brief visit, Mrs Wah told Third Uncle how she had just been talking to her dead husband before we arrived.

"Of course," Uncle said.

"I was worried about food," Mrs Wah said.

It was noon. The blinds were drawn against the stagnant heat, and the hallway door stood a little open for any slight movement of air.

Mrs Wah put her thin hand into the lacy pocket of her apron and took out a hanky-wrapped cluster of cash. My eyes widened. She pulled away the elastic band and tilted her hand to let the silver coins reflect a beam of sunlight. She scrupulously selected a shiny new nickel and held it up before me.

My right palm came up of its own accord.

"For you," she said with a laugh, gathering my fingers closed. "For your piggy bank."

Third Uncle protested on my behalf, saying I was being too spoiled, insisting I give back the coin. He made a motion to take the nickel away.

But according to the family telling of this incident, I jammed my clenched fist into my pocket and stared hard at the hall door. It suddenly swung wide open, hinges creaking, as if someone were stepping into the room with us. Then it flew shut. But no one could be seen. I looked back, sternly, at Third Uncle.

"Wah Bak!" I said, startling myself. "Wah Bak says, '*Piggy hungry, too!*'"

Both Third Uncle and Mrs Wah gazed wide-eyed at the shut door.

At five—innocent, surely, of greed, though not of selfishness—
I had invoked a ghost of Chinatown. Before I realized what had
happened, Mrs Wah bent down and hugged me against herself
and seemed, for an eternity, unable to let me go.

Whenever I wear the gold ring set with the jade stone, its milk-
cloud centre seems to reflect back to me a sand castle, and the
stern face of Third Uncle.

———

OLD CHINATOWN AUNTS and uncles made me aware of the invisible world, and of how transitory the visible one can be. It's one
thing to be aware of ghosts. It's another to *be* one.

I told Garson Lee over a dim-sum lunch with his sisters, Lil
and Shirley, that I would be writing my childhood memoir. He
would be in it.

I wanted his permission to write about that evening when he
was attacked in the alleyway by a paedophile.

"Do you remember that horrible night?"

Through the steam rising from a bamboo tray of Fortune
House dumplings, my question seemed a little bit out of place.
Garson, now a successful accountant, didn't seem to mind.

"I was eight then," he said. "You were involved, too, Sonny."

Lil said, "And it was all my fault."

"No, it was my fault," Shirley insisted. "I sent him out to the
store that night."

The four of us—Garson, Lil and Shirley, and I—had come
together to talk and laugh about my boyhood years. I had not
been with Garson that evening. If I were facing a steel-eyed monster who was willing to kill his prey, I probably would have peed
in my pants and fainted.

"I can still feel how rough his skin was," Garson said. "I can still smell that rotten breath. He just kept pushing me against the railing."

Garson took a deep breath.

"Take some tea," Lil said.

"Let's all drink some tea," Shirley said.

The tea in the pot had been refreshed, but brewed longer, tasting more bitter than sweet.

For a minute, no one said a word. We shared the Old Chinatown attitude that you could talk about anything as long as you had food to eat, tea to drink—a pause to catch your breath—as long as you knew you would never starve, never thirst . . . and therefore, never surrender. We drank. We paused.

But Garson had said I was involved. How could that be? Of course, he meant I was there the next day with my mother, both of us staring silently at his bruises, his swollen eyes, and the purple welts along his neck.

Finally, Garson said, "It was awful."

"Terrible," Shirley said.

"What was?" I asked. "He did something else?"

"The bastard started to."

"That really got to you," Lil said. "That was when you started fighting back."

"I don't know." Garson looked confused. "I just started reacting. I started flailing, hammering the guy with the pop bottle."

"Good for you!" Shirley broke into a broad smile. "Hit the bastard!"

"Use everything!" Lil cheered.

But the attacker proved stronger and pushed Garson backwards, *hard*, grabbed his neck, twisted his head sideways, and started to squeeze.

"I kept bashing him, but I couldn't breathe," Garson said. "I started blacking out. My arms, my legs, everything started to give way. I heard the pop bottle bouncing off the steps. And that smell of the guy, like sour beer . . ."

Garson sat back in the restaurant chair and slipped back into that moment. His face grew childlike, thoughtful. "I knew I was dying." He seemed to be weighing what he wanted to say next.

"Tell him," Lil said.

"Tell me what?" I asked.

"Look, Sonny, I never told you this before . . . but at that point, just when I thought I was going to die, I actually saw *you* standing in front of me."

I started to laugh.

Garson shook his head. "No, don't laugh. It's true. I saw *you*, Sonny." He lifted his hand as if to take mine. "You held out your hand. Like this." He gently closed his hand. "We were going out to play."

"Tell," Shirley said. "Tell Sonny what happened next."

In those seconds when Garson was blacking out, a sedan noisily drove up the Dunlevy end of the cobblestoned laneway and stopped at the back of the icehouse, engine running. The headlights shone down the length of the alley. Startled, the stranger choking Garson let go and fled.

"Next thing I know I'm breathing and choking and sliding down onto the wet ground."

Four housewives out to buy blocks of ice for their iceboxes saw Garson stumbling down the lane towards them. If they had not arrived at that exact moment . . .

"I was ready to die," Garson said. "I saw you, just as I was giving up. Do you understand, Sonny?"

"You thought of me." I laughed. "What a crazy coincidence!"

Garson shook his head: I had missed the point.

"But don't you understand?" he said, his voice solemn. "It was *seeing you* that let me know everything would be fine."

I felt unsettled, to say the least.

"You were there," Shirley said.

"Yes, of course," Lil said. "Oh, Sonny, thanks to you we still have Garson today!"

The three of them beamed, breaking into generous laughter at my perplexity.

For a moment, I was speechless. Their interpretation made me think of folk tales, the ones the Chinatown elders used to tell, tales in which loved ones, distant or recently dead, appeared to forewarn of disaster or to intimate good fortune.

Garson glanced at his watch. It had been a two-hour lunch. Time for him to get back to his corporate accounts and numbers; time for Shirley to return to her insurance work, Lil to the care of Mrs Lee, Leong Sim, now ninety-four.

"We'll talk some more the next time you visit Vancouver," Garson said. "Good to see you."

Garson's appalling experience had finally been told, and was now done.

"*Friendship*," Garson said, raising his cup of tea.

We lifted our cups.

Like a good mystery novel, I thought to myself, one's life should always be read twice, once for the experience, then once again for astonishment.

———

SINCE HEARING FROM Hazel, I have thought often of "the endless knot," the decoration I salvaged from those wind chimes, a knot without a beginning or an end. The many ways to understand life, to fathom love, cannot be counted. I have thought often of the Cantonese opera.

"My aunt Helena says that your real father was a member of the opera company," Hazel had told me.

Alas, there was no more information; at least, no more was revealed by the elders. Shirley asked her mother, Leong Sim, Mother's lifelong best friend, if she knew who my real parents were. Leong Sim visibly hesitated, then shook her head. So much you can know, and no more.

"I could keep asking," Hazel said. "There have to be others who know the truth. They might——"

"No," I said, "I feel I know what I have to know."

It's true. Time and chance, for now, have told me as much as I need to know.

As a child, I dreamed of fabled opera costumes. They swirled to glittering life. I flew acrobatically through the air between red banners and clouds of yellow silk, and heard the roar and clanging of drums and cymbals. And I fought off demons and ghosts to great applause. Were those dreams in my blood?

I cannot help myself: I imagine the man who fathered me, dressed in imperial splendour, sword in hand; he is flying above me, majestic and detached. If I were seventeen, and not, as I am now, sixty, would I weep to know that this man gave me up?

"Best to let the stories rest," Hazel had said.

But my mind races on, unstoppable. I had always thought of my family, my home, in such a solid, no-nonsense, no-mystery manner—how could I possibly think that no more stories waited to be told? I listened for clues and watched for signs. One after another, they came.

During one of our long talks together, Aunty Mary told me about a dinner party that she had attended in Victoria when she was seventeen years old, one year after Grandfather's death. She recalled how one of the visiting Vancouver Tuey relatives commented in her sweet, malicious voice how odd it was that, when Choy King was alive, he never said he had ten children, only nine.

"That's certainly odd," she said, reaching for the soup.

Before her spoon touched a drop, Father's fists smashed onto the table and his face flushed with rage. Cousin's spoon plopped into the soup; her mouth fell open.

"*Why*," Father roared, "*why was First Son never counted!?*" He stood up so abruptly, his chair overturned and crashed against the restaurant wall. "*Tell me why I was never counted! TELL!*"

Mary said everyone sat still. People in the restaurant turned to look. No one said anything. The issue had eaten at my father all his life. Now one joking remark had hit its target hard. The silence that followed revealed nothing.

"I didn't know what was wrong," Mary continued. "Maybe some of the others did. Your mother wouldn't look up. No one said anything. It was awful."

Dinner was finished quickly, silently. Mary sat at the table with her cousins; Father's chair sat empty.

The long unspoken periods between my father and my grand-father came back to me. I had never thought those silences held a mystery; I assumed that was the way things were.

"It was very strange," Mary recalled. "Our father and your father never seemed to be close at all, not like a normal father and son."

There was nothing to say. I recalled the silences between them when the old man lived with us, but mostly I remembered Grandfather as a perfectly docile companion for his five-year-old grandson.

Out of the blue, Mary asked me, "Did you ever know your father had two older sisters back in China?"

My mind raced back to Father as a nine-year-old boy, to his mother disappearing with him after her adultery. I thought there had been only the two of them, mother and son. Now, suddenly, *four* ghosts drifted into view.

"Right after she was caught in adultery, First Wife took the three children and fled to a distant village. Since your Grandfather was away in Gold Mountain all those years, your father's two sisters and his mother were the only family he ever knew as a boy."

I saw Father as a child shadowed by Grandfather.

"The old man hunted First Wife down and took your father back with him to Sunwui. What could she do? In those days a father was entitled to the First Son."

I cannot imagine what it might have been like for my father, a boy torn from his mother and sisters by a stranger claiming his rightful property.

"Your father never told anyone he had sisters," Mary said. "But Harry Young told me before he died that was what happened."

I think again of Father's breaking down in the kitchen when I asked him about his mother. Now I knew other ghosts had come back to him that afternoon, not only his mother but also the two sisters who had sheltered him.

————

AS A CHILD OF CHINATOWN, I never heard a single bitter word spoken against Grandfather or Grandmother. The dramas that split the family between Victoria and Vancouver never touched my child's consciousness.

After Grandfather had his multiple strokes and Yune-Shee would not allow him back to their Victoria house, the old man came to our house to die, in 1945, to the house of the First Son he would not acknowledge in his counting.

In 1968, it was Yune-Shee's turn to be bedridden; at seventy-three, she came to be sheltered and cared for in Aunty Freda's house on Victoria Drive in Vancouver. Her Victoria sons and daughters shared the cost of her rented hospital bed and private nurses, and visited now and again; but it was the daughter she first disowned who comforted her with twenty-four-hour care. Aunty Freda, assisted by Aunty Mary, saw the tiny woman to the end.

Similarly, though Mother and Father lived apart so often when I was growing up, and had their bitter disagreements and misunderstandings, in the end they did not leave each other. For the last twenty years of their marriage, they stayed together under the same roof, disgruntled and affectionate, until death.

A few days after Mother's funeral in 1977, I told Aunty Mary that one of the two pineapple-shaped evergreens that decorated each side of our front steps had suddenly died. The pair of clipped trees decorating our house on 62nd Avenue had been Father and Mother's pleasure. Father had gardeners regularly tend our small front lawn, and they had groomed the two front evergreens perfectly. A third, left to grow tall, stood in the far corner of the yard.

Aunty Mary touched the dead tree's rough yellowed boughs. She looked askance at me, but said nothing. A neighbour explained to me that a blight could cause the sudden death of an evergreen. Meanwhile, the other half of the pair remained healthy, and the third one at the corner of our front lawn stood green and robust.

"Nothing to worry about," he said. "Very rare."

Six years later, in 1983, ten days after Father's funeral in Vancouver, the remaining evergreen of the pair turned yellow as quickly as the first had after Mother's death, and as mysteriously withered.

Aunty Mary and I stared at the vacant spot where the first evergreen had been, then at the dying tree. The third tree, the one at the corner of the front lawn, still seemed healthy. She looked at it, then looked at me, appalled.

"Sell the house," she urged. "Sonny, sell the house right away."

The lone evergreen was still green and healthy when the young Korean couple signed the papers and bought the two-bedroom house. Aunty Mary sighed with relief.

———

I MARVEL THAT MY childhood in Chinatown should raise questions I never thought to ask, heighten mysteries and reveal threads weaving back and forth within my life with neither a beginning nor an end.

My childhood in Chinatown is like a Chinese box that opens in a variety of ways, revealing different levels, each sliding compartment secret. I didn't know when I revelled in the Chinese opera as a child that my natural father was a member of it. I had no way of knowing that Grandfather accepted his adopted grandson as his own, but somehow found a cruel way to reject his own First Son, the man who became my father. All the Old Chinatown men and women who surrounded me in my childhood, who cared for me, all their histories still hidden, beating against the silence like ghosts.

And that time when Sum Sook picked me up and threw me bodily into the air, how could I have known how deeply and sensually I would respond to his touch? Forever after, I knew—without shame—something about my sexuality that I was not able to fathom until fifteen years later. I love, as Dante wrote, the other stars.

And how does anyone come to think of parents and family and

home, as if there were no mysteries, really? How do people contrive for decades to speak neither of the unknown nor of the knowable?

"Don't you want to know everything?" a friend asked me.

"It's surprising we know anything," Aunty Freda once said. "The old Chinatown people were so secretive."

Before our leaving Chinatown to travel by train to Ontario, I stood beside Mother in front of a bonfire in our backyard, tossing into its flames the remains of Choy King's calligraphic writings, his diaries and journals; and my dog Winky snapped at the grey fragments floating down from the sky. Fire and ashes claimed our family history.

When Aunty Mary and I searched my parent's trunks for documents and pictures, she said, "Why did they throw so much away?"

I have no answer.

There's nothing to be done about the unknowable—the intricate shadows and silences between the facts that one feels so certain of—except to pause and be astonished. All lives are ten *times* ten thousand secrets. Even those who are quite sure of themselves, they, too, are made up of mystery, defined by secrets told and untold.

Whose life, I wonder, is not an endless knot?

# Acknowledgements

This memoir depended upon the generosity and knowledge of many people; they are not all listed below, but have made their appearances in Paper Shadows. Other persons appear under informal names as they or their families have requested.

I would like to thank Dr. Elizabeth Johnson of the B.C. Museum of Anthropology for access to archival materials on the Cantonese theatre companies in Vancouver, and for her generous assistance in guiding my research; Dr. David Chuenyan Lai of the University of Victoria for his impeccable studies of Canadian

Chinatowns; Carol Haber of the Vancouver City Archives; Donna McKinnon of the Vancouver Historical Society; the personnel of the Nanaimo Chinatown Museum; and the helpful staff of the Vancouver Public Library and the Strathcona School Library; Sushan Chin, of the Museum of Chinese in the Americas, New York; Chris Lee and Larry Wong for their assistance at the Vancouver Chinatown Museum and the Chinese Cultural Centre Archives, and to Saintfield Wong, curator; authors Maria Coffey, Lynne Bowen and Marilyn Bowering for sharing their writings and research materials; for their Masters' theses from the University of British Columbia, Joanne Mei-Chu Poon and Paul Richard Yee. Many thanks to Larry Wong for answering my calls to help verify details, for generous assistance, and for locating family documents.

For access to invaluable Chinatown directories of the period, for news clippings, photographs, for access to their private collections, and for copies of family diaries and mementoes, I thank John Atkin, Dr. Wallace B. Chung, Nancy Hee, Fred John, James Lee, the David Lee family, May Leong, Imogene Lim, Wesley Lowe, Beverly Nann, Albert and Ann Plant, Jake Sweeney, Tony Fong, Robert Mills . . . and most especially the generosity of Robert Yip, Victoria Yip and her Wing Sang family members.

For their identification of Chinese dialects and sayings, and for their translations of documents, my thanks to Tony Cheung, Dorothy Chin, Jack Chin, Ronnie Leung, Evelyn Leong-Cheung, Richard Seto, Alfred and Chun Shin.

For their patience during detailed interviews, I would like to thank Allan and Phoebe Chan, Winnifred (Wynne) Chang, Mr. and Mrs. Harry Chow, Lena Chow, William and Lena Chu, Elinor Denton, Randy Enomoto, Nancy Hee, Art and Lil Iwata, Terry Jang-Barclay, Bevan Jangze, Fred John, Jo Ann Law, Betty Lee, Gar Lee, Garson Lee, Gary Lee, King Lee, Lola Lee, Spike Lee, Valerie Lee

Whong, Alex Louie, Toy and Mary Lowe, Ng Moh, Carol Ann Soong, Freda Schroeder, Kay Sun, Joey and Shirley Wong, Norman Wong, Wally Wong, Victoria Yip and family; and others who wished to remain anonymous. Above all, my thanks to Hazel Young.

My appreciation for very specific assistance and encouragement during my research and sabbatical assignments, especially to Kenneth Dyba and his pal Lilly, who gave firm advice and organized my files; Doris Tallon; Antanas Sileika; Joyce Eagle; Lynda Hill; Dennis Yandle and Jean Stackwick; Philip Berke, Jack and Madeline Berke; Beverly Yhap; Kelly Mitchell; Hazel Yee; Mel Tuck; Jerry and Thora Howell; Joy Trenholm; James Lowe; Dr. Alan Li; Keeman Wong; Carol Shields; King and Cindy Anderson; Lorraine Krakow; Mike Dragvik; Mary Bredin; Sylvia Carter; Jean Yoon; Almeta Speaks; Ann McNeil; Pak Fai Wan and May Wan; Verna Mar; Deanne Wong; Lloyd and Ada Yee; Steve Wright; Betty Lee and Gary Lee; Marilyn Waller; Walt and Berenice McDayter; Art Campus, Kimberly Wood and Joe Costa. Special thanks to the families of Joe and Helen Kertes and to H.H. and Linda Au, and to Ben Labovitch.

And for so unreservedly offering home and family life, my heartfelt thanks: in Vancouver, Jacob and Alice Zilber, Randy Enomoto and Lynn Westwood, Marsha Ablowitz and Laura Chapman; in Caledon, Gary and Jean Noseworthy; in Victoria, King Lee and Linda Denton; in Toronto, Karl and Marie Schweishelm, Jean Jablonski, Tony Cheung and Evelyn Leong-Cheung; in Ottawa, Robert and Lisa Yip; in Minden, Susan Stephens; in Amherst, Mass., Angela Fina; in New Jersey, Sharron Harris, Sheila Sannes; in Hawaii, Wing Tek Lum and Chee Ping Lee Lum; in Canton, N.Y., John Hunter and Ghislaine McDayter; and in New York City, James and Lillian Lee.

For encouraging creativity at Humber College, thanks to Dr. Robert "Squee" Gordon, President, and to Joe Kertes, Director of the Humber School for Writers; Pamela Hanft, Dean of Liberal Arts and Sciences; John Maxwell and Crystal Bradley, Chairs of the General Arts and Sciences, and not least, Carol Bueglas and Cynthia Wilson. Thanks also to friends and colleagues who were supportive and generous with their time and understanding.

For extra assistance and their reading of parts of this manuscript and their frank comments, thanks to Judy Fong-Bates, Richard Harrison, Michael Glassbourg, Margaret Hart, Larry Wong, Garson Lee and family, Shirley Wong; Marie, Karl and Kate Schweishelm; Lil Iwata, Nancy Wade, Maureen Wall, Gary Noseworthy, Dr. H.H. Au, Miriam Mittermaier, and not least, Alice Zilber.

For their astute criticism during different stages of this book, I am most grateful to Joe Kertes, Alan Hepburn, Ray Jones, and copy-editor Beverly Beetham Endersby. My appreciation to Jacob Zilber and Kitty Wilson-Pote for their sensitive contributions and invaluable suggestions; and to Mary Jo Morris, whose constructive instincts for my work continue to lead me from being stuck in a chapter, to moving on, at last, to the next one. Thanks to my agent, Denise Bukowski, for her energy and enthusiasm. Appreciation for their thoughtful design and detailed work to Laura Brady, Susan James and Cathy MacLean.

Finally, my thanks for the inspired, risk-taking faith of Jackie Kaiser, for her editorial skills which helped me to shape this book, and for her dedication in seeing through this evolving, ghost-haunted volume from its first to last page: I remain astonished.